# A DIFFERENT DEFINITION
# OF POVERTY-STRICKEN

If this book appears to be speaking only
of children in penal institutions and children
in the poorer public schools, then its
appearance is deceiving. For the kind of
poverty that identifies the child who is
the true subject of this book, is a poverty
of experience—a poverty which can afflict
lives lived at $100,000 a year just as readily
as it curses the $1,000-a-year existence.
The poorest man in the world is the man
limited to his own experience, the man who
does not read. This book is about every
child who may become such a man.

# Hooked on Books: Program & Proof

Daniel N. Fader, Ph.D.
Elton B. McNeil, Ph.D.

A BERKLEY MEDALLION BOOK
published by
BERKLEY PUBLISHING CORPORATION

BERKLEY MEDALLION EDITION, JANUARY, 1968
2nd Printing, March, 1968
3rd Printing, July, 1968
4th Printing, January, 1969
5th Printing, April, 1969
6th Printing, December, 1969

SBN 425-01508-4

*BERKLEY MEDALLION BOOKS are published by
Berkley Publishing Corporation
200 Madison Avenue, New York, N.Y. 10016*

BERKLEY MEDALLION BOOKS ® TM 757,375

Printed in the United States of America

# Table of Contents

PART ONE

HOOKED ON BOOKS

by DANIEL N. FADER, Ph.D.

## PART TWO

### HOOKED ON RESEARCH

### by ELTON B. McNEIL, Ph.D.

# *Part One*

# ONE FOR THE STREET

THIS IS A HARD STORY TO TELL RIGHT. IN FACT, IT'S A hard story to tell at all:

The principal and I had been to lunch. As we stepped out of our air-conditioned car into 90 degrees of September heat, he said he'd only be a minute and walked across the narrow street into the shade of a very small, two-story, flat-roofed house. My vision was blurred by the reflected heat, but I could see a pretty young girl in the window. They talked, she smiled and showed him something that I couldn't see, and then he came back across the street.

"Pretty little thing," I said. "How come she's not in school?"

"She's working," he said, shortly, and I let it go. But it wasn't gone for good, because when we got back to his office he turned to me and asked, "Did you see what she showed me?"

"No," I said. "You were in the way."

"It was one of our paperbacks. Judith Scott's *The Art of Being a Girl.*"

"Well?" I said, when he didn't say any more. There was a point to what he had told me, but I didn't know what it was.

"Like I said, she's working today." When he saw that I didn't know the language, he told me straight. She was thirteen years old and she worked two days a week as a prostitute to help support herself and her family. The other three days she came to school. It was something, he said, to see how the students treated her. Especially the boys. The girls, so far as he could tell, treated her like any other girl. But not the boys. They *never* fooled with her and they cooled any new stud who pawed her ground. They were good to her, he said, and that was the only way

1

to put it. They were considerate. They knew how it was with her and they didn't try to make it worse.

That's all there is to the story, but I can't get it up and it won't go down. It's not that I haven't known thirteen-year-old prostitutes before. I just never knew one who read *The Art of Being a Girl* while waiting for business, and I never knew any junior high school boys who knew enough to be kind to her. But it's more than that.

Maybe it's the pap we feed them. Maybe it's the peeled and overripe bananas we feed them in the schools, when they've got the teeth to bite through tough fiber and scaly skins. How can we offer them Dick and Jane and the castrated classics when fourteen-year-old Dick protects the peace of thirteen-year-old Jane on Mondays, Wednesdays and Fridays, and purchases a piece of the same Jane on Tuesdays and Thursdays? How can we get them to believe that we're for real when we spend our hours from eight to three eluding them in a ground fog of words, and they spend their time from three to eight plus Saturdays, Sundays and holidays bumping and scraping against HOW IT IS? We can't. We're not for real; they know it, and they've put us down.

Who are the unreachables? Who are the unteachables? Do they have any reality other than in the blind eyes of the beholder? Is their existence a function of our failures as teachers rather than their failures as students? How does a boy make it all the way down to the bottom tenth grade class in a large high school in a very large city when, with emphasis in his voice and excitement in his face, he can tell one of his classmates, "I don't care if you seen the movie. You *got* to read the book!" Does the I.Q. of the average child in a Harlem public school *deteriorate* 4 points between the third and sixth grades because the child can't learn or because we can't learn him?

The child *is*. We've never managed to find out *who* or *what* he is because we've been so fatally distracted by who *we* are and what *we* want him to be.

The stories begin to run together. Have you heard about the sizable town (with a college) not very far from Ann Arbor, Michigan, where no child in the public schools uses or may possess paperbound books in any classroom "because they are shoddy and they contain literature that is

2

shoddy"; or the large high school library in the Detroit area where *Inherit the Wind* was removed from the shelves by the librarian "because it has the word 'damn' in it"? Or the high school in the Chicago area where the principal ordered the librarian to remove *all* the paperbacks because he had received a phone call from *one* irate parent whose child had told him that "James Bond and all that trash" was actually available in the school library?

You hadn't heard, you say? Where have you been? Where have we all been? Where were we when the intelligent, upper-middle-class boy got so traumatized in his California public schools that he had to be put into a very special reading class staffed by psychologists from the University of California at Los Angeles? Summoned by the teacher from his seat in a rear row, he began to walk directly toward the front of the room; suddenly he stopped, backed up a few steps, turned about and walked around the periphery of the room to reach his teacher. What had stopped him? An open book lying on a desk halfway toward the front of the room. Who knows what horrors it symbolized for him, after ten years of scarifying failure in the public schools?

Has anybody told you about all the desperate children, no longer children but unable to become adults, who inhabit the Job Corps camps? What do they want? A job, a trade, a way to buy a decent piece of the world they never made. We'll give them the currency of a vocation, we say, and they'll be able to buy that place in society. But how do you teach a boy to become a man who drives big rigs or repairs cars and trucks or cooks in a restaurant kitchen, if the boy can't read? You can't hold a job as first or twenty-first cook if you can't read the recipes. Put paperback books in their Job Corps classrooms; the immediate and overwhelming favorite becomes *30 Days to a More Powerful Vocabulary*. They know where they hurt the worst.

If this book appears to be speaking only of children in penal institutions and children in the poorer public schools, then its appearance is deceiving. For the kind of poverty that identifies the child who is the true subject of this book is a poverty of experience—a poverty which can afflict lives lived at $100,000 a year just as readily as it

3

curses the $1,000 a year existence. The poorest man in the world is the man limited to his own experience, the man who does not read. This book is about every child who may become such a man.

# HOOKED ON BOOKS

BEFORE POVERTY BECAME A GOOD THING TO SOME WHO
have never known it (and to some who have), I spent a
day as University Accreditation Visitor in the English
classrooms of Poverty-Stricken High School. Though I
don't know the average family income in P.-S.H.S., I do
know that only about 5 percent of its graduates get any
formal education beyond high school. Since we all know
that one test for the quality of poverty is the quantity of
education, I know enough to recognize a Poverty-Stricken
High School when I see one. I tell part of its story now because that story is a prelude to the program for teaching
reading and writing which occupies these pages.

One of the two most striking features of P.-S.H.S. was
its undefeated principal and undiscouraged teachers. Having read neither widely nor deeply in the lore of the poor,
they did not understand that "educationally unaspiring"
means "essentially uneducable." Instead of conducting a
holding operation, with the principal as warden and the
faculty as screws, this high school was actually convening
its classes on the assumption that students who are not
going on to college can profit from their education. If this
appears to be a commonplace assumption, then the following evidence may place it in a clearer light:

In the many secondary schools I have visited where
some students go on to college and some do not, I have
often asked the principal or the head of the English Department to send me to the teacher who does the best job
with noncontinuing students (an awkward phrase for an
awkward situation). I have invariably been directed to the
teacher who keeps the best order in the classroom. *Discipline* is clearly the criterion of success, and if the price is
the child's pleasure and enthusiasm—well, order comes

high. In this case, so high that nothing is valued beyond it and classes in such schools (they are legion) are convened with the tacit understanding that little will be taught and less will be learned. The optimistic working assumption at P.-S.H.S. was remarkable by comparison.

The second of the school's striking characteristics was as negative as the first was positive: In spite of the good feeling between teachers and pupils, and in spite of the pervasive notion that both occupied the classroom for some useful reason, very little teaching or learning occurred in the English classes of P.-S.H.S. The discovery was especially disturbing because the children were happy in the corridors, were affectionate and respectful to their teachers, were apparently clean, rested and well fed . . . were, in fact, everything but successful learners. And the English faculty was pleasant, enthusiastic, reasonably knowledgeable and well paid . . . everything but successful teachers. The mystery embodied in the mutual frustration of teacher and pupil in P.-S.H.S. was one of the major causes of the research and development that have gone into the experiment called *English in Every Classroom*.

Four o'clock came and our team had been at the school for seven hours. The first hour had been spent listening to the principal tell us something about the school, the middle hour had been sacrificed to eating Home Economics Class meat loaf, and the last hour had been spent telling the faculty about our day's observations. In between were four hours of class visiting, two or three classes per hour; then, as Accreditation Visitors from the University of Michigan, each of us was to write a report to the university's Bureau of School Services appraising the quality of the school's instruction in our special subject.

As we drove back to Ann Arbor, I tried to formulate the report I would write. To write that the school was doing very badly in English seemed somehow unfair, but the day's inescapable truth was that they were doing very badly indeed. And yet, by comparison with the Highly Recommended High School (more than 50 percent going on to college and most performing well) which I had visited during the preceding semester, P.-S.H.S. deserved to be praised. In H.R.H.S., the English classes for students not going on to college were travesties, mocking the very cause

6

they were meant to serve. Instead of freeing and augmenting the student's store of language, English classes there served an inhibiting function.

It was shocking to see the apparent change in the English teachers between the time they dismissed a class of academic students and convened a class of general students. Stevenson could have created Henry Jekyll and Edward Hyde from the schizophrenic model embodied in the average H.R.H.S. English teacher. Dr. Jekyll in the academic classroom changed to Mr. Hyde when dealing with the "other" students. Creative, compelling teachers of students who were going on to college altered their countenances and personalities in a matter of minutes to become little better than jailers of children who could not respond so easily or so well to the language and literature their teachers valued. I had seen the same sorry scene enacted in a dozen schools. Today, in P.-S.H.S., the feeling had been very different, and yet the results had been largely the same. No easy report phrases took shape in my head.

My companion on the journey back to Ann Arbor was Ray Kehoe, Associate Director of the Bureau of School Services. When I had told him of my day at the school, he told me of a problem he faced which might have something to do with the day's experiences. In the name of the Bureau he had accepted a commission that had become unexpectedly difficult to fulfill. On the surface it appeared to be simple enough: Engage members of the Bureau and of the University faculties to construct a meaningful curriculum for the W. J. Maxey Boys' Training School, then being built in Whitmore Lake, Michigan. But only the appearance was simple; among other difficulties, he had been unable to find anyone to write an English program for a school full of noncontinuing students. Would I be interested? We were both surprised, I think, when I accepted the commission.

A few days later I met with Bureau officials and the two men who were responsible for organizing the new school. Bud Maxey and Stanley Black were to be director of the entire facility and supervisor of instruction, respectively. We were to come to know each other very well in the next three years, but at that point we were strangers. To ease the moment of meeting, Ray Kehoe said something about my familiarity with juvenile delinquency. No adult, he said, could shoot pool like that and not have led a misspent youth. We all laughed, but the damage was done. I left the meeting confirmed in the belief that my experiences as a pool hustler and high school stayaway would make it easier for me to write a program for boys who were more of the same.

That belief was foolish, and it cost me months of mistaken research. My original assumption was that language training was a matter of discovering and effecting techniques for making lasting changes in performance. Like so many other would-be innovators, I looked more closely at myself than at my subjects. I had had a mild case of juvenile delinquency; I had only to remember myself and I would have a point of departure for writing a program. Now I know how wrong-headed that assumption was, but the realization was long in coming.

My kind of delinquent was the product of a hopeful society. No matter whom or what we hustled, bashed or lifted, we did not view the past as desperate or the future as hopeless. Shooting pool, gambling, fighting, staying out of school or breaking into it—all were temporary accommodations to a world that was going to be *much better when we grew up*. That was our credo, and we held to it in spite of everything.

Misled by irrelevant memories, I visited elementary schools, junior high schools, senior high schools, juvenile homes, and training schools. During the first three months of school visiting I caught only occasional glimmers of light that would not fit under the bushel I had built for them. But as weeks of traveling and questioning wore on, the occasional glimmers became intrusive beams with deep shadows. In the shadows were all the faces in all the classrooms where language, though the apparent subject of the class meeting, had obviously gone out of style. If I saw one, I saw a hundred teachers addressing themselves to four students (usually girls) in a class of forty empty faces with vacant eyes. Better than any written evidence, those eyes and faces testified to the irrelevance of what was happening in English classes.

Their teachers told me that gaining the attention of those blank eyes became more difficult with each year, and that holding their attention was impossible. As I returned from daily school visits and tried to write about what I had seen, I began to realize how much I knew about the teachers, their methods and their materials, and how little I knew about the children.

How could I set up a school program when I knew so little about the students it was meant to serve?

I began again. This time I went to the students. What's wrong with your English class, I asked, that causes you to turn it off the way you do? You're out to lunch during your English class, I said, and I want to know why. They told me why: They told me that it didn't make any difference about them. That the teacher didn't like them so they didn't like the teacher. She didn't talk about anything that mattered ("Sentence diagraming? Shoot! What do I care about that?") and she didn't talk like she *wanted* you to understand. And never nothing to read that was any good, even if you wanted to read. What difference does it make anyway?

What difference does it make? The words are repeated so often that they become part of the litany with which the burial service for school is conducted. For the student not going on to college, school is dying and the English class is dead. We must exhume the body for examination.

Listening to students rather than to teachers had given me a new starting point: Who or what was responsible for the murder of the English class? Could it be revived? Was revival important? Could English in a school context ever matter to the student who saw no purpose in schooling and little hope in anything else? With six more weeks and sixty schools behind me, no closer to the right answers and wondering if there were any, I began school visiting again. But this time I began with one firm piece of information.

Children are rarely indirect or misleading about what they feel. Unlike adults, children seldom learn to mask, postpone or abrogate the effect of any cause that moves them. Just as the living language is never wrong, so are children always accurate in reflecting things as they really are for them. Therefore I knew there was no use identifying the children as causes of what was wrong in the English class. They may be all that they shouldn't be, but they

9

*are,* and must be met where they are before they can be led to where they *should be* (i.e., where *we* are).

If not to the children—their lack of manners, their lack of interest, their deficient home environment etc., etc., etc. —then where to attribute the cause? Where else but to their teachers and the materials and methods they use? One advantage of identifying the source of the trouble in this way is that here at least it may be remediable. Remedying children is something else again; adult logic has a way of being persuasive only to adults, and lines of communication between teachers and parents are practically nonexistent.

The first step seemed to be to find out what teachers were doing in *all* classrooms, with the purpose of translating the successes of math, science and social studies into the English curriculum. My first efforts in that direction turned out to be my last, for visits to a dozen schools and conversations with some forty teachers led me to understand that the failure of the English teacher was only one part of the failure of the schools to meet the needs of the unpromising student. Programs in all areas were no more hopeful than the students themselves.

Having eliminated the children as cause and the successes of other subjects as remedy, I returned to the person, the methods and the materials of the English teacher.

## The English Teacher

In my next round of school visits, and in discussions with teachers outside the school environment, I remarked again and again that the most serious deficiency of the English teacher is her exclusivity. Why, I asked, do only English teachers teach English? What a silly question, I was told. Only English teachers teach English because only English teachers are qualified to teach English. *Everyone* knows that. If *everyone* knows that, I replied, then surely *everyone* must also know that English teachers have failed to teach their subject, no matter how it is defined, to hordes

10

of students for a very long time. And *everyone* must also know that a child without a functioning and willing literacy—the minimal responsibility of the English teacher—cannot successfully be taught any other subject in the academic curriculum.

Surely if *everyone* knows all this, then *surely no one* can expect the English teacher alone to teach English. But that is exactly what everyone seems to expect. We're history teachers (or math or science or shop or music or . . .), they told me, and we have enough to do to teach history, let alone English. Or—we do *our* jobs—why can't the English teachers do theirs? Whatever the posture of friend or antagonist, the result was that the English teacher was exclusive indeed. Her responsibility was the student's literacy, and the responsibility was entirely hers. After all, I was told several hundred times, no one asks the English teacher to teach history (math, science, *et al.*). Why should teachers of other subjects be asked to teach English?

Because the reasons seem very compelling for having *all* classroom teachers teach English, the first part of this program, originally intended to promote literacy at the Maxey Boys' Training School, is based upon the idea of DIFFUSION, which describes the expansion of responsibility for teaching reading and writing to each teacher in every classroom. First among the compelling reasons for making such a change in customary practice is the failure of that practice.

It is a remarkable fact that I met not a single principal or teacher who cared to argue that students who were not going on to college were being adequately prepared in the English language. This silence is all the more significant when contrasted with the sound of success which accompanies any discussion with the same people on the subject of college preparation. In that area, high schools are now generally rated by their most severe critics—the universities—on a scale employed almost exclusively at its upper end. And teachers know it. Turn conversation from the general to the academic student and high school English teachers rightfully expect to be praised. Their expectations are very different, however, when they talk about their less malleable clay.

A second and equally powerful reason exists for making

11

*English in Every Classroom* the philosophical and operative basis of a new program in literacy. That reason is the nature of the children themselves. "Practical" is the adjective recurring most often in language used by secondary school teachers to describe their nonacademic students. The word seems to have a wide variety of meanings, at least some of which are pejorative. But where it is used with a favorable meaning it seems to refer to the unusual (in middle-class terms) need of such students to perceive and to be able to judge the immediate relationship between cause and effect before they can be successfully motivated. Satisfaction of this need is the lever most frequently employed by this program to raise the "practical" child toward literacy.

Put yourself in the place of the "practical" student: What lesson would you learn if your English teacher were the only teacher who consistently required something more of your literacy than a minimal display? You would learn exactly what generations of "practical" students have come to know so well: that the English teacher can be effectively ignored, for only she really cares about your use of language. Since language is not easy for you—one reliable criterion of the intellectual difference between general and academic students—and since it is apparently unimportant for all the other teachers who shape the bulk of your school day, why should it be a big thing for you? Leave your mind in the corridor as you walk into your English class; put your brains out to lunch and your eyes out the window for forty minutes a day and you've got it made. Why should you strain yourself when nobody but the English teacher seems to care?

Now change the situation: Every day in every major subject classroom you enter, you're required to read and write as though reading and writing really mattered to every one of your teachers. "Everywhere you turn there's writing" was the half-exasperated comment of one District of Columbia schoolgirl after the program had been in action for six months in her junior high. Her exasperation was her teacher's hope. Being a "practical" child, she had learned that the coolest survive longest. Before English had assaulted her in every classroom, she had managed to

12

freeze it into quiescence. Now she was losing her cool, and her teachers were being warmed by the thaw.

The exclusivity of English teachers is not a condition reserved for those poor sufferers alone. Though they may be doubly isolated, they share a significant part of their condition with all other members of the teaching profession. And that is the word, "profession," which seems to me to be at the dark heart of the problem.

Who with any interest in the world inhabited by teachers can have missed the overwhelming frequency of "professional" as an adjective used with a certain touching hopefulness by all members of that community? No other word in the mouth of teacher, principal or superintendent bears the poignancy of that one. And yet, so few of its users have any clear idea of what it means; and even less fulfill its requirements.

Though I do not claim the two parts of the following definition to be exclusive, or even sufficient, I am certain both parts are necessary in defining the professional man. First and larger of two unequal portions is adequate knowledge of an intellectual discipline. Even as the lawyer and doctor use their specific knowledge as a prism through which to view their world, both professional and private, so the historian, grammarian, and social scientist possess specialized knowledge which orders their lives as well. For example, language teachers reflexively classify almost everyone by their speech. Certainly the classification is unconscious: equally certain, it happens in most of their human encounters.

This ordering of one's life within the structure and premises of a particular discipline is the first requirement of the professional. But taken alone it is incomplete and unproductive. I would like each reader of this sentence to shut his eyes and recall the last professional convention he attended. Any lawyers or doctors among my readers will see a vision substantially different from that seen by teachers. That substantial difference has been illustrated at every teachers' convention or conference I have ever attended, usually in the ritual of paper reading. Here's how it works:

Typically, either by invitation or through competition, three papers are selected for a particular program. The audience, attracted either by the subject of the session, the titles of the papers or the personalities of the readers, usually hears one reasonably good paper, one fair paper and one that ranges from barely acceptable to terrible. An impartial bystander, having wisely remained within range of the applause but out of reach of the words, would find himself unable to distinguish best from worst. Furthermore, were he then given a tape of the audience's questions and comments, he could only conclude that all three papers had been rather good and reasonably well received.

Is it professional courtesy that causes so even a reception of such uneven work? Does our charity overcome our critical instinct and confuse our search for truth? It does nothing of the sort. Unlike conventions of other professions I have attended, where the wolves eat the rabbits at one bite, the teaching profession convenes only rabbits and nobody eats anybody. The few teeth sharpened are sharpened privately on reputations rather than publicly on work. In short, public criticism of one teacher by another is as little encountered in the so-called profession at conventions as it is in the so-called profession in schools. It is exactly this remarkable absence of interior criticism that causes the profession to remain so-called.

This is the second part of the professional condition: A willingness to speak and to hear the voice of criticism. I have used the example of typical behavior at teachers' conventions because I believe it is symptomatic of the destructive insularity which afflicts every teacher in every classroom in public (and all other) schools. The program called *English in Every Classroom* aims to violate that insularity by requiring close and continuous cooperation between teachers *in every classroom* as a means of assuring the literacy of every student.

### The Materials and Methods of the English Teacher

The title of this section is an index to the prejudices of its writer. "Methods and Materials" is the customary phrase; its implications for teacher and student have been very unpleasant indeed.

Having asked hundreds of English teachers and instructors in other subjects why only English teachers teach English, I had exhausted half my stock of questions. The second half of this meager armory was, "Why do you use the materials and methods you use to teach English?" Responses were as various as the responders; all could be summed up in the following fashion:

1—For methods: "The methods I use are those I have found through experience to be successful."

2—For materials: "The materials I use are those made available to me by the system"; or "I use the materials I use because those are the materials I've got to use"; or "I use these materials because these are the materials I've built my lesson plans on"; or "Ask the principal [supervisor, superintendent]. Don't ask me. They order the stuff. I just use it"; or "These are the best materials available. We have the newest and the best, and we're proud of them."

The one response I never heard, however, was this one: "I use these materials because they are effective with my students. They like the textbooks and other materials I use, and they learn well from them."

This missing response is illuminated by the phrase, "methods and materials." The order of the words reflects the order of their appearance in the field of education. According to this order, methods do not rise out of materials; rather they *are,* and the practices they produce lead to the types of materials selected for use in English classes. But if not from the materials, then whence do methods come? From the needs of students? Hardly, since not even the most optimistic schoolman claims much language success with the general student. From the needs of the abstract subject called "English"? Far more likely, and far more likely therefore to result in the painfully limited success such methods have known with the general student.

The argument for their inevitable failure goes something like this:

A subject taught for its own sake, rather than for its utility in meeting real life situations, may or may not be fascinating, depending upon the teacher's and the student's ability to understand and enjoy its content. On the student's part, at least, this enjoyment is directly related not only to his capacity for perceiving and enjoying abstraction, but also to his capacity to apply abstractions once he has mastered them. This may show itself in his ability to turn abstract grammar into good speech, or it may be nothing more exotic than mastering the difference between spelling and defining words in lists and using them in sentences. For instance, English teachers are all too familiar with the child who can spell words in a list correctly, but who cannot spell them when required to use them in sentences. Perhaps even more relevant to my argument is the legion of children who can define words by rote but who can only use them meaningfully in self-defining sentences.

The point is this: Pages of grammar rules and sentence diagrams, and lists of words to be defined and words to be spelled, have become part of materials which arose from archaic methods long proved ineffective. Furthermore, and far worse, precedence of methods over materials inevitably causes undervaluation of the materials selected. The implicit and underlying assumption *must* be that the materials don't really matter very much if the methods are efficient. What other assumption could conceivably account for the books, the incredible books, presently in use in the schools?

But what happens when the materials used in classes for the general student are selected to meet the practical needs of the student rather than the more abstract needs of the subject? In English, for example, rhetoric takes precedence over grammar, and utility becomes more important than beauty. When such criteria become the new basis for selection of materials, a radical change is inevitable. For example, such extremes of the same language as Shakespeare and the daily newspaper are found to have much in common. In terms of the practical needs of the student, the newspaper takes precedence. Because it begins more nearly where he is, it may prove to be the bridge across which he crawls, stumbles and finally walks, erect, to where he should be. If he finds Shakespeare at the other end of the bridge, then the simple, inelegant news-

16

paper, magazine or paperback book has become a legitimate and necessary means to attaining a complex, eloquent end.

When the goal of the English class is redefined in terms of rhetorical ease and willing expression, the ancient methods of the schools become as irrelevant to the subject as they have generally been to the student. Ease in understanding newspapers and pleasure in reading magazines cause both to replace the grammar texts and workbooks of time-dishonored usage. Instead of a student who spells according to rules, we may now have a student who spells by the image of words which have a hundred times impinged on his reading consciousness.

Because the reasons seem as compelling as those for asking teachers *in every classroom* to teach English, the second part of this program is based on the principle of SATURATION, meaning the replacement, whenever possible and in whatever classroom, of customary texts and workbooks with newspapers, magazines and paperbound books. The object of this is to stir the sensibility of the practical child. Even as he learns to be reticent in a world of words he cannot fathom, so may he learn to be receptive in a world of words he can understand. Because he finds newspapers, magazines and paperbound books in every classroom, and because he *can* and *will* read them, he may yet be brought to compromise with a verbal world he cannot avoid.

# PREFACE TO THE PROGRAM

HOGMAN WAS SWEATING AND SO WAS I. THE MORNING was hot, and we had hundreds of paperbound books to unload from the rear of my Volkswagen sedan. Why hadn't we boxed them before putting them into the car? Why my car? Why me at all—a teacher of English literature, a lover not a mover of books? We talked as we waited for some cartons.

"That a mighty tiny sheen," he said.

"Mighty tiny," I said, looking at the pile of books filling up the rear.

"Them's tiny books," he said, asking me to talk.

"We get any of yours?" I asked. The principal of the school and I had spent two hours in Cottage Unit A searching the boys' rooms for books. Those we had found were now sprawled in the back of the car. Hogman had come with us from the cottage, where he had helped to collect the books and load them into the car.

"Had all them James Bondys, but I done read 'em a couple times."

"We get anything you weren't done with?"

"I reckon."

"What?"

"The chuck what makes hisself into a splib."

*"Black Like Me?"*

"That the one."

I reached back and shuffled through the pile until I found one of the many reclaimed copies of Griffin's book. "Here. Bring it back when you're done."

He ducked his chin and half turned his big body away from me. Then he took the book and slipped it into his back pocket. We were both sweating through our shirts, but he didn't have to be back in Ann Arbor to give a two o'clock lecture. I was thinking about that lecture when

Hogman turned toward me, a broad smile on his face, and said kind of low and chuckly, "Like reading, man. You know—it ain't so bad."

You know, it ain't. The program for teaching English in the public schools, outlined in this book, is based upon the idea that reading ain't so bad and it's time more people learned how good it is. Since everybody agrees that people never learn better than when they're children, this book describes a school program suitable in some measure to all children in all American school systems from kindergarten through twelfth grade. Though suitable to all, this program is particularly concerned with the student whom educators have identified as "general," meaning all too often that the school system has few specific programs to satisfy his educational needs. This is the same student who can sometimes be identified as disadvantaged and can more often be characterized as impoverished. He is disadvantaged if he is poor, but he may be impoverished and be rich. He is impoverished if he does not read with pleasure, because if he does not read with pleasure then he is unlikely to read at all.

Big Bill, Superduck, Hogman, Lester—all were students in the W. J. Maxey Boys' Training School at Whitmore Lake, Michigan, a few miles north of Ann Arbor. Their routes to the school were as varied as the faces of poverty; but if their pasts were various, their futures were alike: they would return to Maxey or to another penal institution, whether state or federal, juvenile or adult. They spoke of Jacktown (Jackson, Michigan, State Penitentiary) like an old and reliable acquaintance. They were boys, they were old men, they were tough, they couldn't fight their way out of a Girl Scout meeting. Sometime during the first weeks of my work at the school I said to one of the physical education teachers, "You must get some pretty fair athletes out here." I'll never forget his answer:

"These boys ain't good at nothing. If they was, they wouldn't be here."

I watched them fight. He was right—they didn't have anything but hate going for them. Awkward right-handed leads from flat-footed stances; long, looping punches that landed, when they landed at all, on shoulders and tops of

19

heads. More than one teacher and cottage supervisor told me that he'd just as soon let them fight because they seldom hurt each other. Basketball, football, softball—sadball. They were society's losers. The hate they had as their sometime ally was as likely to be directed against themselves as against others. "Man, what's the use?" The words were engraved on their lips.

On this hot September morning, Leon Holman (principal of the Maxey School) and I, Daniel Fader (Assistant Professor of English at the University of Michigan), were holding a shakedown. Criminals' cells and delinquents' rooms have, in the history of penal institutions, been shaken down for everything from money and drugs, to knives, guns, files and blunt instruments, but this may have been the first time they were shaken down for books. The wingman went ahead of us, unlocking the doors; Hogman followed, pushing the cart. We knew we'd find books, but we never thought it would be like this. Books were everywhere: on their shelves, on their desks, their beds, their washstands. Their teachers said they were reading; the books they carried with them, stuffed in their pockets, said they were reading; the number of books missing from the library said they were reading . . . but here, suddenly, was evidence we couldn't question. It was a perversely happy two hours for both of us, faced as we were with the stolen evidence of our program's success.

That program, as it has been developed and tested, is described in this book. The children and young adults for whom it is intended usually need to perceive an immediate relationship between cause and effect before they can be successfully motivated. Their questions about literature are often put in terms of "What does it mean to me?" which is only a more specific version of their "Why should I?" in answer to the demands of reading and writing. The purpose of the program called *English in Every Classroom* is to help those who teach such students give them useful and satisfying answers.

This approach to learning is designed to provide the general student with *motivation* for reading and writing, at the same time giving him appropriate materials with which to practice and reinforce his literacy. Its potential significance to education lies in its systematic expansion of what good English teachers have done, or tried to do, or wanted to do in schools and classrooms everywhere: convince their colleagues in all subjects that English must be taught by each teacher in every classroom with materials that invite the general student to learn.

All aspects of this curriculum proceed upon the assumption that the chief problem in teaching reading and writing is not intellect but motivation. The program further assumes that a student's desire to learn makes learning probable.

Members of the Departments of English and Psychology and of the School of Education at the University of Michigan have been engaged for the past four years in shaping and testing a curriculum for the teaching of English in the W. J. Maxey Boys' Training School at Whitmore Lake, Michigan. The English program at the Maxey School, which has also been implemented under experimental conditions in the Garnet-Patterson Junior High School in Washington, D. C., and is now in use in some form in thirty-seven states and three foreign countries, is the source of methods for teaching English described in these pages. Incredible as it may seem, this is apparently the first schoolwide approach to the language problems of the general student. Equally revealing is a discovery made by the psychologists who have been testing the program: within the varied and subtle spectrum of devices invented and validated for testing literacy, almost no work at all has been done in the vast area of testing *attitudes* toward reading and writing. The implications of this discovery are remarkable:

In the modern history of education, attitudes of readers and writers toward the processes of reading and writing have been regarded—when they have been considered at all—as no more important than the attitude of any mechanical object to the work it performs. Who would ask if a computer likes its work or if a can opener likes the act of opening or the can it opens? Judging by their policies, American educators believe that most children are well disposed toward reading and writing and that they will so continue, independently of the methods and materials used to teach them. No alternate explanation is available. Either the reader/writer is like a mechanical device, to

21

be rated in terms of the relation between input and output (performance), or educators have believed that attitude does not really matter very much after all. One apparent resolution of this unhappy choice was offered me by the former chairman of one of Michigan's largest and most successful (very large percentage of graduates doing well in college) high school English departments: "Reading and writing are *necessary*, don't you see. If we get the performance up, we know we've got a child with the right attitude."

This is the same man who gave me information he felt I would be glad to have in my role as Accreditation Visitor in English for the university: *His* staff of English teachers was so cooperative and sensible that he had been called upon only once to ban their use of a book—*The Catcher in the Rye*. But of course we *both* understood about *that*. Though in fact we both did understand about *that*, we both did not understand about attitude. Attitude follows performance only where children are performance-oriented, and even with such children the attitude may not be the one that educators intend to foster. When reading and writing are merely means to the end of school success, what happens to performance-oriented children when that success has been attained? To put the question another way, what happens when the performing child becomes the school-graduated (performance-certified) adult? Any librarian or bookseller will tell you that the average modern adult avoids bookstores and libraries as though they were leprosaria. Had the goal of modern, performance-oriented education been the creation of unwilling readers and writers, it could not have succeeded more completely. All the supporting evidence is bottom-rooted in front of television screens across the nation.

If this is true of the performance-oriented child, what of the child whose environment and training aim him elsewhere? I am using "performance-oriented" to describe the child, usually middle class, who is taught that time-saving, orderliness, and self-control, all elementary in the process of gratification deferment, will lead him to eventual joy. But what of the child, usually lower class, whose ethics make "live for tomorrow" a joke today? His causes must have very immediate effects, and the devil (who has

22

a school text in his hand) take the foremost. What of this child, to whom "performance orientation" generally has meant mediocrity or failure? At least one part of the answer is clear: We must first re-evaluate our goals as educators before we can hope better to profit our students. In the case both of performance- and other-oriented children, we must admit that performance orientation is not now—and probably never has been—enough. We must take careful and unremitting aim at the child's *attitude* before we can expect to see any lasting effect upon his performance. The plan for teaching English which is introduced here takes the child's attitude as its primary, and sometimes its sole, object.

# THE PROGRAM

"ENGLISH IN EVERY CLASSROOM" IS AN APPROACH TO learning based on the dual concepts of SATURATION and DIFFUSION. The first of these key concepts, SATURATION, proposes to so surround the student with newspapers, magazines and paperbound books that he comes to perceive them as pleasurable means to necessary ends. The advantages inherent in selecting such materials for classroom use are very great. First, and most important, all newspapers, most magazines and the great majority of paperbound books are written in the knowledge that commercial disaster is the reward for creating paragraphs that people *should* read. With the choice a clear one between market success and business failure, publishers, editors and writers know that survival depends on producing words that people *will* read. This program advances the radical notion that students are people and should be treated accordingly.

A second and perhaps equally important advantage in saturating the student's school environment with newspapers, magazines and paperbound books is their relationship to the world outside the school building. No one believes that we are training children from any social level to be performers in school; everyone believes that students come to the schools to learn skills they will need when they leave school, no matter at what level they leave. And yet, instead of importing materials from that world for teaching the literacy that world requires, we ignore such materials as unworthy of the better world we teachers are dedicated to creating. This program yields to none in its desire to help make a better world. It is equally strong, however, in its desire to educate students to deal with the world as it is. No literature better represents that world than the various periodicals and softbound books which supply the basic materials for the SATURATION program.

The third advantage of these materials is closely related to the second. Not only do newspapers, magazines and paperbound books *enable* the student to deal with the world as it is, but they *invite* him to do so. All educators are only too familiar with the school-text syndrome, that disease whose symptoms are uneducated students and unread materials. School texts often go unread just because they are school texts and apparently have very little to do with the nonschool world. One certain way to break the syndrome is to remove the proximate causes—in this case traditional school texts—and substitute newspapers, magazines and paperbound books.

A warning to those who follow the foregoing advice: You'll have at least three unhappy types on your hands when you remove traditional school texts and substitute paperbound materials. Least important will be the parents who want to see their children with traditional texts because paperbound books (or magazines or newspapers) "don't look right." "They were never used in *my* day in school!" Yes, you may reply, and look what we turned out.

Most important of the unhappy types will be the teachers who won't change "and nobody's going to make me." Whether they act from the pressure of invincible ignorance or forty (or four) years of lesson plans, they will prove to be immovable and should be fired. But since removal is the prerogative of employers whose staff members take responsibility for their products—a description in no way applicable to the business of education—such teachers must be ignored. In my experience, they are very much in the minority and the harm they do can be greatly mitigated by their colleagues.

Last among those who will be predictably unhappy at the change in texts will be certain students. These are the ones who have built up a careful and relatively complete system of defenses against the varied apparatus of the school world. We see the worst of them in Maxey and in a few of the big-city public schools where parts of the program have been installed. They are immediately recognizable by their anger, which is very funny in a bizarre way. They are angry because they have been given paperbound books, magazines and newspapers instead of the customary texts. "Where are the *real* textbooks?" they ask. What they are really asking is—"Where are the recognizable symbols of a world we know how to resist? Make us comfortable with the old texts, and we'll be able to fight back because we'll recognize the enemy."

The fourth and final asset of softbound materials reflects a new sort of hope. Though it's not exactly what I had in mind when I first advocated replacing classic school texts with paperbound material, it is an asset which can hardly be overlooked. Its spokesman is a former English teacher who, in the best tradition of a peculiar profession, has been rewarded for excellence in teaching by being removed from the classroom to the position of administrator. He speaks here in the reduced voice of a principal:

"If you couldn't say anything else for newspapers and magazines for teaching our kind of student, you'd have to say that they get a mighty important message across to him. Maybe the most important. No matter how bad he feels about his world, he has only to read a newspaper or magazine to know that somebody else has got it worse."

SATURATION applies in principle not only to the selection and distribution of periodicals and softbound texts throughout the curriculum, but to the explosion of writing in the student's school environment. This explosion is based upon the practice of DIFFUSION, the second of the two key concepts in the design of *English in Every Classroom* and the concept implied in its name. Whereas SATURATION refers to the materials used in every classroom to induce the child to enter the doorway of literacy, DIFFUSION refers to the responsibility of every teacher in every classroom to make the house of literacy attractive. In discharging this responsibility, every teacher becomes an intermediary between the student and functional literacy. In order that the student may come to view writing as a means to all ends, all ends which he pursues in a scholastic context must insist upon writing as the means through which they can be approached. In short, every teacher becomes a teacher of English, and English is taught in every classroom.

## (A) Writing

One of the most interesting yearly statistics made available to many university faculties is the number of incoming freshmen chosen from the top 10 percent of their high school classes. The number has recently grown so large at some universities that their faculties are now more concerned about good students who are excluded than about poor students who may still be admitted. Though this improvement in quality in the entering class has been nowhere more marked than in Freshman English, the promised land of no Freshman English course is not yet at hand. In spite of the notable increase in intelligence and accomplishment which characterizes the average freshman, he still writes miserably when he enters the university. Because of his wholly inadequate preparation in composition, he must take an English course designed to teach him how to write at least well enough to survive four years of college. There can be little doubt that, at many schools, Freshman English is successful in realizing this aim. The reason for this success is of crucial importance in establishing an effective program for teaching reading and writing to students at all levels.

That Freshman English is usually very effective is partially attributable to the quality and predisposition of its students. But these are also the same students who learn so little about English composition before entering college that a course like Freshman English is necessary to their survival. What, then, effects so powerful a change in their performance as writers during their initial collegiate semester? The answer is embarrassingly simple—for the first time in their school experience, they write. They write a small mountain of out-of-class papers, in-class papers, exercises, paragraphs, sentences . . . they write and they write and they write. With very few exceptions, they write more in one semester than they have written before in their lives. And they learn how to write. They

27

have learned to write through the one method they have never before been subjected to, the one method which can be expected to succeed—the constant practice of writing itself.

This view of the dynamics of the learning process in Freshman English is twice relevant to the proposals found in this program of reading and writing. Freshman students in effect teach themselves how to write. Though the teacher and his texts are important, the one indispensable element is the continuous prose output of the student himself. He is asked to do what he has always been capable of doing; soon he finds that he rather likes the experience. The typical college freshman likes his English class, he likes to write (though he probably doesn't know it), and he's able to produce ten thousand words of deathless prose for one class in one semester. In these predispositions and abilities he is likely to be very different from his school counterpart, who too often barely endures his English class and is sometimes stricken by mental paralysis at the very thought of having to write for any reason. The college freshman learns much from his English class because his previous experiences and developed aptitudes combine to predispose him favorably to the English-class situation; many grade and high school students learn little from their English class because previous experiences and language disabilities conspire to cause them to reject any learning experience called "English." If this argument is valid, then the following three propositions are significant: (1) the public school student can be taught to write by writing (in quantity and on subjects appropriate to his individual level of attainment); (2) this teaching and writing must not be confined to the English classroom, which has so often been for him a scene of failure and a source of frustration; (3) the nature of the English classroom must be radically altered if it is to play a meaningful part in his education.

On the basis of these three propositions, certain conclusions seem inevitable. The teaching of English in the public school should be viewed as the primary responsibility of the English teacher and as a secondary responsibility of every other teacher with whom the student has regular classroom contact. This division of responsibility, with its resultant diffusion of reading and writing throughout the entire curriculum, should have a number of salutary effects, most important being communication to the student of the sense that reading and writing can be as natural to his existence as walking and talking. His previous experience has assured him that only English teachers demand constant proof of his literacy; he can hardly avoid assuming that reading and writing are special functions reserved for special occasions, in this case the English class, and that they have no normal relationship to the rest of his world. It is to dispel that damaging illusion that this recommendation is made.

Implementation of the practice of shared responsibility for the student's training in English has proved not only relatively easy in the Maxey Boys' Training School and the Garnet-Patterson Junior High School, but also unexpectedly pleasant for the faculties involved. When I first met with the full faculties of the Maxey and Garnet-Patterson schools for three-day training seminars in August of 1964 and 1965, respectively, I was uncomfortably aware on both occasions of how cold a welcome my program might receive. For it proposes an approach to the teaching of reading and writing which challenges two of the dearest and most ancient misconceptions of the profession. These are the myths, customarily paired for strength, of the teacher as individualist and the classroom as castle. Together they have done more harm to the profession of teaching than any other combination of ideas or events. The myth of the teacher as individualist serves as an example; because of it and the mental set it represents, meaningful cooperation among teachers is essentially nonexistent. Each teacher is so concerned with perpetuating the values and conditions of his own preparation, so concerned with protecting his feudal rights as a free man, that he effectively isolates himself from his peers. Teachers have *no* peer group in the functional sense of that term. They may attend professional classes, taking courses during the academic year and during the summer, but they tend to be speakers and auditors of monologues rather than participants in dialogues. *They do not profit from each other* because they are the true inheritors of the modern theory of compartmentalized education, a theory which declares each man sufficient unto his subject and each subject sufficient unto itself. General practitioners are as little respected and as meagerly rewarded in teaching as they are in medicine.

The inevitable corollary to the idea of teacher as individualist is the theory of classroom as castle. Without the second, the first could hardly be as destructive as it is. Part of our feudal inheritance is the notion that a man's home is his castle. Sanctified by law and custom, this theory has become a practice imitated in the schools. Like most imitations, the shape of the thing has undergone subtle change. Whereas in the home a man has the freedom *to* order his life and raise his family, in the classroom this tradition has been interpreted as freedom *from*. Rather than exercising freedom *to* experiment and freedom *to* criticize (both self and colleagues), teachers distinguish themselves by a process of in-gathering which frees them *from* all criticism to a degree foreign to any other profession. I would be the last to deny that public criticism—often reflecting only ignorance and prejudice—has given teachers one very good reason for insulating themselves from further shocks. But the insulation has become a burden rather than a protection. Teachers now suffer most from their inability to hear each other.

The program I proposed to the faculties of both schools asked them to hear and to help each other. Within this program, each English teacher at Maxey and at Garnet-Patterson became both leader and servant of a team of teachers and every teacher except the physical education instructors became a team member. Teams have been formed as much as possible by grouping an English teacher with the other instructors of that teacher's pupils. Where, because of the varied curriculum in the public school (foreign language instruction, for example), such grouping is not completely feasible, teachers of subjects other than English are assigned to the team which instructs the majority of their students. Teams meet weekly in the Garnet-Patterson School and less often at Maxey, where the teachers have now had three years of work within the program. These meetings are meant to be supplemented by and—as in the Maxey School—eventually replaced by the personal interaction of the English teacher with individual members of his team. In order that the English teacher may have sufficient time to devote to coordination of team effort, he is assigned one class less than the school's normal teaching load. Where an English Department chairman is designated, he is relieved of a second class in order to coordinate team teaching efforts and materials distribution throughout the school.

Team teaching is an old phrase which this plan hopes to invest with new meaning. In return for lightened classroom responsibility, each English teacher acts as a resource person and a guide for his colleagues in the diffusion of English throughout every classroom in the school. He assists each member of his team to set up a writing schedule which produces at least one piece of writing every other day in all subjects other than English. Writing in mathematics class about processes of arithmetic or practical applications of algebra; writing in shop or art classes about particular skills and necessary procedures; writing in science classes about the physical nature of his environment—all these occasions serve not only to make the student master of a significant portion of his verbal world, but to reinforce his special knowledge of that particular subject. Since in this view of the English curriculum the frequency of written exercises is far more important than their length, they vary from a few sentences to an occasional page. They are never unpleasantly long, they are not always read, and their grammar and rhetoric are not corrected by the subject instructor unless he strongly desires to do so.

First, let me explain the unusual practice of requiring students to write papers that no instructor will read. The purpose of written exercises in all divisions of the curriculum is not so much to get students to write correctly as it is simply to get them to write. The radical aspect of this approach to teaching writing does not lie in some Utopian notion of making prose stylists of all public school students. The real innovation is that it depends far less upon the teacher and far more upon the student than do more traditional methods of teaching writing. Instead of a few papers covered with his own corrections, the teacher has many papers at least partially covered with students' prose. Of the five sets of papers received in every two-week period by instructors in subjects other than English, one set per week is read and commented upon for content by the class instructor, one set every two weeks is passed on by him to the students' English teacher who corrects grammar and rhetoric, and one set per week is filed *unread* in the students' folders. This treatment of one set of papers each week in every classroom recognizes and encourages the idea that the practice of writing may be distinguished from its performance. It offers the student opportunity to condition himself for performance by allowing him time to exercise his writing muscles. Filing one set of papers each week without either reading or correcting them serves as a constant reminder to English teacher and subject teacher alike of the real purpose of these continuing exercises—to develop the student's prose-writing muscles to the point where he can use them without fear of aches and strains. Until that point is reached, practice will be far more beneficial to the student than correction.

The idea of unread papers has long been rejected in American education on the basis that "children must have some tangible evidence that their efforts are appreciated or they won't work." Translation of this unchallengeable truth into the notion that everything a student writes must be read, or otherwise he won't write, is a tribute to the human capacity for the illogical. And whoever thought that "appreciation" and "reward" could be equated with papers covered by red-pencil corrections?

The unsurprising fact is that a child can be taught to practice writing, both in the classroom (brief papers) and outside of it (the journal), just as he can be taught to practice a musical instrument or an individual sport. Just as in music and sports, the key to practice in writing is expectation. Our experience at both the Garnet-Patterson and Maxey schools has been that even the worst students take some pleasure in the idea of uncorrected writing when they have been conditioned to expect and value their freedom to practice.

I should like to emphasize here that this approach to the teaching of English does not envision making English teachers of instructors trained in other specialties. It recognizes that only in the best of all possible worlds will instructors of all subjects perceive the partial dependence of their disciplines upon the verbal adequacy of their students, and take appropriate steps to insure that adequacy. Meanwhile, until such a millennium is upon us, this program is built upon the expectation that only the English teacher will correct the grammar and rhetoric of student papers, but that all teachers will be encouraged to make simple corrections where the necessity for such corrections may be apparent to them. Since this procedure depends on the good will of the subject instructors who help to effect it, they must not be made to feel uneasy about their own mastery of the language. Much effort has been expended in both schools to make teachers of other subjects clearly understand that they may regard their role, if they wish, as that of passive intermediary between their students, on the one hand, and functional literacy on the other. In making this point clear, great emphasis has been placed upon the *quantitative* importance of these written exercises.

The speed and thoroughness with which teams formed and began their work at both the penal and public school have been attributed to a surprisingly narrow range of causes by the teachers and supervisors at both institutions. Foremost in this very brief list is a feeling of growing failure and lessening hope which pervades the faculty of every school with a considerable percentage of students who will terminate their education at the end of high school (if the system can manage to keep them that long). In the many public schools I have visited in the past five years, the song of success has always ended in a dirge: We believe we are reasonably successful in the first three grades with most of our children; we know we are doing moderately well with our bright students at almost all levels and better than that in our college-preparatory and advanced placement work. But our results with the general student vary from bad to shocking. We need help. Where can we get it? We need help. . . .

The other reason for the speedy inauguration of this program at both the Maxey and Garnet-Patterson schools is the schoolwide, nationwide awareness that the greatest failure in the education of the general student lies in his

33

language preparation. He is so difficult to teach, say teachers from other subject areas, because he is so difficult to communicate with. Stripped of its social implications, this complaint often reduces itself to the basic problem of literacy. The child who can't or won't read or write or listen well cannot be educated in any subject in the school curriculum. Because he is essentially unreachable in every teacher's classroom, and because teachers in every classroom recognize his language deficiencies as a great part of his problem, the majority of his teachers are ready to aid the English teacher in giving the student the language to deal with his world. That readiness, born of frustration on the part of *all* the teachers, has played a very large part in leveling the customary barriers that might have impeded the progress of *English in Every Classroom.*

In concluding this section on the teaching of writing as a responsibility of the entire school faculty, let me quote from comments made about the program by those who have been asked to teach within it:

"I haven't got time to teach English and math. You'd better tell me which I'm supposed to do."

"Their vocabulary seems to have about doubled. They really go for those dictionaries."

"I've noticed a big improvement in their history spelling. I don't know if it's due to the program or not."

"I find that the pupils show much greater freedom of expression than they did at the beginning. The papers most recently written are much more interesting to read than the earlier papers."

"I've taught for a long time and I know you can't get kids to write if you don't correct their papers. Their parents would complain too."

"Every member of my team has said how much better our students are writing. It's important to the students that all of their teachers are working on their writing together. They like that."

"It makes the child aware of the consolidated efforts of the teachers."

"It gives the English teacher opportunities to evaluate her own effectiveness by the quality of work done by the child in other classrooms."

"I like the democratic way we plan."
"It's a wonderful method of teaching."
"It stinks."

## (B) The Journal

Of the many and varied encouragements and inducements to writing within the scope of *English in Every
Classroom,* none has been more consistently successful
than the journal. The journal has been used in schools
before. English teachers and teachers of other subjects
have occasionally turned to it as a support for more formal
writing assignments. I have seen journals in public schools
used for continuing book reports in English classes, for
observations upon municipal government in civics classes,
and as diaries in social studies classes. Wherever they have
been included within the school program, they seem to
have pleased teacher and student alike. Taking their own
inclinations and their students' pleasure as a guide, the
faculties at Maxey and Garnet-Patterson have used the
journal with a breadth and freedom not found in other
schools.

In addition to the two paperbound books from the
library that each entering student is allowed to choose for
his own, and the paperbound dictionary he is given to
keep, he also receives from his English teacher at the beginning of the school year a spiral notebook. This is identified as his journal, an appropriate name for a notebook
intended for daily use by every student. When he is given
his journal, the student is told that quantity of production
will be the only criterion for judging his writing. Content,
style, grammar, rhetoric—all are insignificant compared
to quantity. This journal, the student is told, has only one
reason for existence: to provide you with a field upon
which you can practice your writing. You will be required
to write a minimum number of pages each week (two
pages a week at Maxey and Garnet-Patterson), and you
will be asked each Thursday to turn in your journal to

your English teacher who will return it on Friday. Your teacher will read your journal only if you invite him to read it. Under no circumstances, however, will your journal be corrected. It will be assessed for quantity, nothing else.

The use of the journal in the Garnet-Patterson Junior High School differs in one important way from its use at the Maxey School. Journals are given a cursory reading by the teachers in the public school. This is very different from the procedure of the training school, where the fact that the journal is never read by teachers, except by specific invitation, is one of its most attractive aspects from the boys' point of view. Journals can remain unread in the training school because a penal institution, no matter how progressive and enlightened, is still a closed system designed to remove offenders from society. Each member of the training school staff teaches and counsels there precisely because he understands that vituperation and obscenity are methods by which disturbed children may free themselves from some of the frustration and fear that shackle them to illiteracy. In the public schools, however, this problem must be handled very differently because of the public nature of all the students' school language, spoken or written. The simple expedient of telling the students that their notebooks will be glanced at each week, though neither read carefully nor corrected, largely solves the problem of preventing the use of publicly unacceptable words and ideas.

The quantitative view of writing has as a necessary corollary the permissive handling of journal entries by the teacher. Whether written inside or outside of class, whether legible or barely intelligible, whether a sentence, a paragraph or a page—each entry is another building block in the structure of the student's literacy. If the teacher can bring himself to regard the journal in this way, he will be equally satisfied with prose that is original and prose that is copied from a newspaper, a magazine or a book. And both he and his students will be more than satisfied with work which is evaluated by no one. If this permissiveness in the nature of the entry is closely coupled with an unvarying weekly check on the amount of production, then the formula for success in much of human enterprise—a little license with accompanying obligation—can make the journal an exceptionally useful teaching tool.

Teachers in the program have found that varying the pace of the journal's use by varying its place has been an especially successful teaching strategem. One teacher alternates weekly periods of using the journal in the classroom for brief writing assignments with having his students write outside of class. He has observed that he gets a good deal of personal writing outside of class, but that the diarist recedes into the background when the students are called upon to write in their journals in class. Furthermore, he has found that he gets surprisingly creative production when he reserves the last ten minutes of the hour rather than the first ten for journal writing.

In the early stages of the program at the Maxey School, a disappointingly small number of boys wrote more than the required minimum of two pages in their journals. We had half expected that the journal would be used by many as a kind of private stamping ground where they could work over their enemies, work out their fears, and work at the habit of writing. We were wrong; now, three years later, we know why. The journal became all we had expected it to be, and more, but instead of taking its anticipated and immediate place as a cause of change in student attitudes, it became a result of that change. As language took on real value, as speed with a dictionary and ability to write for the school newspaper and literary magazine became means for achieving peer esteem, the average weekly production in the journal increased slowly but surely. A page a day, once highly remarkable, became more usual, and five pages a day became the average output of one young man, who confided to his teacher that he'd written that much in the first fifteen days just to see if the school would really give him another notebook when he filled the first one. It would and did; he filled eight notebooks before he left the school.

Among the many creative uses found for the journal, one of the most interesting is the "good listening" device employed by one of the English teachers. The more she spoke with her students, the more she had come to believe that though they appeared to understand what she was saying—and, when asked, would claim that they did —they did not in fact usually understand her spoken directions. With this realization came the inspiration to employ the journal as a dictation workbook in which "listening good" became a challenging pursuit. A few days of this practice every two weeks has become a popular pastime with her students as they concentrate upon reproducing exactly what she is saying. She believes that the interest in her exact words which this exercise fosters carries over into closer attention to her words when interpretation rather than mere transcription is the requirement.

A discussion of the journal would not be complete without the story of Lester. Lester came to the penal school by the surest of several possible routes; he got himself born a Negro. Having managed that, he proceeded to increase his chances greatly by growing up in his mother's care in Detroit's Negro ghetto. Get born a Negro, get raised by your mother on Detroit's East Side, and you've done about all you can to make it to a training school. The rest is a matter of luck.

Lester had the luck, all of it bad. If you're a white boy from a rural area, just drag race your car, badmouth the sheriff, and WHAM! B.T.S. But if you're a Negro or white boy from Detroit, you've got to go some to make the scene at Maxey. Lester went some. When he arrived at the school, he was sixteen years old and a habitual criminal. He had to be, to get one of the places reserved for Wayne County boys.

During his stay in the reception center at Whitmore Lake, Lester underwent testing designed to produce a sufficient paper identity for juvenile penal authorities to classify and assign him to one of five available programs throughout the state. The sum of the testing was that Lester was passive, that he would like to be in a school program, and that he functioned on a fourth-grade level at the age of sixteen. With that identity, Lester came to Maxey.

Perhaps the experience he remembers most clearly from his first day in class at B.T.S. is the large spiral notebook he was given and the accompanying directions for its use. He remembers being told that he would be expected to write at least two pages a week in that notebook, and that under no circumstances would anyone correct what he wrote.

"Suppose I can't think of two pages worth?" Lester may have asked the question. Someone always does.

"Then copy from a newspaper or a magazine or a book."

"Copy? ! ! !" The boys are always shocked and incredulous. In school, COPY is the dirtiest four-letter word they know. Punch your teacher in the nose. Break the windows and destroy the books. What can happen to you? Suspension? Probation? But whatever you do, and by all that's damned and dumb, *don't copy!* Because for that you get thrown out. They'd rather scrawl almost any other four-letter word on the walls of the toilet or locker room. But COPY! That's a word right out of the darkness. And a teacher just said to —— (It's hard to bring yourself even to say the word.)

But they *do* copy. They copy and they copy and they copy. Then they copy some more. The modern, no-holds-barred record for copying at B.T.S. is forty-five pages in the first week. Teachers are grateful, however, if they get two. One youngster, who had never read it before, was fascinated by *Time* magazine. For weeks he copied from the same well-worn issue. His teacher was delighted. Not only had he probably written more in that brief period than he had written before in his life, but his conversation was full of the things he was reading. During that period he passed from truculent reserve to something like happy participation in his English and social studies classes. (Our suggestion to the courts that, having copied an entire issue of *Time,* he had been punished sufficiently for his crimes, did not receive the attention it deserved.)

A few boys with remarkable stamina copy the bulk of their journal work throughout the entire academic year. Most get tired of copying, however, especially where no teacher renews its attraction by forbidding it. And so most go naturally to the next stage of journal usage—the diary. For almost all the boys this second stage is also the final stage of their journal development. Like the majority of his fellows, Lester filled his journal with the thoughts and happenings of his daily life. Unlike his peers, most of whom wrote little more than the prescribed two pages each week, Lester wrote and wrote and wrote. Fourth-grade attainment on a test validated upon white middle-class children by white middle-class adults would have meant nothing to him. He liked to write; he discovered he liked to write by writing.

What Lester wrote at first gave his teacher bad dreams. The truth is that most of the teachers at the Maxey School (and at other training schools where the *English in Every Classroom* program has been adopted) occasionally do read their students' journals. But no comment is ever made to the student, *no matter what he writes.* The journals are sometimes read, in spite of the teachers' original promise, because the information they contain can be so helpful to the psychologists and social workers who must deal with the child's welfare outside the classroom and, eventually, after he leaves the school. Precisely because a boy's increasingly erratic conduct had sent his English teacher to his journal, in an attempt to understand his behavior, we have had the experience at B.T.S. of being able to anticipate and to treat the causes rather than the symptoms of a boy's "going high."

Lester filled his pages with the sickness of an adolescent tortured by every confusion and every desire—magnified unbearably by intelligence and incarceration. One obscene word repeated six to eight times on each line for seven full pages is an index to the depth from which Lester viewed the world above him. He was striking out with the only weapon he had. With patience and understanding, the only weapons *she* had, his English teacher waited. And waited and waited and waited. Neither she nor any of us could have said exactly what it was she waited for. But we all knew that Lester had to get that sickness up and out before anything good could come from him.

Then, before class on a Thursday morning (the journals are collected each Thursday and returned the next day, after having been checked for quantity), Lester brought his journal to his teacher and told her to read it. She reports that her knees got weak and she felt suddenly queasy as she tried to guess what he had spilled onto the page. "Lester," she began, "I don't think that I . . . uh

. . . well, that I should. . . ." She had intended to say that she would read it later or that evening or next year . . . but she knew he meant *now* and she had to read it *now*. She remembers the sensation of narrowing her eyes against the shock as she opened the notebook.

It was a poem. A nice, inconsequential piece of verse carefully divided into four stanzas of four lines each and painstakingly rhymed on alternate lines. Some sixth sense reserved for teachers in a bad spot told her not to ask him why he wanted her to read a poem she recognized as having been copied from a daily newspaper. Instead, she praised it. And she praised poetry. And she praised the writing of poetry. Her praise included the people who write poetry, because they find it helps them to say what they mean. She was fishing, and he was watching her like a hawk waiting for the right catch before he swooped. She was running out of words and ideas when he suddenly reached inside his shirt and drew out a sheaf of papers covered with his own handwriting.

It was poetry. Some of it. Some was just doggerel verse. And some was nothing at all. But Lester had been trying to write poetry for months, not quite knowing how, not knowing whether or to whom to show it, failing often, giving way to emotions he couldn't control and couldn't express, and, occasionally, succeeding. His teacher praised it as much as she dared. Now that he had come out into the open, she had to be careful to give him no cause, including effusiveness, to return to heavy cover.

Lester brought in new poems before every English class. The poem copied from the newspaper, his own sheaf of poems finally revealed, the teacher who didn't snigger or patronize—all had combined to break the wall Lester had been building for all his sixteen years. The breach became a spillway down which Lester poured.

"Miss Farnell, can I publish my poems?"

Put yourself behind the teacher's desk. What do you reply? But Lester didn't mean that he wanted to publish a book. He only wanted to make a mimeographed booklet —a sheaf of papers prefaced by a title and his name—for distribution within the school itself. Certainly a booklet like that should be easy enough to make, even in a training school? Yes, and easy to distribute. But impossible to recall, once distributed.

Lester was in the midst of the most significant change-process of his life. The changes were so radical that they hardly seemed real. A relatively few months of accomplishment—perhaps the first unqualified success of his life—had begun a process powerful enough to change a passive, effeminate, obnoxious boy into an aggressive, masculine, obnoxious boy. But the process was reversible. And the fearful vision that haunted his teacher was the reception those poems might receive in the school.

For what is a poet in a training school? He walks with a certain lightness of foot, you can hear him swish as he passes, and, baby, in a training school that is VERY BAD. So bad that we would have given a great deal to spare Lester the experience. He had been promised an answer to his request on the following day. Our collective decision to publish the poems was based, finally, on the simplest of reasons—none of us had the strength to say no. But our "yes" was weak and worried. The poems were mimeographed and distributed throughout the school. We held our breath.

Of all our private predictions, varying from hot disaster to cold indifference, none dared to be as hopeful as reality. None of us, barricaded within the assumptions of our middle-class worlds, foresaw the eminence that poetry would bring to Lester at B.T.S. And we were even less capable of foreseeing the value that Lester's writing would give to poetry at B.T.S. One type of book we had omitted completely from our original paperback library was the poetry anthology and the book of poems by a single author. If we were collectively certain of anything, it was that these boys had never willingly read poetry in their lives and were unlikely to begin at B.T.S. We think somewhat less now of collective certainty. Lester's poems were published. Lester was lionized. And we were overwhelmed by the discovery of thirty-five poets in the Maxey School population.

Lester published two further collections before he completed his stay at Maxey. With each publication, the group's view of Lester and poetry (and Lester's view of himself) changed profoundly. Lester saw something in himself to value, and his peers saw something in poetry. Lester is long gone from Maxey, but the librarian is still having trouble meeting the demand for books of poetry.

What began as an improbable story ends as an impossible fantasy. As Lester underwent the dramatic change from a passive to an aggressive human being, from a local laugh to a local leader, his aspirations changed as well. To him, the world of the W. J. Maxey Boys' Training School at Whitmore Lake became even smaller than it was. Lester wanted to copyright his extensive production of poetry. Acting upon the advice of his English teacher, Lester wrote to Congressman Weston Vivian, Democrat, then representing Michigan's Second District, of which Whitmore Lake is a part. Lester sent along his poems with a letter inquiring about copyright. Mr. Vivian's response was predictable—if you still believe in the Age of Miracles. All this remarkable Congressman did was to read one of Lester's poems into the *Congressional Record,* get Vice President Humphrey's autograph on a copy of that edition of the *Record,* fly to Detroit, motor to Whitmore Lake, and present the autographed copy to Lester at an assembly of the entire school. No one will ever be able to assess accurately what Mr. Vivian's visit did directly for Lester's ego, vicariously for those of his fellow students, and incidentally for the causes of poetry and literacy at Maxey. The results of that visit are still being tallied.

Because improbability is boundless, Lester's story has a sequel. After his release from B.T.S., Lester called his teacher regularly to report on his activities. A few months after his release I walked into the school library one afternoon to find her staring vacantly past the spinners full of paperbound books.

"Lester called this morning." I could barely hear the words.

"What's wrong?" Nobody makes it, I thought. Even Lester.

"He says he just got a five hundred dollar check from a publisher for his poems."

It was true. Improbable. Impossible. Nevertheless true.

Another B.T.S. alumnus who keeps in touch with his former teachers came to visit the school sometime after

Lester's telephone call. He was able to verify the story with the best kind of evidence—he had *seen* the check. It was no surprise to him, he said. "When that cat come from Washing Town," he told us, "everybody *know* Lester going to be *the man.*"

## (C) Reading

No student is likely to learn to write if he believes that writing is an affliction visited upon defenseless students solely by English teachers; nor is he likely to learn to read unless reading is made a part of his entire curricular environment. Therefore this program requires that *all* teachers base a significant part of their course content and a portion of their written exercises upon textbooks designed to *invite* reading. These textbooks are the newspapers, magazines and paperbound books which import the nonschool world into the classroom.

An acceptable text in this program is one which is not an anthology and does not have hard covers, for the hardbound text and the anthology have a number of serious defects in common. To the unsuccessful student both are symbols of a world of scholastic failure, and both to some degree are causes of that failure. No hardbound text was ever thrust into a child's pocket, and no anthology was ever "read" in any meaningful sense of the word by anybody. The student fed a steady diet of highly selected collections is not being encouraged to read so much as he is being trained to survey, to mine, and to collect shining nuggets of precious literature. The discrimination he is taught by reading a typical school anthology is greater than it need be, while the actual quantity and continuity of his reading is less than it should be. The use of such an anthology testifies to a lack of effort or imagination, or both, on the part of the educator, and the surrender of inspiration to convenience. Furthermore, the anthology shares with all other large, hardcover books in the desktop-and-locker disease which so often afflicts these less

44

portable and digestible texts when they are given to poor and mediocre students. Such books were obviously not made to give companionship to immature students; recognizing this, these students usually give them the minimal attention they appear to deserve.

In emphasizing the importance of softcover, easily portable texts, I wish to point out two of their greatest advantages. First, the traditional, limited sense of "text" should be expanded to include any appropriate paperbound book and periodical now being published. Certainly the attention given by educators to *what* a child reads has proved, by its exaggerated emphasis upon "quality," damaging in the extreme to *how much* he reads. Generations of students, nurtured solely on anthologized and authorized classics, have become the parents of children who, like their parents, lack the reading habit because the typical school program neither stimulates nor breeds a desire to read in the average student. In teaching all children, but most especially in teaching the environmentally disadvantaged child, attention should be refocused upon the *quantity* of supervised reading they can accomplish. This argument makes the strongest sort of case for materials which are from the world outside the school and classroom. The greatest possible use should be made of newspapers and magazines in every class in all curricula, and softcover books should be preferred to hardbound texts wherever choice is possible.

The second great advantage of softcover, easily portable texts lies in the invitation to possession and casual reading inherent in their very form. In many less fortunate children, the need to possess is unusually strong. Softbound books and magazines are an ideal means of satisfying this need, for the full possession of them involves more than mere ownership. The physical possession of books and magazines is the most likely method of encouraging a child to read, especially when reading materials closely resemble those with which he is at least vaguely familiar outside the classroom.

Speaking of portability and possession, one of the most remarkable facts to come to our attention during the history of *English in Every Classroom* at B.T.S. is the attrition of library books that we now identify in our records as the "walkaway factor." The Maxey School attempts to rehabilitate its wards within a minimum security program. Among many other implications, minimum security means that anybody who really wants out can find a way. One result of such a policy is that many of the boys make genuine progress toward personal responsibility in their brief period of incarceration. Another result of minimum security, however, is that a significant number of boys become "walkaways." Their motives are various, their plans nonexistent, their futures alike (almost all are returned to the school), but their companions on the road bear a certain resemblance to each other. Though a boy may leave everything else behind, including his friends, he takes along some or all of the paperbound books in his possession at the time. Which, says the librarian, is not the worst way to lose books.

If paperbacks are a bargain, newspapers are a wholesale delight. The most telling recommendation of the newspaper, repeated in many forms by English teachers who have taught from it at least three times a week for periods varying from three months to three years, is that it is *warmly welcomed* by the students who use it. Again and again teachers have said that the newspaper "gives me something to do all the time; I don't have to worry about how I'm going to hold their attention." As any teacher knows who has had to deal with reluctant readers (as which of us has not?), the first step is the most important in moving them toward literacy. Once they willingly take that initial step toward reading, their literacy will be as functional as the fingers that turn the pages.

Occasionally the overture toward reading is played in strident tones, as it was in an English class of eight boys at the Maxey School. The teacher had planned the class around the newspaper. The boys had written a paragraph summary of a lead story on the front page, begun a letter responding to a controversy in the "Letters to the Editor" column, and answered a series of questions about a number of brief articles in the sports pages. They had been subjected to the newspaper for almost an entire hour when the teacher told them that the class was over and

46

the time had come to pass in the newspaper. Their rising growl of protest had brought me quickly down the hall from the library. The sight and sound of eight sixteen- and seventeen-year-old "nonreaders" complaining loudly because their English class was over for the day was so unexpected that I stood in the doorway, confused and un- certain, until I saw the smile on the teacher's face. As he said afterward, he knew he should do something beside grin at me, but nothing else seemed to fit his feelings.

The newspaper is no more the answer to a teacher's prayer than any other inanimate teaching tool. But it is a superior tool when coupled with the animating force of the teacher's confident use, because it contains within its pages something to engage and reward the in- terest of every child. Like all novel devices, however, it must be protected from overexposure. The best pro- tection we have discovered is to alternate its use with the magazine. The average we have striven for in the English classes of the Maxey and Garnet-Patterson schools is to use newspapers three times a week, and magazines twice. This pattern can be varied, of course. Most important, however, is the recognition that any tool may have its cutting edge made dull through overuse.

A question often asked is, "Is it better to use a local newspaper or one with a nationwide circulation?" Since the purpose of using the newspaper in the classroom is to place before the student materials which are likely to *in- vite* him to literacy, a local paper is easily the better choice. *The New York Times,* for example, may be in every way superior to the local rag dominated by an edi- tor-publisher who may be a moral idiot and a grammar school dropout. Limited though he may be, he neverthe- less fills his paper with local news of every description. Because of this, the reluctant reader is very likely to find his product more attractive than any big-city journal, no matter how famous.

The choice between local papers is not so easy, im- plying as it does a selection likely to create ill will if the school system purchases any considerable number of pa- pers. In such cases, the use of more than one newspaper can be a boon, since two newspapers offer opportunities for comparative study of everything from style to accuracy. Practical arguments can be cited for using either the morning or the evening paper. The evening paper is useful because of the time it allows teachers to review it for teaching purposes. The morning paper is equally useful, for the fresher news it contains. Whether published in the morning or evening, however, the newspaper communicates a sense of vitality and immediate excitement equaled by no other public writing of our time. It is just that sense of excitement which has been so sadly missing from the texts of our public schools.

Because the magazine captures the reader's attention in a way quite different from the newspaper, it is an excellent complement to the paper's use in the classroom. Whereas the newspaper does very little to make itself visually attractive, hoping instead that the topicality of its contents will lure the reader, the magazine can afford to stress form and color because of its longer life and the more leisurely reading pace it invites. Magazines have proven extremely successful teaching devices at the Maxey and Garnet-Patterson schools. After much trial and some error, teachers at both schools have discovered which magazines are most welcome and most useful to their students. Though the list is reasonably exhaustive, it is not exclusive. Other magazines may work as well or better in other circumstances.

One more important matter before listing recommended periodicals—how many magazines and newspapers are enough? After a great deal of experimentation, we have discovered that one set of papers per day for each English teacher is a very workable arrangement. The size of the set should equal the number of students in the English teacher's largest class, plus one for the teacher. In a public school with 840 students, for example, all of whom are taking English every day in classes of thirty-five, with teachers handling four classes each, six full-time English teachers would be required. Each of these teachers would receive thirty-five papers each morning for her students plus one for herself, a total of 216 papers a day. These papers would be used by the English teacher three times a week in each of her four classes; they would be available to the members of her team for use at all other times. In practice this means that the papers are in use in

English classes for about half the teaching periods of the week and may be employed for an equal period of time in all other subjects combined.

Magazines can be ordered by a somewhat similar formula. For each magazine that the school decides to use, the number of copies should equal the number of students in the school's largest homeroom class. This arrangement has worked very well with the exception of a few children's magazines found to be extraordinarily helpful in teaching unusually slow readers. These are *The Golden Magazine, Jack and Jill* and *The Children's Digest.* In spite of the title of *Jack and Jill,* painfully reminiscent of the world of Dick and Jane, all three magazines are so successful with both teachers and children in the junior high school that we have had to double our purchase of each to satisfy demand.

*Highlights for Children* and *Humpty Dumpty* complete the list of publications we have used with younger children. These five magazines serve to introduce twenty-five additional periodicals which fall conveniently into eight categories. The two largest categories are car and scientific magazines, and sports magazines; together with the publications for younger children, they account for almost half the periodicals on our list. *Hot Rod* and *Motor Trend* represent a type which attracts some children to reading who might otherwise read nothing at all. I once sat in an English class for "terminal" students where a high school junior (who couldn't read, according to his teacher) was covertly reading a copy of *Hot Rod* spread on the seat beside him. How do I know he wasn't just looking at the pictures? Because we talked about it, he and I, when the class was over, and I'll swear that this boy who couldn't read had read that particular issue of *Hot Rod* and plenty of other car magazines as well.

Completing the car and science magazine list are *Popular Science, Popular Mechanics* and *Scientific American.* All appeal strongly to our "practical" children, with *Popular Mechanics* apparently most desired. Next to publications for the younger children and those of a mechanical and scientific nature, the largest single category is that of sports. *Field and Stream* and *Outdoor Life* are read, as is *Sports Illustrated,* by a respectable percentage of our students, but none of the three is as popular as *Sport*. The explanation seems clear enough. Both the outdoor magazines generally appeal to readers who know something about fields and streams and want to know more. As for *Sports Illustrated,* it deals, in part at least, with more familiar subjects, but its prose is often too sophisticated for inexperienced readers.

The six smaller categories in our periodicals list are picture, news, digest, teenage, home and prose magazines. The names are used for convenience of grouping; they are not complete descriptions, nor do they always describe discrete groups. *Life* is a good example. Clearly it is a picture magazine, most valuable for its photographs. But it also reports the news, and belongs partially to that section of the list as well. *Look* and *Ebony* complete the list of picture magazines we have used, while *Jet, Newsweek* and *Time* comprise the news magazines. In addition to *Children's Digest,* also listed in another category, *Negro Digest, Reader's Digest* and *Science Digest* form the group of monthly summaries, with the last named belonging equally in the company of car and science magazines.

*In, 'Teen* and *Seventeen* are the three teenage magazines we have used with good effect in various schools within the experimental program. As for publications aimed directly at the home market, *Good Housekeeping* and *HairDo* have attracted the greatest number of readers in the Ludington Reading Rooms, which have attempted to relate the program to various Detroit-area communities. Finally, in the omnibus "prose" category, *American History Illustrated* and the *Saturday Evening Post* have been most successful.

Magazine distribution throughout the school is the responsibility of the English chairman in the junior high school and of a selected teacher in the training school where no chairman has been appointed. Both employ approximately the same methods: Teachers are asked to reserve those magazines they know they will want to use on particular days in ensuing weeks. During the week before the reserved magazines are to be used, a list of magazines with unreserved days is circulated throughout the school. When magazines arrive at the school, they are held out of circulation for one or two days to allow all teachers to become familiar with their contents. At the end of that period, a final list of available magazines is circulated throughout the school.

The formula for minimal usage—at least twice a week in the English and social studies classroom, at least once a week in every other classroom—guarantees a considerable classroom reading of magazines within the program. But no formula can guarantee *meaningful* usage of materials, no matter how reasonable the formula and how attractive the materials. The success of magazines within the plan of *English in Every Classroom* is due entirely to the discovery by teachers in every classroom that magazines are good for learning and good for teaching. As with newspapers, magazines are in constant use because students will learn from them and teachers can teach from them. No higher recommendation is possible for any textbook.

Speaking of guarantees and recommendations, all recommendations for the adoption of paperbound materials as substitutes for conventional texts carry guarantees of failure, if such changes are not made within a program which also makes meaningful changes in the methods of teaching English. No child, no matter how disadvantaged, is so imperceptive that the mere substitution of one format for another will permanently raise his opinion of the essential processes of the classroom. Before very long even the slowest will recognize that he has been had again, and newspapers, magazines and paperbound books will come to symbolize for him the same irrelevance and frustration that he has always known in school.

### (D) The School Library

#### (1) A Philosophy of Use

The concept of the school library requires the same sort of basic reconsideration that this program advocates

51

for the teaching of reading and writing. Many observers have remarked the depressing lack of visual appeal and the even more disturbing absence of reading activity in public school libraries. Most depressing of all, however, are the schools so overcrowded that they have no room for a library. The following recommendations are aimed particularly at alleviating these three problems of space, visual appeal and reading activity:

Where change is most badly needed is in the ideas of economy which dictate the selection of books and methods of display. For what reason other than economy of space are books displayed with their spines out? The spine of a book, with its Dewey decimal notations, is no more attractive than any other spine with such markings would be. And yet we expect the partially literate child, who relates to very little through words, to relate to books through words printed on their spines. This is the same child, remember, who is *always* attracted to pictures, whether found in comic books or on the television screen. Why then do we not make the most of his tastes and predispositions, give up the false economy which shelves large numbers of unread books, and attract him to books through bright pictures on their covers? Let us replace the typically drab, unread books of our school libraries—libraries full of books with pictureless, unopened covers—with paperbound books that attract children (just as they attract adults) by the bright covers that commercial artists and advertising men have made inviting.

School librarians should take a useful lesson from operators of paperbound bookstores, who have learned to let their merchandise sell itself by arranging their stores so that customers are surrounded by colorful and highly descriptive paper covers. But what of the expense of purchasing paperbound books to begin with, and of maintaining a steady supply to replace the easily tattered, broken and lost paperback? What of the expense? Two questions must be asked in return: What is more expensive than the waste of human intellect implied in a library of unread books? And what sort of destruction is more admirable than that of the book tattered and finally broken beyond repair in the hands of eager readers? We have had too little such destruction; the time has come for our school libraries to invite it.

Perhaps nothing more clearly reveals the school librarian's antiquated and insular view of the world than the relatively small use made of paperbound books in school libraries. "Why don't you have more paperbacks in your library?" I have asked the question of several hundred librarians in many sections of this country. In general, where they have not pleaded simple poverty—a plea becoming more and more difficult to defend now that the Federal Government has discovered social action can be influenced through the schools—they have in effect pleaded simple ignorance. There are exceptions to this generalization, but they are still painfully few. Public school libraries are disaster areas, and librarians who do not display books attractively must share the blame with teachers who do not make reading pleasurable.

The simple ignorance of so many librarians is best illustrated by the widespread notions that paperbacks are too perishable and that visual appeal is relatively unimportant. Both ideas are dead and should be given the interment their ancient bones deserve. For three years now we have been using paperbacks and nothing but paperbacks at the Maxey School. For 280 boys our library has 2,200 titles and 7,500 volumes including titles in class-size sets available to all the teachers. No group of boys anywhere is more capable of destruction or more willing to destroy. Yet we have failed utterly in what appeared to be one of our simplest testing objectives: To determine the average life expectancy of a paperbound book when that book is circulated repeatedly among hands unaccustomed to giving or receiving gentleness. As far as we can tell, our books seem likely to last forever. Read heavily, handled incessantly, they are proving virtually indestructible—not, mind you, because they can't easily be ripped or destroyed, but because they have become something of value to the boys and are treated accordingly.

So much for the outmoded notion of financial disaster through the destruction of the books. But another bogeyman hides in the dust of unread library books—a kind of high-minded drawing back on the part of school libraries from the successful vending practices of commercial booksellers. How can school libraries refuse to use every means at their disposal to attract *their* clientele—the students? In this case, the means available are the expensive, graphic covers of the paperbound trade. Any magazine or paperback publisher will tell you how much good covers mean to his sales, and how happy he is to pay well for such covers. Do we dare refuse any advantage available to us in the battle to win children to the world of books? One of the clearest advantages is the cover of the paperbound book—an advantage proved effective in bookstores across the nation.

If reading activity follows visual appeal as effect follows cause, what about space problems of shelving books with their covers showing? The answer lies in the wall racks and free-standing spinners traditionally used to promote paperback sales in corner drugstores and other places where space is at a premium. The problem of library space has another interesting solution—the combination classroom and library advocated by this program. In order for the library to become an organic part of the English curriculum, it should be available as a classroom to all teachers and should be designated as the meeting place once each week for every English class. Where no better room is available, as is so often the case in the old and seriously overcrowded buildings where the disadvantaged child finds his education, a larger classroom can be easily adapted to the minimal space requirements of revolving wire racks for paperbound books.

An alternative to the formal school library or the classroom library has recently been made available by book distributors in some areas of the United States and, I am told, would be made available in many more if requested by school officials. This alternative can be used alone or, far better, as a complement to the school's own resources. I refer here to the mobile bookstore, a trailer purchased by the local book distributor at his own expense and stocked by him with titles suggested by a committee of teachers from local public and parochial schools. Yes, commercialism certainly does rear its thick wallet here, for the books are *sold* to students, with school and distributor sharing in the small profits. Mobile book-rooms will make neither school nor distributor wealthy, but they do represent an ideal example of identity of interest in the public and private sectors of our economy. Schools must train willing readers to justify their existence; book distributors (and publishers) must create readers in order to survive. One book purchased from a mobile bookstore by one reluctant reader represents a significant double accomplishment for education and industry alike. Educators simply cannot afford the luxury of ignoring the products and the knowledge of the commercial world. The very idea of an inviolate "school world" is worse than indefensible; it is damaging in the extreme to the very concept it seeks to perpetuate and protect.

Fundamental to the malaise from which conventional school libraries suffer is the universal assumption that students will use them because they are there. Were this assumption applied to other human activities, ranging from toilet-training to the use of tools, only catastrophe would result. Regarding the library as something less than an irresistible attraction to students is a useful first step in revitalizing it. Implicit in this approach is an objective review of its lending procedures. Instead of placing the responsibility for first (and, too often, last) acquaintance upon the student and/or the teacher, the responsibility should be put where it rightfully belongs—upon the books themselves. *Give* each child a paperbound book or two to begin his school year. Let him understand that he may have any other paperbound book in the library by the simple expedient of trading a book he has for a book he wants. Then *schedule* him twice each week for the opportunity of book borrowing, and if our experience at the Maxey and Garnet-Patterson schools has been any guide —stand back and enjoy the sight of children reading.

*(2) Selecting the Books*

Just what selection procedures create the best paperback library? The youngest boy at B.T.S. is twelve, the oldest eighteen; the average boy reads as well as a

55

fourth-grader, and most are in junior high before they come to the Maxey School. Almost all have lived materially disadvantaged lives; almost all have come from culturally impoverished worlds. At the age of twelve they know more about physical man—from sex of some kinds to violence of all kinds—than any child should and most adults ever will. At the age of eighteen they know less about the world outside the neighborhoods in which they have lived (all alike; moving often is easier than paying the rent) than middle-class children half their age. Everybody knows *about* them. But who *knows* them? And who knows what kind of books they might read?

Haunted by the specter of our own ignorance, we took refuge in a copy of the 1964 *Paperbound Books in Print*. We tore the title list into six equal sections, one section for each English teacher. In his section, each teacher placed a check beside each book he thought the boys would like to read, and two checks beside each book he thought the boys would like to read and he would like to teach. Then he exchanged sections with another teacher and, using crosses instead of checks, did the same with the second section he received. Next, each teacher found a section he hadn't yet read and no third reader had marked; this section he marked with small circles in the same way. Finally, each teacher took the last section in his possession, made a list of the books with three kinds of marks beside them, and a list of the ones that had at least one of those marks twice. When the last step had been performed, we had our library list. In addition, we had a list of books the teachers would like to have in class-size sets for teaching purposes.

Now for appeal to the final authority—the boys. First we had to arrange for the books to be obtained with the privilege of returning them. We knew that our list was intelligent, democratic, inclusive, unique. What we didn't know was whether it contained books the boys would read. If we spent the little money we had on books that would go unread, we might just as well have stocked our school library with all the hardbound books that nobody ever reads anyway and saved ourselves a good deal of trouble. Out of our need came the best experience we were to have at the Maxey School. We discovered the wise charity of Ivan Ludington Sr. and his Ludington News Company of Detroit.

The letter I wrote him was something less than a masterpiece. Only college presidents and skid-row bums are really good at begging. But the answer I got would have made a president proud and a bum delirious. Two days after I mailed the letter the phone in my office rang. Ivan Ludington speaking—what did I need and where did I need it? He would be glad to come to Ann Arbor to make arrangements. No, I would come to Detroit. Somehow that seemed to be the least I could do. It was. It was also the most I could do. Since then, Mr. Ludington has been supplying the school for almost three years with all the paperbound books and magazines we request—absolutely free of any charge. Thus far the numbers are upwards of 10,000 paperbacks and 25,000 magazines. Combine these figures with the equally remarkable generosity of that excellent paper, *The Detroit News* (one hundred copies a day, seven days a week), and the principle of saturation is vividly illustrated. But more about the Ludington story later.

Those of us who participated in selecting the original 1,200 titles for the Maxey paperback library will never again have to be reminded of how little we know about the students we teach. None of us will forget the untouched 700 titles that decorated our gleaming drugstore spinners while the boys read and reread the 500 they liked.

My private prediction for our list was that some 200 books might go unread, largely because they seemed to me to be either too difficult or too passive for a sixteen-year-old boy with a ninety I.Q. who reads at a fourth-grade level. But I had no doubt whatever that the remaining thousand were books the boys would read if we could display them attractively within an effective language program. I could hardly have been more mistaken. Not only was I one hundred percent wrong in my estimate of the number of successful books on our list, but seventy-five of the books I had thought would be ignored proved to be popular with the boys. The 500 winners of our book Derby are included in the Reading List (pp. 148-173).

The schools in which these books have been used, in

addition to Maxey and Garnet-Patterson, now include training schools and juvenile homes in states as various as Michigan, Massachusetts, California, Illinois and New York, and public and private schools in many very large cities and a few very small towns.

The 500 paperback titles that originally proved to be such effective inducements to reading for the boys at B.T.S. have been expanded to 1,000, as the somewhat differing demands of girls and public high school students have been taken into account. Each of the books has undergone the most rigorous testing to which we could expose it—continuous scrutiny by students who have full freedom of selection or rejection. Our highly eclectic list represents a winnowing of perhaps five times the number of titles it presently contains. It also represents books so attractive to young people that the average boy at B.T.S., who arrives with a reading rate of no books per lifetime, is reading one library book every two days by the time he leaves. And that *average* includes all the boys— those who still never read anything as well as those who devour a book a day. However, it does not include the large number of paperbound books used as texts, or the immense number of newspapers and magazines devoured by newly awakened appetites.

Speaking of newly awakened appetites, what do *you* do at a basketball game? Play or watch, you say? Well, that's only because you haven't recently discovered the world of paperbound books. Sam Sublett, director of the Boys Training School at St. Charles, Illinois, tells the following story:

After days of grapevine publicity, a shipment of paperback books, along with their spinner racks, arrived at St. Charles. By Friday morning they were ready for distribution and by Friday afternoon the boys had them out. Only one condition for their presentation to the school had been set by Charles Levy, president of the Charles Levy Circulation Company, who has followed in the Chicago area the lead of Ivan Ludington in Detroit. "I'll give you all the books and magazines you want and your boys can read," he said, "if you'll promise me to handle them as though they were expendable. Get them out of the rack pockets and into the kids' pockets as soon as you can, and, if you can, keep them there." By Friday afternoon, Mr. Sublett and his staff had kept the first part of their bargain.

Friday evening's game was not just another horserace, reports Mr. Sublett. The teams were evenly matched and hot. He and other staff members were held spellbound by a real contest. Midway through the second quarter, up on his feet and yelling, Sam suddenly had that lonely feeling. Only then—for the first time since the game began—did he look around him instead of in front of him. "How," he asks now, "do you tell anybody who wasn't there that *half* those kids were reading paperbound books while a red-hot ballgame was burning up the gym they were reading in?"

Some of those same boys were among the twelve who signed the waiting list for Joseph Kane's *Facts about the Presidents*. Of all books, why that one? And *twelve* boys? One of the staff said it: "Before, we couldn't get twelve volunteers to sign up for anything short of a breakout."

### (3) The Reading List: An Analysis

Warming up the cold list of a thousand paperbacks are the sparks of light and heat given off by rubbing children against books. On a Monday morning, just before the first class of the week, an English teacher is about to close the door to his room as a seventeen-year-old runs past to a classroom farther down the hall. The boy turns, pulls out of his shirt Dick Gregory's *From the Back of the Bus,* waves it at the teacher, and shouts, "I bought it, man, I bought it! Bought four more while I was home. Didn't steal none!" Bought or stolen, those five books were the first that boy had ever owned. Home for a weekend as part of the school's rehabilitation program, he had been able to think of no better use for his time and money than to spend both on paperback books from the corner drugstore. Even if he had stolen them, this would certainly have been the first time he had stolen *books*.

Or the Case of the Bonds Going Out of Stock. The boys wanted the James Bond books. What's more, they wanted them loudly and often. Our usual enthusiastic response to their desire to read books we didn't have was considerably tempered in this case by the covers of the Ian Fleming novels and by our limited knowledge of what went on between those covers. Most of us had seen *Goldfinger,* but few of us had read any of Bond's adventures. My own response had been to suspect the usual book–movie relationship, i.e., if Pussy Galore was a character in the *movie,* how much cleaning up had the producer done to make the author's work acceptable on the screen? That suspicion, plus the undressed covers, had kept the Bond books out of our library.

Like all other censors, self-appointed or otherwise, I was unequal to the job. When it occurred to me—as the howl for Bond grew—that I might at least read the books I was banning, I read them all as a kind of penance. I was embarrassed by their contents; I was embarrassed by the discovery, for instance, that *Goldfinger* is far sexier to see than to read. Henry Miller at the age of ten could have spotted Fleming-Bond two red lights and three double beds, and won the race in a crawl. We asked for a dozen copies of every Bond adventure that Ivan Ludington had in stock.

The books were delivered to the librarian one morning just as she was going into the hall to help a teacher separate a couple of featherweight battlers. Ten boys from the same class were in the library at the time. The bell for change of class had just rung, and the boys were at the door, preparing to leave, when the teacher with them told them to remain inside the library until the fight in the hall was under control. In the confusion that followed, the ten boys were left alone in the library. The librarian says she was gone long enough to walk fifteen feet from her door, see that the situation needed a man, and turn back to get the male teacher who had been in the library with his class. When she saw him coming, she returned immediately to the library. She could not have been gone more than three minutes. As she entered the library, the ten boys were leaving by the other door to go to their next class. She called to the last one to shut the door, and how he jumped when she called his name!

Not until half an hour later, when she began to catalogue the Bond books, did she realize why he had been so startled. In the brief time she had been out of the room, eighty of the 007 adventure stories had disappeared. A little arithmetic led her to the realization that each boy had taken one complete set of the eight titles she had received. Though impressed by such a feat of distribution, and pleased by so evident and massive a desire to read, she felt that the least she could do was to catalogue the books before they were stolen. When she entered their classroom, the boys were upset only because she had discovered the larceny so soon. Nobody had gotten to do any reading. Leaving questions of crime and punishment to philosophers and psychologists, the librarian promised the boys they could each borrow two of Fleming's books if they'd come in at the end of the day when she had the books catalogued. Her final comment was that she had made the promise because their disappointment was so real. They had taken the books because they wanted to read them.

Though our thousand paperbacks are far more interesting to read than to analyze, analysis does teach some valuable lessons to those responsible for stocking reading rooms and libraries like those at Garnet-Patterson, Maxey and Detroit's Northwestern High School.

Nearly two-fifths of our list is given over to action stories of four different, though closely related, kinds. Of that 40 percent, about 25 percent is divided evenly between science fiction and more earthly adventure. The remaining 15 percent is split between spy and detective stories, and war books of every description. Of these four categories, science fiction has had the most interesting history over a period of three years in the Maxey School and two years at Garnet-Patterson. Two years ago I reported in *Hooked on Books* that we had watched a self-selection procedure at work on the science fiction books:

Paperbacks of science fiction are generally the best-written books in the library [at Maxey]. S.F. got quite a play when our library first opened, with authors like Isaac Asimov, Ray Bradbury, Robert Heinlein, and André Norton, and editors such as J. W. Campbell and Groff Conklin having their stories and collections often read. But the best S.F. is a kind of intellectual ballet, and our boys dance the monkey, the jerk, and the frug. As Asimov, Bradbury, and Heinlein declined, Norton's star rose. Specializing as she does in simple action rather than complex imagination, Norton's adventures were read while far better writers languished. Today, S.F. is the least read of the major categories in our library.

Now, two years later, a very different report must be made. Of 125 titles describable as science fiction, approximately 100 are divided into two almost equal parts. One part is the work of eleven highly regarded practitioners of the craft, while the other part (approximately fifty titles) is produced by two indefatigable writers. The group of eleven ranges through such modern masters as Asimov, Bradbury, Heinlein, Sturgeon and Leinster to Pohl, Simak, Knight and Leiber, back to nineteenth-century romantics like Jules Verne and H. G. Wells. The two most prolific S.F. authors, whose output nearly equals that of the other eleven, are Edgar Rice Burroughs and André Norton.

Who that knew them will ever forget *Tarzan of the Apes* or *Beasts of Tarzan?* But who remembers that Tarzan's creator was as comfortable on Mars and Venus as he was in the jungles of Africa? It comes as something of a surprise to discover that Burroughs devoted as many of his fifty-odd books to other worlds as he did to this one. Together, he and Miss Norton provide almost half a hundred titles for readers of science fiction in the rough. Their books are no less read in 1967 than they were in 1965. Rather, the change has come in the increasing number of readers attracted to the more polished S.F. novels, such as Asimov's *Currents of Space,* Bradbury's *Martian Chronicles* and *Illustrated Man,* and Heinlein's *Green Hills of Earth.* Are the boys (and girls) learning the *pas de deux?* Not exactly. But they are learning to appreciate its performance.

Increased attention to more sophisticated science fiction writers by readers who formerly ignored them is evidence confirming other phenomena which have been recorded during the course of our experiment. For example, Mrs. Ruby Gillis, reading coordinator at Northwestern

High School, reported a marked increase in the use of the regular library after the school's reading room, a separate installation, had been open for six months. No accompanying decrease in the use of the reading room was observed. Mrs. Daisy Saffell, librarian at Garnet-Patterson, reported "a 100 percent increase" in the demand for conventionally bound books six months after paperbounds in great number had been installed in the library. And Mrs. Janet Saxe, librarian at Maxey, discovered that the shape of her collection and the reading habits of her students were undergoing similar changes:

Boys who had confined themselves to cartoon books were now adventuring into other and more demanding areas. Boys who had once been entirely satisfied with the vicarious violence of Mike Hammer and James Bond were now turning toward social action and self-improvement books. As a result of their developing interests, the Maxey book collection underwent radical alteration. First of all, it changed in breadth as explanatory texts like *How and Why Wonder Books,* which we had once been so sure would languish on the tables and shelves, led the way in the rise of *serious paperbounds,* a phrase heard from students in our experimental schools with increasing frequency. Mrs. Saxe says now that our next list of best-liked books, if expanded again by 500 titles, will include a remarkable proportion of books generally conceded to be of a "substantial" nature. She points out that such an expansion of scope grows directly from the clearly stated desires of many boys *who have learned to like to read.*

Accompanying the change in breadth in Maxey's library collection has been an increase in the number of books needed in various categories. Though the school's population has not expanded significantly in the past year, its demands for certain kinds of books have suddenly exceeded the library's capacity to satisfy them. In three loose categories—nature and animal books; history, biography and autobiography; poetry and music—the assortment of titles has remained more or less stable. But we have had to increase the number of copies of each title as the boys discover that adventure, like Cassius Clay, may be the greatest, but constant adventure, like continuous braggadocio, is more than either boy or boxing buff can bear.

Unforeseen problems can arise, however, when you decide to enlist the aid of Ray Bradbury in making reading attractive to your students. An English teacher in a large metropolitan high school decided to use *Fahrenheit 451* as a classroom text. She was influenced in making her decision, she says, by the two most important criteria: she had read it, and the bookroom had enough copies for her entire class. Furthermore, those copies would be available for her use when she finished her present teaching unit. With everything nicely arranged, she was considerably less happy than an English teacher should be when she discovered that the voracious reading habits she was working so hard to build had led most of her students to borrow and to read *Fahrenheit 451* when friends of theirs were using it in another class. It was a good book, they reported, but they sure didn't want to waste time reading it again when they could be reading something new.

One of the most interesting observations about our book collection was made originally by the first librarian at Maxey, confirmed by the second, and since reinforced by librarians and teachers at various schools: an inverse relationship exists between size and usage of our six largest categories of books. In descending order of size these categories are science fiction; adventure; spy and detective; war; self-improvement, exploratory and facts-of-life; and social action. Though small in number, the books in the last two categories bulk large in their attraction for boys and girls who not only want to know how it is, but want things—including themselves—to be a whole lot better than they are.

Sometimes, however, wanting a thing and getting it can be frustrated by the ancient problem of "face." Who can look tough with a book by Ann Landers sticking out of his hip pocket? One young man solved the problem to his own satisfaction by informing the librarian, as he borrowed *Ann Landers Talks to Teenagers About Sex,* that he was only bothering with it "because this here guy axed me to get it for him."

The same guy who axed him to get Ann Landers would also be likely to axe him to return for Ralph and

Shirley Benner's *Sex and the Teenager;* Maxine Davis' two books, *Sex and the Adolescent* and *Sexual Responsibility in Marriage;* or Evelyn Duvall's pair on *The Art of Dating* and *Facts of Life and Love for Teenagers.* If that weren't enough, and it wouldn't be, he would return (with a different story) for Winston Ehrmann's *Premarital Dating Behavior,* Havelock Ellis' *On Life and Sex,* Aron Krich's *Facts of Love and Marriage for Young People,* and Rhoda Lorand's *Love, Sex and the Teenager.* Being sensitive to our students' tastes, we have begun to get the impression that implications of sex in a title will guarantee the popularity of any book.

At Maxey, one of the funniest and most meaningful examples of this guarantee involved *The Scarlet Letter.* On a Friday morning, an English teacher watched one of his poorest readers choose Hawthorne's novel from the rack. Knowing how difficult the boy would find the book, and fearing that he would be discouraged by the experience, the teacher suggested that perhaps he had mistaken *The Scarlet Letter* for something else. "Ain't this the one about a whore?" asked the boy. "And don't that big 'A' stand for whore?" When the teacher had to admit that this description was more or less correct, the boy had heard enough. If it was a book about a whore, it was a book for him.

Three days later, on Monday, the same boy came to his English teacher with *The Scarlet Letter* in hand and two sheets of notebook paper. On those two sheets, front and back, were all the words—and their definitions—the boy hadn't known in the first eleven pages of the book. He had clearly spent the weekend with Hawthorne and the dictionary, and he was looking for praise—which he got, lavishly. His English teacher was amazed; the two sheets of notebook paper represented at least six hours of work. According to the teacher, this was a boy who may not have spent six hours reading since he was nine years old, and had no apparent idea of how to use a dictionary when he came to the Maxey School. Motivated by Hawthorne's whore, he fought his way through the entire book. He produced no more lists but he kept at the book (between other novels) for months; during that time, and long after, his conversations with his English teacher were full of his view of what was happening to Hester

Prynne. Proceeding as slowly as he did through the story of her life, she took on dimensions of reality for him which authors dream of imparting to their readers and teachers despair of conveying to their students. His valediction on Hawthorne's heroine may not have been couched in the author's own phrases, but it conveyed an understanding of the book that no one could improve upon: "That woman," he announced as he returned the book, "she weren't no whore."

One implication of this boy's experience is especially interesting. Hawthorne's vocabulary is difficult for *college* students. I have taught *The Scarlet Letter* to freshmen and sophomores at two universities where more than half the students come from the top 10 percent of their high school class. I have invariably followed the first reading assignment of the introductory chapter with a ten-minute written quiz asking for definitions of ten words chosen from the first three pages of that chapter. Each time, I caution the students to "read the introductory chapter *carefully*." Every student is allowed to use his textbook and any notes he may have prepared. Only the dictionary is forbidden. Full credit is given for the barest suggestion of knowledge, *e.g., bark:* some kind of boat; *truculency:* meanness; and even *prolix:* says a lot. But no matter how ominously I emphasized the word "carefully" in the assignment, and no matter how undemanding my standards of definition, no more than one-fifth of the students in any of the classes managed to define as many as five of the ten words.

My ringing, rhetorical, unfair question as I return the quizzes at the next meeting of those unfortunate classes is always, "How can you claim to have *read* anything when you don't even know what the words mean?" The question is unfair because I know perfectly well that they could read with great understanding without knowing what all the words mean. The quiz is merely one method of forcing a slower and more careful reading practice upon students convinced that fast reading is the best reading.

But what has this to do with a juvenile delinquent struggling through *The Scarlet Letter?* Just this: Semiliterate readers do not need semiliterate books. The simplistic language of much of the life-leeched literature inflicted upon the average schoolchild is not justifiable from any standpoint. Bright, average, dull—however one classifies the child—he is immeasurably better off with books that are too difficult for him than books that are too simple. But this generalization involves a whole theory of education. All I want to emphasize here is what teachers have observed at the Maxey, Garnet-Patterson and Northwestern schools and what I have experienced as a teacher of students of a considerably different type—"reading" is a peculiarly personal interaction between a reader and a book, an interaction differing in each case as widely as readers may differ from each other in breadth of experience and quality of mind. But *in no case* does this interaction demand an understanding of every word by the reader. In fact, the threshold of understanding—of meaningful interaction—is surprisingly low, and even in many complex books can be pleasurably crossed by many simple readers.

While it is true that nothing succeeds with our students like sex—whether scarlet or otherwise—the subcategories of explanatory and self-improvement books also attract considerable attention. We have books on drinking, smoking, driving, studying, reading, spelling and job-geting. We have other books on glamor and personality, popularity, dancing, doing your hair, choosing your clothes and surviving adolescence. There are books that tell you how to care for your parents, your children and yourself in a variety of circumstances including pregnancy, birth and military service. You get to choose the book that fits your needs. The librarian in one of our participating public schools promised herself to have a talk with one young man who took Jack Raymond's *Your Military Obligations and Opportunities* at the same time that he borrowed Alan Guttmacher's *Pregnancy and Birth*.

Though we were all believers in the power and importance of sex and self-interest before we began our research, we were surprised at the interest in self-improvement among the boys at Maxey and the students at many other schools. Who among us would have bet on Wilfred Funk and Norman Lewis' *30 Days to a More Powerful Vocabulary* or Ruth Gleeson and James Colvin's *Words Most Often Misspelled and Mispronounced* as best sellers in *any* school? Why should Adrian Paradis' *From High School to a Job* get almost as much action as certain lesser war, spy and detective novels? Actually, any mystery lies only in the eye of the beholder. Teachers, librarians and administrators who have participated in programs like *English in Every Classroom* have good reason to know that, given half a chance, the adolescent is more than likely to choose a balanced reading diet.

The smallest of the six major categories in our list of a thousand popular titles is the social action group. Containing approximately sixty titles, this section of our reading list is only half as large as the science fiction or adventure collections. Amazingly, however, as a group, it gets the most use; furthermore, it includes the most widely read single title—John Howard Griffin's *Black Like Me*. Although composed almost entirely of books by or about Negroes, the social action category attracts readers without regard to their color. We have looked for a difference, but none is observable so far. White and Negro children alike are attracted by the intense reality of books by Richard Wright, James Baldwin, Louis Lomax, Chester Himes, Dick Gregory, Warren Miller and Martin Luther King.

The foregoing seven authors have all contributed more than one book to our list. A fairly common reaction of students who suddenly discover the novels of Baldwin, for example, is to read them *all* and then to read *all* the books by the other six authors in this category. That's twenty-two books, and that's a lot of reading for anybody, especially illiterates. And the disease is communicable. An English teacher at Garnet-Patterson was collecting a class set of Booker T. Washington's *Up from Slavery* when she encountered one girl who wanted to know whether she couldn't just pay for the book, as though she had lost it, "because my mother wants to read it so bad."

With the single exception of the James Bond adventures, our most heavily used action books are the war stories, which comprise about eighty titles. Certainly the war in Vietnam has done nothing to depress the market, but the boys' interest in such stories seems to be deeper and more generalized than that generated by the history of any particular war. A boy who begins with Commander

Beach's *Run Silent, Run Deep* is likely to go on to Beach's *Submarine* and Frank Bonham's *War Beneath the Sea*. If he likes *War Beneath the Sea*, he may pause for Bonham's *Burma Rifles*. Such quasi-sequential reading is encouraged by grouping all books that might cater to the same taste on one display rack. Thus Patrick Reid's *Escape from Colditz* usually takes the interested reader to Eric Williams' excellent *The Tunnel Escape*, which in turn may lead to Paul Brickhill's *The Great Escape* and *Escape or Die*. In the same way, one book by Quentin Reynolds is likely to lead to another, as do the various war and combat books edited by Don Congdon.

The students who created this list of a thousand titles by the simplest and most direct procedure—reading the books—have demonstrated again and again that powerful ideas and swinging action can attract them even without the clothing of contemporary language. The language of some of the social action books is as awkward as a ghosted sports autobiography; the language of some of the adventure books, antiquated in its own time, is anachronistic in ours. But the readers plow on, making little distinction between such varied story tellers from other eras as Sax Rohmer, Jack London, Rudyard Kipling, Herman Melville, Mark Twain and James Fenimore Cooper, and an equally varied contemporary group including Charles Nordhoff and James Norman Hall, Ernest Gann, John Hersey, Patrick O'Connor, James Michener and Robert Ruark.

Not far behind the Bond adventures and the war stories in frequency of usage are the two categories of humor and suspense-and-horror. Though it is often difficult to be perfectly clear about categories (is Rod Serling's *Triple W*—Witches, Warlocks, and Werewolves—horrible, funny or horribly funny?), such questions do not seem to disturb our readers. The forty titles in our collection that apparently lend themselves to a suspense-and-horror classification are all popular. In the forefront of this group are modern editors such as Serling and Boris Karloff, joining Mary Shelley and Bram Stoker, authors respectively of the classics *Frankenstein* and *Dracula*. But even Serling, with the advantage of *Twilight Zone*'s great television popularity, is no more read than the long-time king of the crepuscular, Alfred Hitchcock. Maybe it's his titles that grab the kids—*Stories My Mother Never Told Me, More Stories My Mother Never Told Me, Hangman's Dozen, Noose Report*. Whatever the explanation, Hitchcock gets a lot of action.

Charles Addams is the perfect bridge between the two categories, humor and suspense-and-horror. Everybody has a favorite Addams title; mine is the wonderful double pun of *Addams and Evil*. Equally attractive to some of our readers are *Drawn and Quartered, Homebodies, Monster Rally* and *Nightcrawlers*. As with Serling, and Hitchcock to a lesser degree, Addams' currency is in part attributable to the teacher's friend, television. *The Addams Family* does send young readers (and perhaps older ones as well) back to the cartoons from which its characters are taken.

Cartoon books are an indispensable part of our library because they provide a temporary haven and refuge for students who doubt their ability to read. We have observed that many boys at Maxey, a community in which books have value and confer status, try to give themselves the protective coloration of being readers by picking up a cartoon book. More often than not, they're first hooked on the antics of Peanuts and Dennis the Menace and then hooked on the pleasures of reading. Is reading *Dennis the Menace* cartoons *really* reading? It is if you think it is. You may be looking mostly at pictures, but if Dennis and Charlie Brown can conspire to convince you that you're a reader *just like everyone else,* then you become a likely fish to swallow the bait of language when the line is attractively dangled. Experts may carp and the metaphor may flounder, but the child does neither. He reads.

Having canvassed the four action categories of science fiction, adventure, spy and detective, and war books; having examined the immensely popular self-improvement grouping and the social action books; having spoken of the successful groups of humor and suspense-and-horror books—let me strike a balance by identifying the weakest sections of our list. One of the most interesting bits of information we have gleaned from watching students and books come together in a number of different schools and situations is the relative unpopularity of fictional sports

70

stories and Westerns, which together comprise about eighty titles in our collection. Recalling my own adolescent habits, a staple of my reading diet was the shoeless boy from the mountains who just happened to be driving a baseball five hundred feet (a baseball served up by his daddy, who was a former minor-league pitcher) when a major league scout came looking for a jug of mountain dew. And I knew personally every fast gun in the West. But not our boys. They are far more interested in the stories of Mickey Mantle and Cassius Clay than they are in the accomplishments of the greatest imaginary hero, and their lack of interest in Westerns would turn Zane grey.

The one category of books which finds me acting purely as a reporter rather than as a participant contains more than sixty well-read titles. Since we didn't want to push our luck by promoting girls' books in a boys' school—though for a while we believed we could get them to read *anything* just by making it available within our program—we came to the Garnet-Patterson Junior High School in Washington and to the Northwestern High School in Detroit with a great hole in our reading list. Girls, teachers and librarians told us what was missing and proceeded to select the titles to fill the need.

Of the resulting sixty-odd titles that have survived the test with our girl readers, 80 percent were written by eleven authors. Not surprisingly, all are women. Eve Bennett, Sally Benson, Betty Cavanna, Hila Colman, Margaret Craig, Rosamond du Jardin, Anne Emery, Janet Lambert, Suzanne Roberts, Mary Stolz, Phillis Whitney—all have contributed more than one book to our list. Though the books tend to run to titles like *Diane's New Love, Julie Builds Her Castle, First Love, True Love* and *Just Jennifer,* titles guaranteed to make any self-respecting male delinquent feel queasy, they are certainly read by a great many young girls. Which is why they sweeten our list.

So much sweetness can use an antidote, such as Fred Horsley's *Hot Rod Handbook.* Horsley brings us to a type of book limited in number—barely a double dozen in our collection—but virtually unlimited in attraction. In B.T.S. language, it's the hogbook. "You know, man—the hog, the bomb, the sheen. Man, you *know*—you get your vines and your boats from outa your fox's crib and you ease into your hog to slide off and kick some grips. You're gonna jack up that man on account of he took your slat but he didn't bring you no pluck to get your head bad." Hogs, bombs, sheens—cars by any other name ride just as sweet. Vines are clothes, boats are shoes, your fox is your girl, and a crib is a pad—er, a house. "When I kick some grips or I pack you up, you better slide [go away quick], man, because I'm going to fight you." And for a mighty good reason. "You took my money [slat] but you didn't deliver the wine [pluck] to get me drunk [get my head bad]. So there's nothing left for me to do but break out my pack, blow pot, and listen to this here bad jam until I cop some Z's. Ain't this about a willie?" [. . . Open my package of marijuana cigarettes, smoke one, and listen to this good record until I fall asleep. But I tell you, I can't believe this is happening to *me!*]

Undisputed king of the sheens is Henry Gregor Felsen with his *Hot Rod, Street Rod, Crash Club* and *Road Rocket*. William Campbell Gault hits on all eight with *Drag Strip, Speedway Challenge* and *Thunder Road,* as does Philip Harkins in *The Day of the Drag Race* and *Argentine Road Race.* R. W. Campbell employs the magic formula, combining hogs and foxes in his *Drag Doll.* Evan Jones edits the popular *High Gear,* a collection of stories by authors like Steinbeck, Thurber, Mauldin and Saroyan who write about fast cars and their drivers. Robert Bowen and Carl Rathjen capitalize on the drawing power of their titles with *Hot Rod Angels* and *Wild Wheels.* Patrick O'Connor captures readers with his *Black Tiger at Indianapolis* and *Mexican Road Race.* Sterling Moss and Rodger Ward, two of the great racing drivers, collaborate with Ken Purdy and Brock Yates, respectively, on *All But My Life* and *Rodger Ward's Guide to Good Driving.* And speaking of Ken Purdy, "the man who knows more about the great cars than anyone else in America," his very good book called *The Kings of the Road* is presently out of print and therefore not on our list. But Purdy writes so well about the great cars that the names Dusenberg, Bugatti and Mercedes are as familiar to hog buffs as A-Bones, Beasts and Mother-Heads.

What, man! You don't know the difference between an iron that's been frenched, chopped and channeled, and a gasser that's been bull-nosed? It's all right, man, neither do I.

Hogbooks complete the dozen categories which consistently attract the greatest number of readers to our paperback library. A survey of all the books reveals that both their average and their mean retail price is fifty cents, with no book priced higher than ninety-five cents, our arbitrary cutoff point. Furthermore, only 3 percent cost more than seventy-five cents and only 12 per cent cost more than sixty cents. The customary school discount actually reduces the cost of the average book on our reading list to about forty cents, a price which represents the biggest educational bargain since the invention of the underpaid teacher.

# A GUIDE FOR TEACHERS OF SUBJECTS
## OTHER THAN ENGLISH

THIS PROGRAM FOR TEACHING READING AND WRITING depends partially upon you, the instructor whose professional responsibility lies outside the area customarily defined as "English." Making an English program in any degree dependent upon teachers of other subjects may at first seem unusual and unlikely to succeed. After all, what do *you* know about teaching English? But a second look demonstrates that while the program is unusual in its dependence upon teachers of other subjects, it is likely to succeed for at least two very good reasons: all teachers care enough about their own students and about their own subjects to recognize the potential benefits to both of willingness and competence in English throughout the student body.

We are all familiar with the complaint that teaching partially literate children *anything* is doubly difficult because they can neither sufficiently understand oral directions nor adequately interpret written instructions. Though the complaint is often heard, it has never been directly answered. Instead, it has been referred again and again to the English teacher, the one person who has the least chance of finding the answer precisely because he *is* the English teacher, instructor in the one subject in which the partially literate child has always experienced his worst failures. Given full support by his colleagues, the English teacher may be able to help the nonliterate child. Working by himself, he has amply demonstrated that he cannot do enough. The purpose of this plan, therefore, is to help the non-English teacher to help the student. In so doing, every teacher will be helping each child to become a better student in the teacher's own subject area.

The basic assumption upon which this program is built is the nonliterate child's desperate need for language competence. The child who cannot understand oral and written directions becomes the adult who cannot hold any job above the level of the simplest manual labor or household drudgery; in a technocracy characterized by decreasing individual labor, such jobs become more and more difficult to find. Furthermore, and equally important, since partially literate children cannot depend upon a language they cannot use, they must depend upon other means of expression—force, for example—which they are sure they can use. Perhaps if we can give them language, they will give up some of the wordless violence which they use as a megaphone to communicate with a world which they cannot reach in any other way.

Too much emphasis cannot be placed upon the claim that making all instructors in the school teachers of English will be profitable to all subjects in the curriculum. What subject, after all, does not depend upon language for teaching and for learning? In what subject would both teacher and student not be greatly helped if they could understand each other's conversation and if the student could be relied upon to comprehend written directions? The answer of course is that no subject is independent of language; the obvious conclusion, therefore, is that all subjects should teach what all depend upon for their existence.

The role of the teacher in subject areas other than English is clear, for the minimal demands of the program are remarkably simple; by contrast, its maximal possibilities are unknown and lie entirely in the individual teacher's hands. This approach to teaching and learning is hampered by no absolute precedents, no irrevocable traditions and no unchallengeable methods. The flexible methods it advocates are easily encompassed in the following summary:

## (A) Reading

### (1) Use of Popular Magazines and Newspapers

Part of the program to create a new learning environment for partially literate children is the use of familiar reading materials imported from the nonschool world in which learning—especially language learning—was never forced upon them. Since popular magazines and newspapers are not part of the school world that such children often view it with hostility, these materials greatly recommended themselves for use in this approach.

In addition to the appeal of novelty which periodical texts possess, they have another and more important justification: they are easy to handle and easy to read. Each teacher should plan part of his teaching program around newspapers and magazines; they contain matter relevant to every course in the curriculum.

### (2) Use of Paperbound Books

Part of the effort of English teachers to make reading more enjoyable for their students should be very extensive use of paperbound books in their teaching procedures. Since other courses may not primarily be reading courses, other teachers cannot be expected to use these books in the same manner. Instead, the program asks that all other teachers carefully research the materials in their disciplines in the effort to discover and use any paperbound books and magazines having special application to their subject area. Paperback books should be available throughout the school.

The library created as a result of and as an aid to this

program is modeled upon a paperbound bookstore. It is designed to make a wide selection of easily handled, attractively covered books available to the student on a barter basis. If these are books that the students read with pleasure, then they become a vehicle to promote learning with an ease seldom found through the use of other texts. Recognizing this, teachers in subject areas other than English should thoroughly explore possibilities of using the library and of suggesting additions to its collection which will benefit their own teaching.

## (3) Use of Written Directions

The third aspect of this reading program in classrooms other than English urges careful use of written directives. People very often learn to read when they have to. Or to put it another way, when reading seems necessary to survival, then it becomes a process to master rather than an intrusion to resist. Few students ever really cared whether Jack went up the hill or Jill fell down, but all of them want to accomplish something someone will praise, even if that someone is a teacher. If the road to accomplishment is paved with written directions, that road should be made neither too long nor too difficult, so that a student may find pleasure in traveling it.

## (B) Writing

### (1) Scheduled Writing in the Classroom

Just as no one ever learned to read except by reading, certainly no one ever learned to write except by writing. Making the act of writing a normal, inescapable part of the child's school environment is one of the chief aims of this plan. One thing we are certain of: the average public school student has always identified writing as part of "English" and therefore easily avoidable because the English class was the only one in which writing played any noticeable role. Changing this attitude is crucial to increasing the child's ability to write.

Making the act of writing a standard part of every classroom assumes that each teacher will follow a uniform plan. In this case, the plan requires that every teacher in every humanities and sciences classroom collect five *in-class* writing assignments from each student every two weeks. This plan neither prescribes nor is vitally concerned with the length or content of these papers. It assumes that the repetitive act of writing is the only essential element, and prefers to count papers rather than words. It also realizes, however, that the process of making writing an unavoidable part of classes in which writing has been unimportant before may at first be difficult for teachers newly involved. Therefore, the plan is based upon small groups of instructors centered about an English teacher whose responsibility will be to make the new program as easy as possible for the teachers in his group and as profitable as possible for the students.

In addition to acting as a consultant to his colleagues, the English teacher will also handle one of the five sets of papers received biweekly by each teacher in his group. The remaining sets of papers should be handled by the subject instructor himself. Two should be read for content; the other two should be filed *unread* in the student's folder. This latter procedure, unusual in any system of education, is based upon the analogy of exercise: just as the music teacher does not listen to all the exercises practiced by the music student, so should the writing teacher not read all the exercises of his students. This method allows the student to get the practice he needs without overburdening the teacher.

*(2) Unscheduled Writing in the Classroom*

Writing practice of this sort should be a natural outgrowth of learning procedures within the classroom and a natural complement to planned written exercises. Implementation will require improvisation on the part of the teacher. When a student requires a new tool, or asks a complex question, the teacher's reaction should be to ask for the request or the question in writing, just as the child's superior may do in the world of daily employment outside of and beyond public school.

For teachers of industrial arts, home economics, music, and art, student writing is very much less a natural part of the teaching method than it is in some of the other subjects in the curriculum. This new program in English will find a different place in each of their classes. To begin with, it merely asks tolerant support of an effort that touches each of us as teachers—an effort to bring language competence to children who need it as badly as they need good food and steady affection.

This teacher's guide for instructors in subjects other than English would be incomplete without at least one example of how the program of *English in Every Classroom* has been adopted and modified by the needs and capabilities of an independent system. By "independent system" I mean a school or group of schools committed neither to the whole program nor committed as a whole to any part of the program. This description fits Detroit's Northwestern High School, which has made full use of the reading room concept (as it is described in the chapter entitled "The Ludington Story"), and of an interesting adaptation of the classroom program.

In September, 1966, Northwestern inaugurated a limited curriculum change known as the "Integrated Curriculum in English and Biology." Reasons for that change are quoted here from a descriptive paper written by Mrs. Ruby Gillis, the school's reading coordinator:

At Northwestern High School there are several basic problems we must face with our incoming 10B students:

(1) Many of them read far below grade level. Of the 750 in-coming 10B students, 397 were reading two or more years below grade level.
(2) Failure rate in general biology is extremely high. Part of this is attributable to reading levels.

(3) Students lack a sense of identity within the school. They feel lost in an institution of 2,500 students. Time for orientation is limited, making it difficult to reach students individually.

(4) Many of our discipline problems occur with 10B students.

(5) Generally their basic reading skills are very poor. Reading, writing, and study habits are especially bad. There is not enough time to work with these students in the current forty-minute period to help them overcome their disabilities in time to make a success of their high school career.

(6) Most of these students will not stay after school hours for enrichment courses or special remedial help.

These six clear reasons for undertaking a new type of teaching relationship led to the enunciation of six equally clear purposes for the teachers and students involved:

(1) To integrate the reading and writing activities in the English and science classes

(2) To provide the slow student with motivation for writing and reading

(3) To provide the student with varied and appropriate materials

(4) To provide an additional class period to give the students specific help in reading skills under the guidance of a person trained in the teaching of reading

(5) To give the student a sense of identity through the block time approach

(6) To provide an opportunity for a team of teachers to work closely with a class group.

According to Mrs. Gillis' description, the integrated curriculum is organized on a "tri-class" basis with 10B students who average a fifth-grade reading level. "These students are programmed into three classes: English, reading and biology. They meet five days a week for English and biology" and on four of those days they meet in a reading class which intervenes between the two subjects. "The reading class centers on subject material (largely science) and basic reading skills. All teachers involved work together to plan the curriculum. . . . The Reading Coordinator is responsible for coordinating the material as well as [guiding] the English and science teachers in reading techniques."

In her description of the project, Mrs. Gillis observes that "the program in its initial stages has been highly successful. We have been able to get a variety of paperback materials in science. Through our paperback reading room program each student has been supplied with a dictionary. The *Detroit News* gives us newspapers twice weekly." She continues by saying that the "team approach is excellent" and "teacher enthusiasm is high." Noting that each instructor seems to feel an unusual sense of responsibility for these students beyond the confines of the teacher's classroom, she feels that more time than a weekly planning session may be required to direct the program.

Finally, and perhaps most important, Mrs. Gillis observes that this daily, three-hour group experience promotes a sense of unity and identity within the class groups. "Attendance and punctuality [are] better than average. [This is] very noticeable in the Reading Class which students think of as a *Science Reading Lab*. This takes away any stigma of remedial reading."

# THE ENGLISH CLASSROOM

IMAGINE THE SCENE: ELEVEN DELINQUENT BOYS SITTING in an English classroom, each reading intensely in his own copy of the same paperbound book. *Goldfinger? Black Like Me? West Side Story?* What else could generate such attention from a group like that? A dictionary.

Breast, whore, lesbian, prostitute, vagina, copulation, intercourse, etc., etc., etc.—the boys find them all. The dictionary is any fifty-cent paperbound lexicon. After a few days of use it opens automatically to a page with one of the "good" words on it. A boy raises his head to ask of nobody, "How you spell that U-word?"

"What word?"

"You know, man. That good word."

"You mean U-terrace?"

"Yeah. What's a U-terrace?"

" 'At's where you makes a U-turn."

"Oh man you *so* dumb!"

Whatever its original attraction, the dictionary has rivaled the success of the journal in the English program at Maxey and has been transplanted with equal vigor into the public schools participating in this program. The unavoidable conclusion is that children *like* dictionaries when dictionaries are part of a program designed to make language pleasurable as well as useful.

When a student first enters either the public or penal school, he is given, among other things, a paperbound dictionary. He is told that the dictionary is his, that it won't be collected or replaced by the school, and that he can carry it with him or he can leave it at home or in his room or anywhere else he chooses. If he chooses to carry his dictionary with him, he will be able to use it in class —any class. If he does not have his own dictionary available, he will find a set of paperbound dictionaries in every one of his classrooms. These sets range in number from class size in English and social studies classes to smaller numbers in classrooms where the dictionary is less crucial to the subject. They are, according to the teachers, in constant *voluntary* use.

Our expectation at the training school had been that the dictionaries, if successful, would be transported constantly back and forth between the school and the boys' rooms. As a result, paperbound dictionaries were ordered for each student's personal use, but only one or two desk dictionaries were ordered for each classroom. Our mistake was quickly apparent: The boys wanted to use their dictionaries but they also wanted to keep them as part of their permanent possessions, safe in their own rooms. Experimentally and tentatively, we obtained paperbound dictionaries in class-size sets for each English teacher. Almost immediately we began to hear from teachers of other subjects. Why were they left out? The dictionary was as useful to them as it was to the English teacher. How about sets for their rooms? Happily, we purchased more books; now, all over the school, dictionaries are in use. Teachers of all subjects have discovered that an interest in words often becomes an interest in the ideas the words convey.

With the experience at Maxey as our pattern, we ordered individual books for every child and class-size sets for every classroom in the public school. The dictionaries were an immediate and resounding success. In one of her periodic progress reports, Mrs. Sylvia Jones, chairman of the English Department, told the story of the boy who used the word "damn" in class. "That'll be enough of that swearing," said his teacher.

"Enough of *what?*" asked the boy.

Refusing to be baited, the teacher turned her attention elsewhere, but not before she caught a peculiar expression on the boy's face followed by activity at his seat. She had all but forgotten about him when his excited voice broke through the classroom conversation: "Swearing—that's cussing! The dictionary says so!" He hadn't understood the teacher, but he had possessed the means to arrive at understanding. No learning experience can be better than that.

Though the dictionary appears to be equally successful at both schools, the pattern of its usage differs in one important respect—mobility. Where the protective sense of possession inhibits movement of the dictionary from bedroom to classroom at the Maxey School, the sense of pride in possession seems to have the opposite effect in public school. Many of the children are proud of their very own dictionary; as a result, they carry and use it with a pleasure usually reserved for objects more familiar than word books.

"The English Classroom" is the title of this chapter in the book because one of the primary concerns of the program called *English in Every Classroom* is to place the teaching of English in a context within which it can succeed. The reason for this preoccupation is the conviction that English is unique in its dependence upon other subjects for depth and reinforcement. An English class which does not draw some of its materials from other subjects, and which cannot make its influence felt in those subjects, might just as well be a class in Latin as in English. Given the proper surroundings—seeing a reflection of itself in all courses, even as it reflects them—the English class can be the meaningful focus of the student's education. Placed in a context where reading and writing are as necessary and inevitable as nourishment and sleep, the student, the course and the instructor will thrive together.

Of first importance must be an appropriate definition of the general purpose of the English class. This purpose must not be defined in the usual impersonal and exalted professional terms; it must not be defined in the customary platitudes about improving the moral nature and verbal performance of the child through exposing him to the good and the great in literature. Instead, it must be expressed against the restrictive reality of the child's previous experience. Surely the *ultimate* goal of the English teacher must be to make humanists who are competent readers and writers; furthermore, this training must include competence in grammar and spelling. But, just as surely, the English classroom should be the place in which a learning experience of far greater importance than instruction in the mechanics of language takes place. To the means of effecting that end, the following recommendations are made for the philosophy and conduct of the English class:

(a) *That the approach to literature be social rather than literary.*

This recommendation is based upon a pedagogical philosophy which finds "He give me the Buk" a more desirable statement than "He gave me the book," if the former reflects a pleasure in its utterance which the latter does not. Best of all, of course, would be the coupling of the real accuracy of the one with the imagined enthusiasm of the other. But there can be little question as to precedence: pleasure and enthusiasm must be the first (and at times the only) goal of the English teacher. Literature chosen for the English class should be selected by the prime criteria of immediate interest and particular relevance to the students' situation. The important question to be asked is "What *will* they read?" and not "What *should* they read?" If teachers of English view themselves first as purveyors of pleasure rather than as instructors in skill, they may find that skill will also flourish where pleasure has been cultivated.

One of the best examples of this attitude and its results is Gerald Weinstein's English lesson based upon a very small poem called "Motto" by Langston Hughes. Mr. Weinstein was at that time (1963) Curriculum Coordinator for the Madison Area Project in Syracuse, N.Y. A teacher complained to him that her class "practically fell asleep" when she read "The Magic Carpet," a poem from a traditional school anthology. As an answer to the teacher's implied question—"How can you teach poetry to these kids?"—Weinstein reproduced copies of Hughes' poem and distributed them to the class. Here is the poem and a part of the class reaction, as it was quoted in the National Council of Teachers of English publication, *Language Programs for the Disadvantaged* (edited by Corbin and Crosby, 1965):

I play it cool and dig all jive.
That's the reason I stay alive.
My motto, as I live and learn,
Is: Dig and Be Dug in Return.

After the students read the poem, there was a long moment of silence. Then came the exclamations.

"Hey, this is tough."

"Hey, Mr. Weinstein, this cat is pretty cool."

"It's written in our talk."

But when asked the meaning of "playing it cool," the students had difficulty verbalizing the idea.

A boy volunteered to act it out.

Weinstein took the part of a teacher and the boy pretended he was walking down the hallway.

"Hey, you," said the teacher, "you're on the wrong side of the hall. Get over where you belong."

Without looking up, the boy very calmly and slowly walked to the other side and continued without any indication of what was going on in his mind.

That was "playing it cool."

When Weinstein asked a boy to show what he would do when not playing it cool, a verbal battle ensued.

The class began offering definitions for "playing it cool": calm and collected, no strain.

Weinstein suggested another: *nonchalant*. A new word. Next came a discussion of the phrase "dig all jive."

One student told how he once got into trouble because he didn't "dig the jive" of a group of street-corner toughs.

So the message of Hughes' poem, the class discovered, was that he "stayed alive" because he "dug all jive"—understood all kinds of talk.

Hughes' motto was to "dig and be dug in return"—understand and be understood.

The students were amazed at their own analysis.

Weinstein asked the students how many kinds of jive they understood.

Why all kinds, of course.

The Madison Area Project official launched into an abstract essay on the nature of truth, using all the big words he could find.

The students looked blank.

He then asked them to test his understanding of their jive.

They threw the colloquialisms at him and he got five out of six.

The class was impressed.

"According to Hughes, who has the better chance of staying alive," Weinstein asked, "you or I?"

"You," they said, "because you dig more than one kind of jive."

"The jive you have mastered is a beautiful one," Weinstein said. "But you have to dig the school jive, too, the jive that will occur in other situations. That's what school is for, to help you dig all jive and stay alive."

Which brings to mind the story told me by a young woman about her first year as an English teacher in a difficult inner-city high school. One afternoon a group of boys came to her with incontrovertible evidence that she had made it as a teacher. They had been looking at her car in the teachers' parking lot for months now, and they were sorry for how she must feel because hers was the only hog in the pen that didn't have whitewalls. So they had copped four of them—one at a time, here and there —and now her car looked as tough as anybody's.

Because she understood all their language, she knew what they were telling her. Because she dug their jive, she knew what kind of compliment she had been paid. As for what she did about the tires, I leave that to the imagination of the reader.

One result of teaching English from a social rather than a literary point of view is that the English class will combine language training and social studies. This view of teaching literature makes the English–social studies "core" curriculum one of the most reasonable of modern educational structures. It is based upon the realization that all effective literature is related to life in the same way that a portrait is related to its subject. If the living model is caught and accurately interpreted at a vital moment, whether in painting or literature, it will be accepted because of its informing relationship to life. Such a reaction is the pleasurable first step that leads toward further study and understanding. Thus, reading materials selected for their actual and potential relevance to the student's own experience are likely to be doubly valuable: first for the absorbing interest in self which they exploit, an interest bound to promote a greater desire to read; and then for an understanding and acceptance of the social norm, an attitude which is any school's chief business to promote.

Speaking of portraits and their relationship to life, the same teacher who had her hog improved with whitewall tires tells another revealing story:

> I remember trying to explain some insipid romantic intricacy in a sophomore text by drawing stick figures on the board to represent the characters. "This is Frank, this is Susan," I explained. Drawing a line to represent the barrier between them, I asked what problem or conflict kept Frank from his girl. "Well, ma'am," piped up an unchallenged wit in the back row, "that cat's biggest problem is he ain't got no arms."

She also reports that a similar incident confirmed her suspicion that our students often consider *us* "culturally deprived." "Talking one day of Robert Frost," she says, "I hoped to inspire my young writers with a striking photograph, in color, of the old poet's face. "Does that look like your grandfather?" I hopefully asked one of the less inspired boys in the class. 'No, ma'am,' he replied, 'my grandpa's black.' "

A further implication of a combined English–social studies class is reliance upon a daily newspaper as one of the chief texts of the course. The newspaper is in many ways an ideal text for the English class; its format, style and content all qualify it as an excellent vehicle for teaching reading and writing with special attention to the social point of view. The sense of informality and immediacy which the very presence of the newspaper conveys, a sense so useful yet so difficult to achieve in many other kinds of literature, is also communicated in many magazines and softbound, pocket-size books. Each of these three types of literature provides readily available materials designed to engage the interest of the most reluctant reader; each therefore commends itself for considerable and continuing use in the English class.

After a good deal of trial and considerable error, the

English teachers at both the Maxey and Garnet-Patterson schools have derived formulas for the use of newspapers and magazines which appear to satisfy the needs of teachers and pupils at both institutions. With the customary hyperbole of the theoretician, for whom the problems of distribution and collection never existed, I asked myself why the newspaper could not be used every day in every English classroom. Finding no answer that discouraged the idea, I stipulated such usage as part of the original Maxey plan. It worked. When that plan was adapted to the needs of the public school, the formula of daily usage for the newspaper remained unchanged. It didn't work, and the teachers soon told me why.

At the training school, no class has yet had more than twelve boys in it. Although one B.T.S. boy may be a teaching burden equivalent to four public school children, he possesses only one pair of hands (however quick) and he sits at only one desk (however disarrayed). Getting a dozen newspapers out and back is not usually very much of a task even for the inefficient classroom manager. But when that number of hands and desks is multiplied by three and more, the job of distribution becomes formidable. This is especially true when the newspaper proves to be particularly attractive to the less able student, who gives it up as slowly as possible because he seldom has time to read as much of it as he would like to.

A considerable number of teachers in the junior high school found that managing the newspaper in the classrooms was becoming unusually difficult. One result was the increase beyond reasonable proportions of the time spent on newspaper study in the classroom. Allowing the children to continue their reading was easier than battling them for the return of the newspaper, especially when so many of them were reading enthusiastically (or even just reading) for the first time. The answer to the problem was a change in the basic formula for use of both newspapers and magazines. Instead of employing the newspaper on a daily basis, and the magazine twice weekly, the two types of periodicals are now alternated, so that newspapers are used three days a week and magazines two days. To decrease distribution problems still further, in most classes the two are seldom used on the same day.

(b) *That the English teacher be encouraged to select and to create his own reading materials within the limits of type and format prescribed by this program.*

One of the most common and most serious flaws in programs for poor readers is the relationship between the teacher and the material he uses to engage his students in the reading process. If the instructor does not take pleasure in the texts he uses, what then is the likelihood of pleasurable response from the pupil? The answer is not only obvious in the abstract, but all too obvious as well in schools I have visited, where texts were apparently chosen with neither the individual teacher nor the poor reader in mind. With these observations as a guide, I have refrained from prescribing specific classroom materials and have limited my specific suggestions to matters of type, format and style. I do not believe that desirable results will be obtained unless English teachers are offered a freedom of selection which allows them to consider both the students' needs and their own inclinations.

This recommendation also speaks of "creation" by the English teacher of his own reading materials. Stories, plays and essays written by the teacher who knows what his students' vocabularies really are, rather than what they should be; who knows particular facts rather than patent generalizations about their background, environment and aspirations; who knows, in short, his students as individuals rather than types—such reading materials can be of unequaled value in involving students in the process of reading and writing. In response to the objection that few people, even teachers of writing, are effective creative writers, the answer must be made that anyone who can tell a child a bedtime story, or recount a narrative he has read in a newspaper, book or magazine, can create stories, plays and essays appropriate as teaching devices. Any teacher who has not written such materials before is likely to be very pleasantly surprised at the ease with which he can create them and the readiness with which they are accepted by his students. In cases where teachers feel unequal to the demands of such a task, they may find their initial feelings of inadequacy dispelled by undertaking a writing project in cooperation with another instructor.

(c) *That the teaching of language skills be accomplished through organic rather than mechanic or descriptive means.*

This recommendation is meant to alter a great variety of common practices in the English classroom, ranging from spelling lists to workbooks of all kinds and schemes for analyzing sentence structures. What is wrong with one is wrong with all: they represent language *being* rather than *doing*. In that sense they are mechanic rather than organic, and they are self-defeating. They are always inefficient to some significant degree, but their inefficiency increases as the academic orientation of their student users decreases. This conclusion becomes inevitable when one considers the "practicality" of the mind either unaccustomed or unable to abstract and transfer information. For such a mind, real pleasure may be found in working up lists of properly spelled words. But unlike the pleasure of recognition in reading, which is likely to promote further reading and understanding, the pleasure which a student takes in a well-executed word list does not necessarily mean that he can spell those same words correctly in sentences or even use them comfortably in written discourse. The student who can spell words in lists, but who can neither use them nor spell them correctly in sentences, is a familiar phenomenon in all classrooms. If a list is used at all it should be a list of sentences—a list of words *doing* rather than merely *being,* whose "carryover" is guaranteed if only in a single instance for each word. Such a list would be an example of the organic method of teaching language skills which this program advocates.

A consistent employment of this philosophy would bring the workbook under serious scrutiny. To begin with, there is the question of whether most workbooks are in fact cumulative. Do succeeding lessons really depend upon and build upon those which precede them? Or are the skills which the workbooks teach as fragmented as the workbooks themselves? These are unproved accusations, however, reflecting suspicion rather than hard evidence. What is *not* mere suspicion is the generic flaw of the workbook: it is viewed by teacher and pupil alike as a world unto itself, a repository of exercises which develop skills useful only for filling workbooks. Little evidence can be found to support the argument that the workbook participates in any meaningful relationship with the world in which language performs tasks more demanding than its own arrangement. Generations of students have exercised upon them and come away in the flabbiest sort of verbal condition. Therefore this program recommends that the English curriculum replace the workbook with exercises devised by the classroom teacher, exercises which are free of the book-grouping that suggests they have a life of their own.

Schemes for analyzing sentence structures are subject to many of the same criticisms which question the usefulness of the workbook. Most damaging perhaps is the simple question of their relevance. What do they tend to generate? Do they create understanding, or do they in fact merely re-create themselves? Does exercise of the schematic intelligence produce verbal understanding? We have all had students who take great pleasure in their ability to diagram a sentence, just as others enjoy making lists of spelling words. But even as a list of words in sentences breaks down one more mechanical barrier between learning and meaning, so does a sentence analyzed in sentences add organic dimension to a previously mechanical diagram. The making of a sentence diagram is evidence of little more than the student's ability to learn and the teacher's ability to teach the practice of diagraming sentences. The writing of even a one-sentence analysis is altogether more convincing evidence of the student's understanding of sentence structure.

A further illustration of the difference between organic and mechanic philosophies of teaching in the English classroom is the interesting example of the class-written story or play. In the usual curriculum these exercises are remarkable by their absence. Stories and plays are of course employed with great frequency; but since they are the creations of others, they are far more likely to inspire the reluctant reader and writer to an interest in content rather than in form. That this interest in content is desirable, especially in an English class which emphasizes social studies, is undeniable; but that it need be at the expense of an interest in form is not so clear. If the student has a "practical" rather than an abstract mind, give him the first-hand experience he needs in order to learn. Occasionally let the words be his own. Let him witness words *doing* as he uses them to create a story or a play. Let him have the always pleasing experience of creating an art form, whether artful or not. Any reservations on the instructor's part as to the capacity of his students for such a performance are likely to disappear in the face of their enthusiasm. The group nature of the undertaking is usually effective in quieting individual fears, so much so that students who would ordinarily never consider creative expression on their own are sometimes influenced to try a piece of writing themselves. And, most important, many members of the group discover what a sentence *is* by making one, and thus discovering what it *does*.

Because most that is worth remembering in this book is a reflection of the experience and practice of good teachers in classrooms across the country, it seems appropriate to end this chapter on the English classroom with the words of such a teacher. Donna Schwab was a member of the Northwestern High School English faculty when she wrote the following paragraphs:

The classical school texts are a waste of time for a student who is crying out for information about his world, about himself as part of a race, part of a generation of men and women. The students who took part in the "freedom school" during a recent high school boycott in Detroit expressed a desire to know about laws affecting their rights as citizens, about their own history as a race in America, about their own minds' and bodies' workings. They wanted to talk about religion, Africa, and segregation in the South. It was obvious to all those who listened to them that public schools are doing very little to help the urban Negro youth answer his one burning question, "Who am I?"

*Some* classics can help him answer his question. I taught Shakespeare's *Othello* and Steinbeck's *Of Mice and Men* with encouraging results because we discussed the people as real and the social and moral questions in familiar terms. My greatest delight came when the argument over Othello's sanity reached such a pitch that one of my "juvenile delinquents" stood up and shouted— "You put your money where your mouth is, man. That cat's mind was messed up!"

That cat's mind was no more messed up on the Isle of Cyprus than the public schools are in the United States of America. Though Miss Schwab was writing about Negro schoolchildren, she could as well have spoken of all the colors of the poor, the disadvantaged, and those other temporary and undesirable classroom residents who are not going on to college. Until school boards, administrators and teachers can bring themselves to realize that they are elected, appointed and employed to serve *all* the people, and that serving *all* the people does not mean converting all colors to white and all values to middle-class, we will continue to damage and destroy those children, full of need, who want to value themselves even as they struggle to comprehend the values of a world they never made.

# THE LUDINGTON STORY

IVAN LUDINGTON IS ALREADY FAMILIAR TO THE READER of this book as the patron of the Maxey School. Without his charity, there would have been no training school story to tell. But the full story of Ivan Ludington's charity to schoolchildren is hundreds of times larger than the life of one institution and even now is spreading throughout the vast area of Michigan served by the Ludington News Company. This story is typical of the spirit behind the work since undertaken by others all over the United States.

One day in the late summer of 1965, a year after the Maxey experiment had begun, Ivan Ludington asked me how long it might take to spread the practices of *English in Every Classroom* throughout the schools of Detroit and Wayne County. "If you're speaking of curriculum change," I said, "it may take forever." "Suppose we forget curriculum change for the time being," he replied. "Suppose that we try to *give* magazines and paperback books to the schools free of charge. Would they accept our offer?"

I had to answer that I didn't know. What I did know, I said, was that public schools had been lacerated by criticism and burdened by do-gooders for so long that they'd certainly look any gift horse in the mouth to be sure it was toothless. "If you offer them something for nothing," I said, "they're going to examine it mighty carefully *and* they're still going to want to know what's in it for you."

"All right," he said, "I'll tell them. If I invite teachers, principals and other school administrators to lunch, will you talk about the Maxey experiment while I offer them whatever they want in the way of paperbound materials and tell them what's in it for me?" When I said yes, I had no idea that I was agreeing to address fifteen luncheons in five months. Even less, I think, did Ivan Ludington realize that within the year he would be supplying 92 public schools and 41 private schools with their free choice of magazines and paperbound books.

On fifteen Tuesdays, beginning in September, 1965, and ending in January, 1966, we met in Detroit. I reported on mounting evidence of the success of our approach to the reluctant reader and spoke briefly of the theory behind it. When I had finished, Ivan added that his company was willing to supply paperbound books and, through his influence, publishers were prepared to make newsstand magazine returns available to the schools. Of all the schools represented at those meetings, only one declined his offer. But before the other schools accepted, they wanted frank answers from both of us about our real interests. My answer was simple enough and true enough —my interest was in repaying a small part of the Maxey debt to Ivan Ludington. But his answer was neither simple nor true and he modestly concealed his real interest.

The real truth is that Ivan Ludington wants to give back in kind, where it will do the most good, something of what he's gotten from Detroit and Michigan. Because he and his sons recognize that they live in a community of *all* Detroit's people, they also recognize that the child who is diminished by his school experience is a damaged and damaging portion of *their* community. If some part of that diminishment can be remedied by substituting magazines and paperbound books for ineffective texts, then Ivan's view is that he should help make that change possible. The reason he gives publicly—that his business cannot hope to stay healthy if the schools fail to turn out willing readers; and that it is therefore a wise investment for him to persuade his potential customers to sample his wares—is a logical one, and it has since been taken up on a very broad scale by others in many cities and states. Though good, the explanation is not true. Ivan Ludington has spent so freely of himself and his money for only one reason—he believes the children are worth it.

Even if we had captured these fifteen luncheon meetings on tape or film, to whom could we show them? Only the participants would be likely to believe everything that happened. In one early and memorable encounter, the good food left the table untasted as a school principal told the Ludingtons and me and various representatives of other schools and anybody else in the restaurant who was interested, that our idea had no relation to reality. Which is one way of reporting that he said we didn't know what we were talking about.

We grew hot while the food grew cold. No, he wasn't claiming that the schools couldn't do a better job than they did. But he was sick and tired of so-called experts from the universities trying to tell them what to do, and he was getting just as sick of hustlers from big business trying to tell them what to do it with. Until people realized that the schools' biggest troubles were the children's homes and communities, and *not* the teachers, their materials or their practices, nothing constructive could be done. It was all tinkering and nothing but tinkering. He was full up to here with the whole damned thing.

At the end of a bad two hours we left the dining room in two groups and two factions. As I walked out, red in the face from repressed anger, the teacher who had come with me from Maxey—a feisty young woman brought up on the Detroit street doctrine of direct action—turned to me and demanded, "How come you didn't belt him?" I had to admit that I didn't know why, but I did know that it hadn't been much of an introduction to the role of do-gooder in the public schools.

To remember that luncheon and to write now that the principal who gave us such a bad time became one of our ardent supporters has a quality of never-never about it. In the vast correspondence file accumulated by the Ludingtons in the past two years is the following note to Mr. Ludington, written by the man who didn't get belted: "The children of _____ School have taken to the Ludington Reading Room like ducks to water! The teachers and adults in the community are equally enthused."

Accompanying the letter was a description of the reading room's opening and its operation: "The community turned out in numbers which filled the Ludington Room and overflowed into the halls and neighboring rooms. Although the written invitations specified the opening hour to be 4:30, guests had arrived in full force by 4:15. . . . It was amazing to see so many people who were so thirsty for books. Each guest was allowed to select one book to keep and take home. Many an adult and child could be heard asking, 'Can I really keep this book?' "

The principal's report of an "amazing" thirst for books omits an equally amazing event that typifies a great part of the reading room experience. When the announcement was made that everyone was welcome to take and to keep one book or magazine, many visitors who were in adjacent classrooms heard the news from those who had been in the reading room. After the vast rush of books and bodies had subsided, teachers discovered that seventeen *textbooks* had disappeared along with the more expendable Ludington materials. Fearful of spreading the schoolbook disease throughout the community, the very next day they sent home urgent appeals with their students. No one has quite recovered from having *nineteen* textbooks returned in response to the teachers' plea!

Attending the opening ceremonies of this earliest of our reading rooms were a multitude of school and community officers. The response of the children and their parents was so enthusiastic and so genuine that it prompted many of the official visitors to telephone or write the Ludingtons when the evening was over. The moving experience witnessed by so many observers evoked these words in a letter from one of them, formerly a teacher and principal, now in a supervisory position:

I keep thinking about the children and parents who came to the _____ School the other evening. If only we could have captured the way they looked, their comments and their excitement!

I am certain that many persons would feel that we exaggerate when we share this experience which grew from exposure to the printed word. It would be extremely difficult for them to acknowledge the enthusiasm which we saw because they are so wrongly convinced that people from such areas are hostile to books. If ever I saw support for our mutual conviction that the right materials presented in the right way break the barriers, those few hours supplied it.

That mutual conviction, shared by many for so long with so little effect, has had its realization in reading rooms like the one now operating in Northwestern High School. Behind its remarkable success lie the efforts of people as different and as dedicated as Mrs. Ruby Gillis, reading coordinator, and Joe, student.

Northwestern opened its Ludington Reading Room on February 21, 1965. In the first ten days of its operation, over 1,500 of the school's 2,700 students visited the room and 1,850 books were put into circulation. All of us have seen the sudden upsurge of interest associated with a new program fall off to nothing when the newness wears off. But in this case we have comparable figures gathered seven months later. In nine September school days, 1,147 students visited the reading room and left with more than 1,000 books.

Last spring, some weeks after the Ludington Room was opened at Northwestern and its full impact was being felt throughout the student body, seventeen-year-old Joe approached Mrs. Gillis outside the reading room. "Mrs. Gillis," he said, "I got to be in there! Can I be in charge of them books?"

Coming from another seventeen-year-old, the question might not have been so startling. But in Joe's case it was something special. Because Joe couldn't read. He had been the beneficiary (or victim) of the doctrine of the "social pass," a passive philosophy of school advancement which allowed him to reach the eleventh grade without being able to read. And now, still unable to read, having resisted learning the written language with all his strength—having resisted successfully and for so long—now Joe wanted to be a librarian. Why?

The answer is simple enough: Joe wanted to be where the action was. Over half the students in a large school is a lot of action, anyway you figure it. Joe figured that he couldn't keep his place on top unless he made the reading room scene. Improbably, impossibly, Joe became a librarian. He wanted to make it so bad that he memorized the covers of *all* the paperbounds and replaced them in their proper pockets in the wire racks solely on the basis of their identifying pictures. (Someone said it: A memory like that, and he can't read!)

What do you say to a boy who can't read but who has *got* to read Elizabeth Kata's *A Patch of Blue* because his friends "are talkin' 'bout it." You say—read it. And he reads it, somehow, a few pages a day, every day, because he wants to be seen carrying and reading that book. It doesn't matter any more that he couldn't read before. What matters now is that he *is* reading. Knowing that he *has* read, he will read again. On the other hand, just what do you do with a girl from home economics class who is looking for a cookbook specializing in bread recipes and asks for *The Scarlet Pumpernickel?* Is half a loaf better than none?

How do you create a reading room like Northwestern's —a room full of words so attractive that your biggest troubles come when the room is closed for one day for painting and you have a small mutiny on your hands by students—all kinds—who want to know why they can't be in there *with* the painters? ("I already read these two books! What I'm gonna do until tomorrow?")

First of all, you get yourself a principal like Mrs. Jessie Kennedy, a reading coordinator like Mrs. Gillis, and some swinging English teachers like those at Detroit's Northwestern High School. Then you find a patron saint like Ivan Ludington and you're in business. In spite of first impressions, in-school requirements are likely to prove the more difficult to fulfill. I have advised and addressed groups of magazine and paperbound book distributors in many sections of the country. Eagerness to cooperate with public and private schools in their areas is widespread among them. Publishers of almost all popular magazines are willing to make newsstand returns available, through the distributors, to schools in all sections of the country. Distributors themselves are generally willing to invest their own funds in demonstration projects in schools with ideas to match their good intentions.

If so much good will exists, then why has so little action resulted? Why has there been so little real cooperation between private enterprise and public education? Mutual ignorance and suspicion, hardened into tradition, are the unpleasant answers—answers which reflect the worst aspects of business and of educational isolationism. On the one hand, big business traditionally has understood next to nothing of the educational market. Though the very recent flow of federal funds into the schools has been followed by the entry of some of our largest corporations into the business of education, little evidence exists to indicate that these corporations understand anything about this business other than the profits to be made there.

By comparison, big education has been at least equally culpable. Where business suffers from complete ignorance of the educational market, education is afflicted with disabling suspicions of the business world. Perhaps the disease is endemic and untreatable. Perhaps the educational world, whose inhabitants can personally escape the obvious penalties for producing shoddy products, feels it must protect itself from the values of a world whose inhabitants cannot so easily escape those same penalties. If, however, the disease is remediable, then one area for early treatment may lie in cooperation between business and education to produce children who can and will read and write. Within that area, no arrangement seems more promising than the mutual assistance offered by reading rooms to publishers and distributors in one world, and to elementary and secondary schools in another.

The value of that mutual assistance is nowhere more clearly to be seen than in Northwestern's Ludington Reading Room. Highly visible to the public because of its size, location and enthusiastic support by faculty and staff, this particular undertaking represents a private investment in public welfare which has grown to the point where, in addition to their purchases, Detroit and Wayne County schools received 298,000 magazines plus countless paperback books in the month of December, 1966, all without cost. Neither business nor education, working alone, could have gotten results such as these:

> Student response has been overwhelming. Never have I seen such interest shown in reading since my arrival here at Northwestern four years ago. . . . Students are seen reading everywhere—on hall duty, in lunchrooms, in study halls, and even in classrooms (undercover). *The* status symbol is the paperback.
>
> At least half a dozen or more students have asked if they could serve as librarians. Boys seem to outnumber

101

the girls in attendance. One teacher commented, "This is the best thing that's happened to Northwestern since I've been here."

*Reading coordinator's report*

I have watched students who have never before been coaxed into textbooks, pick up paperbacks and carry them around in their pockets for weeks, reading a few pages a day. What a breakthrough! I have watched supposedly slow students get through a paperback book every other day. . . . I am delighted to hear students recommending books to each other and having true literary discussions, even if about James Bond.

*English teacher's letter*

I think this program in our school may do for the teaching of reading what Sputnik did for the teaching of science.

*English teacher's statement*

There is, we must admit, a certain variety of motivation. For example, one young man was heard to say to another, after entering the reading room for the first time, "Man, I thought you say they was only gonna be girls in here!" We would like to report that his visit caused him to become a regular patron of the reading room. Unfortunately, however, Mrs. Gillis says that he hasn't been back since discovering the mixed nature of the crowd.

But for every one that remains away, three appear among the racks full of paperbound books and the tables covered with magazines. One who has changed his mind about "them kind of things" (said with unutterable disdain) is Robert, who last year was the student of a relatively new English teacher at Northwestern. Of all her students who first visited the Ludington Reading Room, Robert was the only one who refused to select a book. When she asked what was holding him back, his retort to her question was a masterpiece of indirection: "I only ever read one a them things," he said, "it was call' *Steel Shivs*. I know all about 'em now, and you better learn about 'em too if you wanna get along around here."

A few days later his journal contained the following statement: "Dear Miss _____, I believe you are the finest chick I ever seen." Following were pages of enamored description of his dear Miss _____. "See me," she wrote on the last page. When he came slouching up to her desk at the end of the day, she still was at a loss as to what to say to him. Suddenly, inspired, responding impulsively to the threat and the need of his presence, she handed him the book lying in front of her on the desk. "Here," she said, "read this. Go see what you can find out about yourself. Maybe you can tell me why you write love letters to your English teacher in your journal." She didn't look up until she was sure he had left the room. The book was *Introduction to Freudian Psychology*.

Sixteen hours later he returned the book. He had read it. "Well, what did you find out?" she asked, surprised at his speed and curious about his response. Looking bored beyond caring, he drawled, "It's all right, I guess. Did you ever see this part?" With that, he opened the book to a section on sublimation and she found herself reading about young women who go into teaching as a substitute for the husbands and children they want but don't have. She smiled and blushed in spite of herself; he grinned, and the crisis between them was permanently resolved. The reading room now stocks many paperbound books about psychology, and Robert was the first to read them all.

Most popular among the paperbacks borrowed in one month was John Steinbeck's *The Pearl* and, in another month, Richard Wright's *Black Boy*. Consistently in the top ten have been George Orwell's *1984*, all the James Bond adventures, Griffin's *Black Like Me*, Lorraine Hansberry's *Raisin in the Sun*, Unger and Berman's *What Girls Want to Know About Boys*, Dick Gregory's *Nigger*, Judith Scott's *The Art of Being a Girl*, any book about *Dennis the Menace*, and William Barrett's *Lilies of the Field*. Yes, Northwestern is an inner-city school with an entirely Negro student body. Free to choose from a vast number of titles, the students select books which speak of problems as close to them as their own skins. Which is why, for instance, *Othello* can be such an effective bridge between sixteenth-century England and twentieth-century America.

Can you guess the titles of the five best-read magazines? I played the game with myself and got two out of five—*Ebony* and *'Teen*. Did you guess *Reader's Digest*,

*HairDo* and *Popular Mechanics?* Can you picture two girls from "incorrigible" families fighting over a copy of *Ladies' Home Journal* because their mothers had asked each of them to bring the magazine home? Or the trouble Ruby Gillis had with *Nigger?* "We've had a hard time getting that one back," she says. "The parents borrow it from their kids, read it, and then pass it along to all their friends at church."

As every teacher knows, the full effectiveness of his work depends upon influencing the child's home environment as well as the child himself. He therefore values especially the reading room practice which makes paperbound books and magazines available to the community at large. One Ludington Reading Room, established for the past year in a Detroit grammar school, has welcomed an average of more than 700 parents per week during the afternoon hours between three and seven. Watching a child progress of his own free will through comic books and Peanuts to *A Tale of Two Cities* is a rich experience for any teacher. Watching an adult, the parent of a "problem family," painstakingly read *Teen-Age Tyranny,* by Grace and Fred Hechinger, over a period of weeks, lips moving with the words, is as powerful and even more poignant. When one child writes, "Thang you for the magazines I like them because they has lots of thing we can do as a family," you know that she knows too much about things that fall apart, things that will not hold together without every kind of help—even that of magazines.

Of all the burgeoning effects of the Ludington Reading Rooms and various other formats for distributing books and magazines to children in Detroit and Wayne County schools, none has been more provocative, more hopeful and more difficult to assess than their effect upon the community surrounding the school. For those of us who have been part of the experiment of *English in Every Classroom* and of its associated community programs, our direction for future action has become increasingly clear. Just as meaningful use of newspapers, magazines and paperbound books in the classroom is impossible unless such materials are set within an imaginative program of reading and writing, so is a truly effective program for teaching literacy in the schools inconceivable without growing support from the community media. To obtain, develop and capitalize upon that support must be the primary work of those committed to the proposition that language is the clothing of life and no child should go naked into the world.

Ambiguous, improbable, difficult to evaluate—and exciting beyond measure. All are rational assessments of the most inconclusive, unexpected and extraordinary of the responses—both apparent and real—provoked by the reading room program in Detroit. To quote from a news story written by Roger Rapoport for the *Michigan Daily:*

> Police officials have gone so far as to assert that the program curbs juvenile delinquency. Detroit police commissioner Ray Girardin points out that when the reading [room] program was used at the Moore grammar school last year, juvenile offenses in the area dropped to 57 from 180 the previous year. "Fader's program is a fine idea," says Girardin. "It is a real help to us and we plan to cooperate any way we can." The commissioner has already offered the use of squad cars to transport the paperback books to the schools.

Yes, there are elements of high comedy in some of the images that the idea evokes—Batman and Robin leading a cavalcade of squad cars. But the laughter becomes sober and reflective as one considers some statistics compiled by Commissioner Girardin's department. In the ten school areas making full community use of their reading room facilities, juvenile delinquency increased significantly in only one and remained approximately level in two others. In the remaining seven, however, total juvenile offenses decreased by an incredible 61 percent below the figure for the preceding year when reading rooms were not available.

As anyone who has ever known juvenile delinquency firsthand can tell you, an enormous proportion of it—maybe even 61 percent—is directly and immediately caused by having nothing better to do. Steal a car, roll a stranger, break into a store or a house—what do you get out of it? Not merely the car, the money or the goods, though all may be useful. You get action, action that is absent from the godawful dullness of the poolrooms, the streetcorners and the public schools. In the latter, even the action that other men have known or imagined—the action contained in books—has gone out of style. Is it possible that kids who read in a community where reading is valued, where adults are eager to read the same books and magazines, become kids who have lost their most compelling reason—the frustration and alienation of pure, unbearable boredom—for breaking the law?

# POSTSCRIPT: "MY EVALUATION"

I THINK I HAVE LEARNED A GREAT MANY MORE THINGS here which i will need on the outside to better my self. When i first came seven months ago i could have died from bore, because it was a boring thing to come every day and don't do one thing. But now i believe that this place can be a wonderful place to get boys who have drop out of school back on the track. See when a boy haven't been to school in a long time like i have it is very hard on him anyway to adjust to this program because this whole program is based on school. But after awhile you start thinking about what will i do. Or where will i work when i get out. And it all adds up and you finds out that you will need an eduaction. An eduaction now adays is needed very badly and without one, you are lost.

Well i have found myself and i really belivie that i am going to make good of my self. I have also learned how to communicate with others and i find that this will be very imporante, and also i know how to make my own decision and i will be doing that the rest of my life. I only hope that the decisions i make from now on will be the right ones and yet ill never know. Well Mr. Williams i hope ill see you somewhere on the outside, and ill do very good in Social Studies for you.

Well thanks for every thing.

# STUDY GUIDES

The following three-week study guide for *West Side Story,*
put together by Miss Ann Farnell for her English and social
studies classes at the Maxey School, is included here as a
model for the use of paperbound books in the classroom.
This particular study guide has the strongest possible recommendation—it works. It has been used by all English and
social studies teachers at B.T.S., with invariably good results.
The premises upon which the guide is based are those upon
which the program is founded: begin with material students
like, then relate that material to their life outside the confines
of the classroom. If, as teachers, we can export general values
by importing particular environment, we have a clear and
present duty to create those environments within our classrooms. No argument for "quality" in teaching materials can
be as persuasive as this conclusion quoted from the report
on *Paperbound Books in New Jersey Public Schools:*

> It was found that the so-called reluctant reader and the
> slow learner were not so reluctant or as slow as certain
> teachers previously thought. Provided with books that inter-
> ested them, they were no longer reluctant or slow. Over and
> over again, these students concluded that they learned more
> by reading something they liked. . . . It was found that the
> near illiterates in many classrooms were now reading whole
> books albeit that many of these selections would not be
> considered meritorious from a literary point of view. Never-
> theless, they were reading and enjoying this new experience.

*West Side Story* was chosen by Miss Farnell as the subject of the first of her study guides because she had seen
it, read it, and liked it. She was, in short, applying the
same criterion of familiarity that she hoped would engage
the interest of her students. Where her familiarity was
vicarious, theirs might be first-hand. But she was sure that
whether read or lived, the experiences of the people in
*West Side Story* were real enough to her students to engage
their interest and universal enough to teach any young reader
(and some older ones) valuable lessons about himself and
his world.

Teachers will notice how careful Miss Farnell has been
to relate the book to the lives of her students. In order to

use her study unit as it was meant to be used—and as it has subsequently proven so successful—"Daily Objectives" must invariably be combined with "Enrichment Activities," which are keyed to the same page divisions as the "Objectives." Where daily objectives focus the student's attention on the book itself, they are less important than the enrichment activities which make every effort to give the book a vitality that can come only from the pulse of reality. If it's "just a story," it's likely to be just no good. Bring alive the situation and the characters who people it, and no book can be resisted by any student with even minimal abilities to perceive meaning.

The last page of the study guide deserves particular attention. This list of over twenty books represents Miss Farnell's attempt to give *West Side Story* wider experiential implications than one novel or one play can itself contain. To accomplish this, she has created a temporary classroom library of books dealing centrally and in every degree of tangent with the concerns of *West Side Story*. Her experience, and the experience of others who have used this guide as a pattern, is that no device more effectively creates willing readers than one good book with others like it easily and immediately available.

# A STUDY GUIDE FOR

## *WEST SIDE STORY**

by Irving Shulman

Ann C. Farnell, Teacher
Roosevelt Junior High School
San Diego, California

### Introducing the Book

Since *West Side Story* has been widely shown as a movie, the sound track played frequently on the radio and as part of personal record collections, and the music sung and

---

* Published by Pocket Books, Inc., New York, N.Y.

danced on television, teachers will probably find that many of their students have some recognition of the title. This can be a handicap, for some students will respond negatively because they feel that they already know the material. The teacher can capitalize on this, however, by encouraging those very students to tell a little about what they know. After brief discussion, the teacher can disclose something unique about this book that most students are unlikely to know: that the book is a novelization of the play which was adapted as a movie. The more usual arrangement is to have the book written first, and then to have a play or a movie made from it. But in this case, the teacher can point out, the play was so good that the public wanted and got a novel based upon it.

This is also a good opportunity to touch on *West Side Story* as a musical play in which the important dialogue is sung and the scenes danced rather than spoken and acted. The teacher can remind the class that even though the situation centers around teenage gangs in a big city and singing and dancing may seem inappropriate to a fight scene, this is just one other way of expressing a real life situation. The reality is simply enhanced by the pace and drama of the singing and dancing. Here, however, lies the big advantage of reading the book for those students who were repelled by the movie. The book of course is entirely without singing and dancing. It is a novel, it is written like a novel, and it reads like any other good story.

## Overall Objectives

1. To show how fear and dissatisfaction with oneself and one's way of living cause:
   A. Some people to try to change the status quo
   B. Other people to fight tooth and nail to maintain it
2. To show that fear and dissatisfaction cause:
   A. Some people to group together in order to protect their interests
   B. Other people to come together to try to better their lives
3. To show how fear and dissatisfaction cause:
   A. Some people to "go along" even though they don't really approve
   B. Other people to try to break away

110

4. To show how the same motivations of fear and dissatisfaction were the conditions that created the two gangs
5. To show how failure to recognize and understand their similarities caused them only to see their differences
6. To show how hatred is a result of dissatisfaction, fear, frustration, lack of love, failure to recognize similarities, and relentless concentration on differences
7. To show how two individuals were temporarily able to overcome their personal fears and group frustrations and to love each other
8. To show how the gang's collective hatred caused them to destroy the individual love of Tony and Maria
9. To show how common hatred led to a common tragedy
10. To show how hate, instead of solving problems, only creates more hatred, more problems, and finally leads to tragedy
11. To show the close relationship between ignorance and prejudice, and ignorance and fear
12. To encourage investigation of one's own attitudes toward other people
13. To encourage empathy or "putting yourself in the other person's shoes"
14. To show how the needs for acceptance, status, and recognition are traits basic to all human beings
15. To show how friendship can be abused and used selfishly
16. To show how vengeance only makes things worse in the long run
17. To show how good intentions, if not thought out carefully, can lead to tragedy for everyone
18. To encourage personal comparison of one's own feelings with storybook characters
19. To show that literature, music, art, plays, and movies are expressions of situations that usually are true to life
20. To encourage oral, written, graphic, and dramatic expression

Study Sheet I
Chapter One, pp. 1–16
*West Side Story*

*Daily Objectives*

1. To see the personal conflicts within the Jets
   A. Action vs. Riff

B. Riff vs. Tony
C. Baby-Face vs. the gang
D. Anybody's vs. the gang
2. To see the conditions that create gangs
    A. Dissatisfaction
    B. Fear
    C. No direction
3. To see the attitudes that permit gangs to flourish
    A. The landlord and other tenants
    B. The police

*Discussion Questions*

1. Who is Riff Lorton?
2. List as many members of the Jets as you can find in the first chapter.
3. How is Tony "different" from the Jets now?
4. How has Tony both disappointed and helped Riff?
5. If Action wants to be the leader of the Jets, why doesn't he challenge Riff?
6. What are both Baby-Face and Anybody's trying to do in reference to the gang?
7. How do the landlord and other tenants feel about the Jets vs. the Puerto Ricans?
8. Even though Sergeant Krupke and Detective Schrank question the Jets about the stink bomb, how do they really feel about Puerto Ricans?
9. How do Schrank and Krupke feel about their jobs and the kind of job they are doing?

Study Sheet II
Chapter One, pp. 17–22
*West Side Story*

*Daily Objectives*

1. To see why people leave their native countries to come to a new country
    A. Living conditions in Puerto Rico
    B. Living conditions in New York
    C. Hopes carried to the new country (Maria)
    D. Reality of the new country (Bernardo)
2. To see how the Puerto Ricans cling together, just as the Jets do, but for different reasons
    A. Family unity

B. Same nationality
C. Lack of acceptance by the majority
D. Protection within the minority

## Discussion Questions

1. List at least three reasons why the Puerto Ricans left their native country to come to New York City.
2. From Bernardo's and Maria's conversation on the roof, what ideas do you get about their family life?
3. How does Maria feel about being in America?
4. In contrast, how does her brother Bernardo now feel about being in America?
5. Do you think Bernardo probably had the same attitude as Maria when he first came? Why do you think so?
6. Since Puerto Rico is a commonwealth of the United States and Puerto Ricans are considered American citizens, do you think Bernardo has a right to be so bitter? Explain your answer.
7. If you were Bernardo, do you think you would feel the same? Why?
8. What do you think the saying "Misery loves company" means? How does this saying apply to the Jets and Sharks?
9. What do you think the saying "Blood is thicker than water" means? Can this saying apply to the Jets and Sharks? How?

Study Sheet III
Chapters Two and Three,
pp. 22-46
*West Side Story*

## Daily Objectives

1. To see how Tony was trying to break away from the Jets
2. To see how Riff used friendship to pressure Tony
3. To see how Doc and Señora Mantanios had similar problems
   A. Doc and Tony
   B. Señora Mantanios and Maria
   C. Their stores
4. To see the basis of Anita's and Maria's friendship
   A. Maria is Bernardo's sister
   B. Both are Puerto Ricans
5. To see Maria's dissatisfaction with Chino

Directions: In the underlined blanks write the letter of the
           answer that the best completes the statement.
1. Tony decides to quit the Jets because_____.
2. Riff gets the Jets' leadership because_____.
3. "Blood is thicker than water" could apply to both
                and_____.
4. Doc complains about iron shutters over the store win-
    dows because_____;
5. Tony attributes the shutters to_____.
6. Riff tells us he's in a gang because_____.
7. Señora Mantanios wants the doors locked and the shut-
    ters closed because_____.
8 All the characters in this section are similar because
    _____.
9. Maria is dissatisfied because_____.

    A. otherwise you don't belong, you're nowhere, and be-
       longing puts you on top of the world.
    B. of Tony's and Riff's friendship.
    C. of discontent at the sense of inferiority, of being
       ignorant, which cool talk couldn't change.
    D. of Tony's and Doc's friendship.
    E. of all gangs and their destructiveness.
    F. Tony has passed it on.
    G. of Maria's and Anita's friendship.
    H. of the Anglos.
    I. others' desires seem more important than her own.
    J. the P.R.'s
    K. they are trying to protect their interests.

Study Sheet IV
Chapter Four, pp. 46-69
*West Side Story*

*Daily Objectives*

1. To see the role of Murray Benowitz, the social worker
    A. His hopes about the value of his work
    B. The realities he didn't expect
    C. His frustrated, but continued will to help
2. To see how Tony's values changed enough to allow him
    to be attracted to a Puerto Rican

3. To see how Maria's prejudice toward Americans was too weak to ignore Tony
4. To see how even passive Chino overcame his fear when his interest (Maria) was threatened
5. To see how Bernardo protected his interest (Maria), but became enraged because she "crossed" the gang line

## Discussion Questions

1. Why had Murray Benowitz's other neighborhood dances failed?
2. How had his experiences with these kids changed his view of the world?
3. If you were Murray Benowitz, would you have kept trying to better things? Explain your answer fully.
4. What emotion did Maria first experience when Tony danced with her?
5. Why was Maria afraid?
6. Up to now, what kind of picture do we have of Chino? How does this picture change when he sees Maria with Tony?
7. Do you think Bernardo should have gotten so angry with Maria? Explain your answer.
8. If you were Tony, would you have left Maria alone rather than get involved? Explain your answer.

Study Sheet V
Chapters Five and Six,
pp. 70-94
*West Side Story*

## Daily Objectives

1. To see how Tony tries to solve the gangs' problems and his personal conflicts
   A. Persuade the gangs to fight one-to-one or not at all
   B. Make Maria happy by arbitrating
2. To see how Riff's loyalty to Tony gave Bernardo the opening to vent his hatred.
3. To see how frustrated love, bravery and friendship add fuel to fear and hatred
4. To see the tragic results of tormented emotions

*Discussion Questions*

1. In the Coffee Pot, how did the Jets act? What was their spirit and feeling about the coming fight?
2. How did Tony suggest the fight should be handled? Why?
3. Why did Tony show up at the fight? What did he intend to do?
4. What events thwarted his good intentions?
5. He soon realized he might have handled things differently. What did he realize he could have done if he had thought more clearly?
6. What were the final results of the fight?

Study Sheet VI
Chapters Seven, Eight, Nine and Ten,
pp. 95-120
*West Side Story*

*Daily Objectives*

1. To see the after-effects of the fight on everyone else
   A. Maria and Tony
   B. Chino and Anita
   C. The other Jets
2. To see how futile revenge is as a problem solver
3. To see how good intentions are not enough
4. To see how the final tragedy was shared by all

*Discussion Questions*

1. What changes did Maria go through in her feelings about Tony after learning he killed her brother?
2. Why did Chino really kill Tony? To avenge Bernardo's death, to avenge his rejection by Maria, or both? Explain your answer.
3. If you had been Chino, what would you have done?
4. How did the other Jets feel about Tony afterward?
5. How did the other Jets feel about themselves and the whole incident later?
6. In Chapter Nine, when Maria and Tony are talking about Riff, what new discoveries do they make about Riff's and Tony's friendship? How do they decide Riff and Bernardo are alike?

116

7. What do they conclude about Riff's and Bernardo's futures if they had lived?

8. Why does Maria feel Tony was not doomed to the same destiny as Riff and Bernardo?

9. Why then is Tony's death the real tragedy in this tragic story?

10. How does Anita try to prove her strong friendship for Maria?

11. Anita's intentions, like Tony's, were good when she left the drugstore. What happened to cause her to change her mind? What was the result? Why did she change the message? What could she have done instead?

12. What is the meaning of the last sentence on page 120, "And if things did not change, was this the way it would always be?"

*West Side Story*
*Enrichment Activities*

A. Chapter One, pp. 1-16
1. Write a character sketch of either Detective Schrank or Officer Krupke. What kind of men are they? What are their goals and ambitions? How do they feel about themselves, their work, the neighborhood, each other, the kids, the city, Puerto Ricans, etc.?
2. Draw a picture illustrating any incident in the first chapter which interests you.
3. Make a list with definitions of vocabulary words from the first chapter which you were not familiar with before. Keep the list up to date as you read. Hand in the list as a vocabulary booklet after you have finished the novel.
4. Describe a time when you felt or experienced thoughts or events like those of the characters in the first chapter.
5. Draw a group or individual picture (in words) of the various characters mentioned in the first chapter.

B. Chapter One, pp. 17-22
1. Write a report on the history of Puerto Rico.
2. Find out as much as you can about the words "prejudice," "scapegoat," and "status quo." Find out for yourself what they mean, then take a poll of the people around you and see how many other people know what they mean. Keep track of the right and wrong answers that you get. Also record the age of the people you poll.

3. Find out what a minority group is and write a report on the history of a minority group in this country.
4. Keep a scrapbook for a few weeks of any incidents you find in the newspaper of prejudice encountered or progress made by a minority group in obtaining their rights.

C. Chapters Two, Three and Four, pp. 22-69
1. Keep a list of the Spanish words you find throughout the story and look up their meanings.
2. Write a description of someone who reminds you of any of the characters in the story without giving his real name.
3. Write a report on Social Work and what social workers do.
4. Draw a map of Puerto Rico giving information as to its size, population, major products, industries and agriculture, government, and distance from New York City.
5. Try to find information as to other locations in the United States with a heavy minority group population. For example, California and Washington have large Oriental populations. Give some statistics such as numbers of people, when most came to the U.S., and why.

D. Chapters Five and Six, pp. 70-95
1. Give an oral or written report on a time when you were afraid. What events led up to the situation. How did you feel? What did you do about it? If you could, would you handle the situation in the same way? If not, how else would you handle it?
2. Write a newspaper article reporting the deaths of Bernardo and Riff. Give a little history as to the cause of the gang fight and how these fights can be prevented in the future.
3. Tell about a time you were involved in a similar incident. What led up to it and what were the results?
4. Tell or write about why Riff's and Bernardo's deaths are considered tragic. How do you think this will affect the rest of the characters in the story?

E. These Concluding Activities cover the whole book:
1. Form small groups and reenact any of the major scenes in the story. Act out what took place in the story, and then act out your own version of how the situation could have been handled so nobody got hurt.

2. Write an analysis of the various friendships described in the story. What is friendship to you? How far does a person go for a friend? How were friendships abused in the story? Compare Anita's and Maria's friendship with Tony's and Riff's.

3. Give oral reports on parts of the story that especially interested you. For example, some of these parts might be: prejudice, love, hate, revenge, dissatisfaction, status, hope, acceptance, kindness. If you choose one of these, you could tell what these words mean to you and use various characters from the story to support your ideas.

4. Write or tell about how you felt when you had finished the story. Did it affect you personally in any way? Did you feel sorry for anyone? If so, why? What parts madè you feel happy?

5. Not much attention is paid in the story to the mothers of Doc and Tony. How do you think they felt afterward? Support your views by including the information available about these people.

6. Write another version of how the story could have ended. How would you have liked to see it end?

7. Give oral or written book reports on any books you read that you think could be related to this story. Tell what you think the relationship is between the book you read and this story.

8. Form a group and draw a mural depicting some of the major scenes from the book.

9. Write or tell about a gang you know and some of their activities.

10. Form a panel to discuss gangs.

11. Write your own version of *West Side Story* using some real life people you are acquainted with.

## SAMPLE DAILY LESSON PLAN

*West Side Story*

### FIRST WEEK

| *Lesson* | *Homework* |
|---|---|
| *Day One:* Introduce book and review Overall Objectives with class. Begin reading Chapter 1. | Finish Chapter 1. |

*Day Two:* Review Study Sheet I. Write out Study Sheet I. Explain Enrichment Activities. Group to select activities to be started tonight.

Start Enrichment. Continue reading.

*Day Three:* Discuss Study Sheet I. Introduce Study Sheet II. Review Objectives. Write out Study Sheet II.

Finish Study Sheet II. Continue reading; work on Enrichment Activities.

*Day Four:* Discuss Study Sheet II. Work on Enrichment Activities. Or, introduce Study Sheet III (if using S.S. III as test, Chapters 1-3 to be read by tomorrow).

Read Chapters 1-3. Work on Enrichment Activities.

*Day Five:* Review Study Sheet III—to be done in class or used as either open- or closed-book test. Pass out Study Sheet IV for homework.

Study Sheet IV and Enrichment Activities due Day Six.

SECOND WEEK

*Day Six:* Hand in Enrichment Activities. Discuss Study Sheet IV. Pass out Study Sheet V and review.

Read Chapters 5 and 6. Complete Study Sheet V.

*Day Seven:* Discuss Study Sheet V. Choose Enrichment Activities again. Work in class.

Work on Enrichment Activities. Read Chapters 7 and 8.

*Day Eight:* Continue Enrichment Activities. Pass out and review Study Sheet VI. Start Study Sheet VI.

Continue reading Chapters 9 and 10; work on Enrichment Activities due Day Ten.

*Day Nine:* Continue Study Sheet VI discussion. Work on Enrichment Activities.

Work on Enrichment Activities.

*Day Ten:* Hand in Enrichment Activities. Finish discussion. Motivate for Concluding Activities.

# THIRD WEEK

*Day Eleven:* Work on Concluding Activities. Begin presentations on Day Thirteen.

*Day Twelve:* Continue Concluding Activities.

*Day Thirteen:* Begin presentations.

*Day Fourteen:* Presentations.

*Day Fifteen:* Presentations.


*West Side Story*

## RELATED READING

The books listed below relate directly or indirectly to *West Side Story* and can be found in the classroom library while we are studying that novel.


| AUTHOR | TITLE |
|---|---|
| Elizabeth Kytle | *Willie Mae* |
| Louisa Shotwell | *Roosevelt Grady* |
| Ethel Waters | *His Eye Is on the Sparrow* |
| John Howard Griffin | *Black Like Me* |
| Richard Wright | *Black Boy* |
| | *Native Son* |
| | *Uncle Tom's Children* |
| Harry Golden | *Mr. Kennedy and the Negroes* |
| Martin Luther King | *Why We Can't Wait* |
| Louis Lomax | *When the Word Is Given* |
| | *The Negro Revolt* |
| Chester Himes | *The Third Generation* |
| Harper Lee | *To Kill a Mocking Bird* |
| James Baldwin | *Go Tell It on the Mountain* |
| | *The Fire Next Time* |
| | *Blues for Mister Charlie* |
| | *Nobody Knows My Name* |

Martin D. Duberman    *In White America*
Ralph Ellison         *The Invisible Man*
Michael Dorman        *We Shall Overcome*

# A STUDY GUIDE FOR
## *ANNE FRANK: THE DIARY OF A YOUNG GIRL* *

Ann C. Farnell, Teacher
Roosevelt Junior High School
San Diego, California

### To The Teacher

*Anne Frank: The Diary of a Young Girl* is a book so rich in material that it can be used effectively in a number of educational settings. The teacher will note that included in this study guide are separate introductions designed for use in the English, history or family living classrooms. The rest of the study guide, however, is completely integrated, with no such distinctions. The purpose of this format is to give the teacher and students a secure beginning within the confines of their particular subject matter, and to enable the teacher to expand her focus when she so desires. Thus, the history teacher may find herself dealing with language activities such as the student journal, and the English teacher relating yesterday's history to today's political events through newspapers and magazines.

A vocabulary is also included for use in spelling, dictionary or reading practice. Along with the vocabulary, there is a compilation of interesting quotations from the book which can be used to stimulate journal writing or impromptu paragraphs. In addition, a list of paperback books deals with the European phase of World War II, the history of the Jewish people, and related current problems. A guide to pertinent periodical literature, available in most public libraries, is also included for possible research by the teacher or interested students.

---

*Published by Pocket Books, Inc., New York, N. Y.

## Introducing the Book In the English Classroom

"I see the eight of us with our 'Secret Annexe' as if we were a little piece of blue heaven, surrounded by heavy black rain clouds. . . . Now we are so surrounded by danger and darkness that we bump against each other, as we search desperately for a means of escape . . . Oh, if only the black circle could recede and open the way for us!"

Anne Frank, age fourteen, wrote the above words in a rare moment of despair. For her, the black circle never did recede, yet through her book, *The Diary of a Young Girl,* she opened the way for countless people of all ages, nationalities, religions, races and occupations to greater insight and appreciation of the human spirit.

The impressive fact is that Anne, despite living at a time when the world was torn by World War II, despite living with seven other people for over two years in crowded and deprived conditions, despite the daily fear of discovery and the concentration camp, wrote primarily as a teenager. Her thoughts, emotions, attitudes, problems and behavior were not unlike those that most teenagers the world over experience.

The difference, however, is that Anne put on paper what so many of us put in the back of our mind or perhaps express in confidence, to another person. Anne's best friend was her diary and because the diary was written in trust and confidence, Anne had no need to be anything less than truthful.

Anne Frank wanted to write. She wanted to write because it gave her pleasure and comfort. She did not anticipate that her words would be published. She wrote because she enjoyed writing, not because she needed readers to read what she wrote. Anne's diary, however, has been published in twenty-one countries and translated into as many languages. In Europe, there are orphanages, schools and streets named after Anne Frank. Her story has been produced as a Broadway play and a Hollywood movie.

Anne Frank was never permitted to become the adult she hoped to be. But her name and the nobility her writing represents will continue to live as long as her book is published and there are people to read it.

## Introducing the Book In the History Classroom

*Anne Frank: The Diary of a Young Girl* was published in Holland shortly after World War II. It is the journal of a teenage girl who, with seven other people, hid for over two years in the upper floors of an office building in Amsterdam. The reason for their isolation was tragically simple—they were all members of the Jewish faith. Adolf Hitler, the tyrant of Germany, had declared that all Jews were to be imprisoned and killed as enemies of the German people. Anne Frank and six million other Jews did, in fact, meet death in concentration camps throughout Germany, Austria, Holland and Poland. Her diary, however, exists today as a continuing reminder that the good in spirit cannot be killed because that spirit will always defy and defeat those intent on persecution and extermination.

Today the world is still in the throes of political and social unrest. In our own country, as well as in other countries, minority groups are engaged in a continuous struggle for full equality. Some individuals and groups continue to insist that people are born superior or inferior on the basis of their race, religion or nationality.

While a cold war is being waged, there are people who justify their pacifism and conscientious objections to war of any kind with arguments based on their reactions to the Nuremberg trials. On the other hand, many people use World War II as a devastating example of what occurs when freedom-loving people fail to take immediate action against an aggressor government.

In the long history of mankind, thirty years is a short time. Almost every phase of our political, economic and social situation today dates back to World War II. When one considers events since 1945, it seems that, if history does teach us lessons, we have not learned them too well. Certainly one of those lessons is that people must be able to live together in a cooperative and mutually beneficial way. In a global sense the world needs to learn much more about peaceful, rational living; the diary of Anne Frank is testimony that people *can* live and interact in a civilized fashion even under the worst conditions.

Anne Frank, in her candid descriptions of life in the Secret Annexe, reminds even the most critical that if her love and faith could survive, there surely is hope for us all.

# Introducing the Book In the Family-Living Classroom

"Why do grownups quarrel so easily, so much and over the most idiotic things? Up till now I thought that only children squabbled . . . I suppose I should get used to it. But I can't . . . as long as I am the subject of every discussion . . . Nothing about me is right. I'm expected to simply swallow all the harsh words and shouts in silence . . . I can't! I'm not going to take all these insults lying down. I'll show them that Anne Frank wasn't born yesterday."

Sound familiar? How many teenagers throughout the world have said something similar during an angry moment. The remarkable thing about the above statement, however, is the conditions under which it was written. Anne, along with her family, another family and a single gentleman, lived in hiding for over two years with very little food, clothing or freedom to move about. These people, all individuals with different needs, attitudes and ideas, were bound together by their common religion and their will to survive.

For these reasons, even though there were frequent quarrels and occasional displays of selfishness, never was there any physical violence among the members of the Secret Annexe. Although they were not true blood relatives, they did identify as one family because of their close proximity to each other and their interdependence.

As in any group-living situation, difficult problems arose. Anne often saw herself as "the central figure in a hypercritical family," a figure torn between her desire to be herself and meeting the sometimes contradictory expectations of her elders.

Anne's diary is not only the expression of a teenage girl striving for independence and maturity, but a human drama of interaction and adaptation to severely frustrating conditions.

It is a study of people and particularly a portrait of the growth of an adolescent girl toward young womanhood. Unfortunately, Anne did not live long enough to reach her goal. Her diary, however, is a lasting testimony to the love, beauty, unselfishness, humor and joy Anne brought to the process of living.

## Overall Objectives

I. To see the events which necessitated the Secret Annexe
   - A. The rise to power of a political madman
   - B. The slaughter of millions of innocent people
   - C. A total war which still divides the world

II. To see how people group together to survive
   - A. The Franks
   - B. The Van Daans
   - C. Dussel

III. To see how other people risked their lives to help the victimized
   - A. Koophius
   - B. Kraler
   - C. Miep and Elli
   - D. The underground

IV. To understand the physical deprivations of confined living
   - A. Little food or clothing
   - B. Crowded quarters
   - C. No privacy
   - D. No freedom
   - E. Little talking
   - F. Guarded movements

V. To understand the emotional deprivations of confined living
   - A. Individual moods
   - B. Personal prejudices
   - C. Unfamiliar habits
   - D. Immature behavior
   - E. Faulty communication
   - F. Constant fear

VI. To appreciate the resourcefulness of group adaptation
   - A. Exchanging presents
   - B. Discussing books
   - C. Writing poetry
   - D. Arbitrating problems
   - E. Establishing schedules
   - F. Assuming responsibilities
   - G. Devising hobbies

VII. To witness the personal growth of Anne from an adolescent to a young adult

A. Understand her moods during these crucial stages of growth
B. Appreciate her personal enrichment in such an impoverished environment
C. Appreciate the sensitivity and beauty of her self-portrait
D. Appreciate the honest efforts she made to understand herself, other people and the world

VIII. To appreciate the strength of Mr. Frank as the leader of the group
    A. Chief arbitrator
    B. Top administrator
    C. Loving parent
    D. Advisor, counselor and teacher

IX. To see the basic similarities between people
    A. Encourage positive comparison of oneself with others
    B. Encourage personal comparison of oneself with literary characters

X. To see how the spirit of love overshadowed the outrages of hate
    A. How faith and hope can dominate fear and despair
    B. How inner beauty can suppress ugliness
    C. How goodness can eventually triumph over badness
    D. How people may die but their spirit can live on

XI. To encourage critical evaluation of the concept of racial superiority
    A. Explore the prevalence of this concept in the world today
    B. Encourage investigation of personal attitudes about oneself and other people
    C. Examine the effects of prejudice historically as well as currently

XII. To show that literature, poetry, art and music are sustaining pleasures for many people

XIII. To encourage oral, written, graphic and dramatic expression

XIV. To encourage the continued reading of books, magazines and newspapers

128

# ANALYSIS AND DISCUSSION OF BOOK

## *ANNE FRANK: THE DIARY OF A YOUNG GIRL*

### Preface–Introduction

*Daily Objectives*

A. To see the intensity of the Nazi effort to exterminate everything Jewish
B. To appreciate the importance of Anne's diary being saved from the Nazis

*Discussion Questions*

1. When were the members of the Secret Annexe finally discovered?
2. What was the mission of the police at that time?
3. How is it that Anne's diary was not destroyed?
4. Why does Anne's diary symbolize "the triumph of the human spirit"?
5. In the introduction, Eleanor Roosevelt said, "War's greatest evil is the degradation of the human spirit." In your own words, tell what you think this statement means.

*Enrichment Activities*

1. "I believe in the good of man" and "My mission is to destroy and exterminate" are statements found in the Preface. Contrast the meanings of both statements. Tell who is being quoted and what you already know about each person. Can you think of anybody today who has made similar statements or whose activities would support either statement?
2. Read the autobiography of Eleanor Roosevelt entitled *My Story*. From the story, write a character sketch of her.

3. Using the *Guide to Periodical Literature* in your school or public library, look up magazine articles on Eleanor Roosevelt and make an oral or written report.
4. Write the Library of Congress, Washington, D. C. 20540, or the Franklin D. Roosevelt Home, Hyde Park, N. Y. 12528, and ask for materials on Franklin D. and/or Eleanor Roosevelt. Make a poster display with the materials you receive.

*Anne Frank:*
*The Diary of a Young Girl*

pp. 1–11

*Daily Objectives*

    A. To see why Anne decided to keep a diary
    B. To get an idea of Anne's personality and way of life before hiding
    C. To see how Jewish people were being treated at this time

*Discussion Questions*

1. What reasons does Anne give for writing a diary? What does this saying mean: "Paper is more patient than man"?
2. Why did the Frank family move to Holland? Do you think they were wealthy people? How does Anne seem to get along with others? How does she spend her spare time?
3. In reference to Jews, Anne said, "Our freedom was strictly limited. Yet things were still bearable." What did she mean by those statements? Give examples.
4. How does Anne perform in school? Did she resent her teacher, Mr. Keptor? What did she do when Mr. Keptor punished her by assigning an extra composition?
5. Why had the Franks been preparing to go into hiding?

*Enrichment Activities*

1. Begin a diary of your own in a composition book. Begin by writing at least ten minutes a day on whatever interests

you. If it is difficult for you to think of something, copy articles from newspapers and magazines.
2. Write a paragraph entitled "Feeling Lonely."
3. Write a description of your best friend. Tell the reasons why you are best friends. What do you do together? How long have you known each other? What makes this friend special?
4. If you had been Anne Frank and the teacher had assigned the composition "Chatterboxes" to you, what would you write?
5. Make a list of the restrictions imposed on Jewish people. Try to imagine what your life would be like with similar restrictions. At the same time, keep a list of people who in some way ignored the restrictions and helped the Jews. What did these helpers do?
6. Make a report on the history of the Zionists.

*Anne Frank:*
*The Diary of a Young Girl*

pp. 12–38

*Daily Objectives*

A. To feel the impact of the call-up notice on the Frank family
B. To become acquainted with the physical environment of the Secret Annexe
C. To understand the effects of this move on the family's emotions
D. To see the increasingly abusive treatment of the Jews by the Nazis

*Discussion Questions*

1. How did Anne react when she learned of the call-up notice? How did the others react?
2. Why didn't they take suitcases instead of wearing as much clothing as they could?
3. Why did the wearing of the yellow star of David make a difference to other people?
4. How many floors did the Secret Annexe contain? What do the initials W.C. stand for? With what kind of mood

does Anne describe the apartment? How did they make the place more cheery?

5. What does Anne say was the most oppressive fact about the Annexe?
6. How does Anne describe each member of the Van Daan family? How do the Van Daans compare with the Franks (likes and dislikes, attitudes, feelings for each other, handling of family problems)?
7. After a month of living together, how does Anne feel about Mrs. Van Daan, and why? What impression do you have of Anne's relationship with her mother?
8. How does Anne spend her spare time now? Do you remember how she used to spend her time before moving into the Secret Annexe?
9. What changes are beginning to take place in Anne's feelings about herself? What has caused these changes?
10. How does Mrs. Van Daan see herself? How do Anne and her mother see Mrs. Van Daan? How did Mrs. Van Daan react when Mrs. Frank disagreed with her self-concept?
11. What information are the Franks receiving about Jews captured and sent to concentration camps?

*Enrichment Activities*

1. Using the floor plan on page 16 and Anne's description, make a shadow box model of the Secret Annexe.
2. Reread pages 1 and 4 through 8. Compare that Anne with the Anne on pages 25–29. How is she beginning to change? Write a comparison of her moods, reactions to adults, and feelings about her family.
3. Think about yourself for a few minutes and write a self-portrait. What are your qualities? What are your likes and dislikes? What do you like most/least about yourself? How do you get along with others? What are your habits and gripes?
4. Read the book *Judgment at Nuremberg* by Abby Mann and write a report on the postwar criminal trials of Nazi administrators of concentration camps.

*Anne Frank:*
*The Diary of a Young Girl*

pp. 39–45

## Daily Objectives

A. To see how Anne is feeling more abused and neglected by her parents
B. To keep pace with the war
C. To appreciate the group's unselfishness about sharing with each other

## Discussion Questions

1. On page 39, Anne describes a situation which caused her to feel hurt. Do you think she has a legitimate complaint? Why do you think Anne is so critical of her mother? Would you agree that her mother is a poor example?
2. Where are Tunis, Algiers, Casablanca and Oran? What do you think Churchill's statement on page 42 means?
3. On what basis did the group decide to take in an eighth person? Why was Dussel chosen?
4. Notice that for the second time Anne has referred to the Van Daans as family. On what page was the first reference?

## Enrichment Activities

1. Write a poem or essay entitled "Mother" or "Father." Try to imagine yourself as a parent. How do you think you would raise your children? What makes a good parent?
2. Write brief reports of Tunis, Algiers, Casablanca and Oran. Tell about their population, government, major religions, climate and products. Draw a map showing their locations.
3. Describe a family you know. What do you think a family should be? In the family-living section of your school

133

or public library, find a book which compares family living in different sections of the world.

4. Look up magazine articles on Winston Churchill and give a report. Churchill wrote many books himself. Perhaps you could make a list of the books he wrote.

*Anne Frank:*
*The Diary of a Young Girl*

pp. 46–72

*Daily Objectives*

A. To notice that a sense of humor still exists in the Secret Annexe
B. To see the changes taking place in Anne's personality
C. To see how Anne is affected by Dussel's presence

*Discussion Questions*

1. Someone once said that humor is truth exaggerated. What are some of the truths contained in the "Prospectus" on page 46? Find other passages in the book which you thought amusing.
2. Anne's moods seem to be getting more depressed. What are some of her problems now?
3. How does Anne describe Dussel? How does sharing her room with him become a problem? Why do you think Anne is feeling so desperate?
4. From time to time, there are events which cause much fear in the group. Be prepared to give an example of one of these occurrences. Why are these incidents so frightening?
5. What kinds of new activities have been added to keep the group busy?

*Enrichment Activities*

1. Write a report on some of the Jewish holidays such as

Hanukkah (Chanukah), Purim, Yom Kippur, and Rosh Hashanah.

2. Draw a mural or set of pictures illustrating the scene on page 52.
3. Describe a time when you were afraid. What was the situation? How did you feel? What did you do? Would you do the same thing today?
4. Make a report on the Netherlands. Find out what you can about Amsterdam before and during the war, and Amsterdam today.
5. Look into the various religious festivals around the world. What various forms of Christmas are celebrated? If the religion is non-Christian, does it have a festival about the same time as Christmas?
6. Write a newspaper article reporting the burglarizing of the Secret Annexe.

*Anne Frank:*
*The Diary of a Young Girl*

pp. 73–91

*Daily Objectives*

A. To understand the significance of Mr. Frank's birthday poem to Anne
B. To note Anne's sarcasm when she is angry
C. To appreciate that Anne's unusual abilities to observe and listen are partly responsible for her writing talent

*Discussion Questions*

1. What does Anne's birthday poem tell us about her parents? Do they really not understand her, as she suggests? What reasons does Mr. Frank offer for disciplining her? In the last few lines, how does Mr. Frank describe Anne?
2. Compare Anne's fourteenth birthday party with the party at the beginning of the book. What is different about the two parties and why?
3. On page 83, Anne describes a scene which depicts her as innocently causing a row with Mrs. Van Daan and Dussel. Make a note of some of the statements Anne makes which could be called sarcastic. How would you

define sarcasm? Why is sarcasm often brutal but funny? What is the meaning of the P.S.?

4. What are some of the details in Anne's descriptions of a typical day and night in the Secret Annexe which demonstrate her unusual ability to observe and listen?

5. Is Anne the only member of her family with literary skills? How do you think her literary skill was developed? What impression are you getting about the educational attitudes of the Franks?

## Enrichment Activities

1. Pretend that you are a close friend of Anne and write a birthday poem for her.

2. Practice watching and listening in your own home or perhaps your classroom for a few days. Then start your own description of a typical day and/or night.

3. Write a description of a person you know who is like a member of your family.

4. Keep a list of all the books you have read lately. Be able to write a sentence or two about each book.

Anne Frank:
The Diary of a Young Girl

pp. 92–120

## Daily Objectives

    A. To note the increasing strain of living in the Secret Annexe

    B. To appreciate Anne's philosophy for offsetting depression

    C. To see the change of tone in Anne's writing indicating her emotional growth

    D. To see Anne beginning to relate to Peter on a more mature basis

## Discussion Questions

1. Through Anne's writing we can become quite familiar with her moods. What are some of the thoughts and scenes she chose to write about which indicate her severe depression at this time?

2. At what point do we see that Anne is coming out of her depression? Why does she think she has been depressed? What kinds of thoughts does she express which help her to overcome the depression? Do you think her depression is natural or not?
3. From page 113 we begin to see a more mature Anne. What kinds of changes are taking place in Anne which indicate she is no longer a child, but a young adult?
4. What is Anne's rationale for deciding to talk to Peter? Why does she prefer him to Margot, her sister? How does this new relationship emphasize the growth in Anne?

*Enrichment Activities*

1. Write a short essay on "My Happiest Moment." Tell what the situation was, how old you were and how you felt.
2. Write a short essay on "My Saddest Moment." Do the same as above, but include what you thought or did to forget your sadness.
3. Think about yourself and the members of your family. How are you alike and how are you different? Why do you suppose sisters and brothers can have very different characteristics? Write a paragraph about your family's individual differences or draw a picture depicting a typical family scene at your house.
4. With two other members of the class, bring family photographs and make a bulletin board display.

*Anne Frank:*
*The Diary of a Young Girl*

pp. 121–140

*Daily Objectives*

    A. To see how Anne is beginning to evaluate people more objectively
    B. To see her begin to develop a plan for interacting with others while being herself
    C. To share with Anne her awakening interest in herself as she physically matures
    D. To see how circumstances can bring people together

*Discussion Questions*

1. What diversions has Anne created lately to pass the time and improve herself?
2. Why is it significant that Anne spends most of her time on creative, constructive activities?
3. Do you think Margot is a much different person from Anne? Explain your answer.
4. How does Anne feel Margot has changed toward her?
5. Anne describes various efforts she has made to become closer to her mother. What were some of these? If you were she, what might you have done?
6. How does Anne decide she is going to operate within the group? Will she be able to maintain her independence?
7. What is so surprising to Anne about the investigation of the cat Boche with Peter?
8. What does Anne tell us of the "underground"? Why do you suppose the people in the underground risk their lives for people like Anne and her family?
9. Contrast Anne's "live or die" attitude on page 139 with her attitude on page 12. What is happening to her? Has she given up?
10. Do you think Anne would be as attracted to Peter if their circumstances were different? Why is this friendship unusually important to both Peter and Anne?

*Enrichment Activities*

1. Think about a person whom you dislike. Write a paper about that person but give him a code name. Tell why you dislike him/her. Does he treat everyone the same way he treats you? Do you think if the person changed you would like him? Is it possible for the person to change what you dislike?
2. Bring in a sample of your own hobby or spare-time activity. Tell the class what sparked your interest and how long you have had this activity.
3. Select two other girls in your class to play the roles of Anne, Mrs. Frank and Margot. Make up a skit which you think demonstrates the relationship of the two girls toward each other and their mother.
4. Be one of four boys in the class who will dramatize the dialogue on pages 132 and 133. The roles would be Henk, Mr. Frank, Mr. Van Daan and Dussel. If you like, add to the scene some appropriate dialogue of your own.

*Anne Frank:*
*The Diary of a Young Girl*

pp. 141–161

*Daily Objectives*

    A.  To see the development of the relationship between Peter and Anne

    B.  To see how this relationship is affecting her feelings about herself as a maturing young woman

    C.  To appreciate Anne's inner spirit and philosophy of life

    D.  To see this book as an example of her inner faith and courage

*Discussion Questions*

1. How has Peter made Anne's life more interesting?
2. On page 148, Anne tells us what her main objectives with Peter are. What are they? Do you think these are the basis for a truly loving relationship? Are these objectives typical of teenagers?
3. How does Anne see herself now in contrast to two years ago?
4. Contrast Mrs. Frank's philosophy on misery and Anne's. Which do you agree with? What are the differences between the two?
5. We have witnessed many of Anne's moods and stages. We have also shared her happinesses and miseries. On pages 149–152, Anne describes her feelings about herself in the past and in the present. She also writes of her philosophy regarding misery. Why is her philosophy so touching? Is Anne realistic? Does she practice what she preaches? Why is her book a symbol of the courage and human spirit of which she talks?

*Enrichment Activities*

1. Write a story or poem entitled "My First Love."
2. Draw a picture of what you think Peter looks like.

3. Think about yourself as a child. How have you changed your ideas, attitudes, and behavior? Write a "before" and "after" comparison of yourself.
4. Two girls and three boys form a group to expand the dialogue on pages 154 and 155. Perform your skit in the classroom.
5. Use the quote "Love often springs from pity" as the theme for either a poem or a short story.


*Anne Frank:*
*The Diary of a Young Girl*

pp. 161–194


*Daily Objectives*

    A.   To see Anne and Margot relating to each other more as friends than rivals
    B.   To see the parents' reaction to the friendship between Peter and Anne
    C.   To see how Anne feels about her ability to write


*Discussion Questions*

1. What does Margot's letter tell us about her feelings? Does this disprove any of Anne's notions about her sister?
2. How would you say Anne reacted to her sister's letter? Was she jealous, understanding, selfish, provocative or what?
3. How does Margot's style of writing compare to Anne's? Do you think she is as bright as Anne? Does she write as well, worse, or better?
4. How have the parents of Peter and Anne begun to view their friendship?
5. What effects is the war having on the general populace, according to Anne?
6. What is so satisfying to Anne about writing? Why is her question, ". . . will I ever be able to write anything great?", significant? What is the importance of her statement, "I want to go on living even after my death!"?
7. How did the burglars cause the routine of the Secret Annexe to change?
8. How is Anne affected by her first kiss? Even though she is happy, she feels many other things too. How would you describe those other feelings?

*Enrichment Activities*

1. Write a paper evaluating the relationship between Anne and her sister Margot. Are they close? Do they act like most sisters act? Even though Anne is younger, what advantages does she have over Margot at this time?
2. Write a paper or poem about your own sister or brother.
3. Describe your impression of Anne's parents. How are they similar to most parents? Do you think they were unduly strict about Anne and Peter?
4. Write a short story of your own about war from a civilian's point of view. Try to imagine what you would do if this country were suddenly plunged into war on our own grounds.
5. Imagine yourself as the burglar of the Secret Annexe who becomes suspicious that Jewish people are hiding there. What would you do? Build a mystery story around this idea.

*Anne Frank:*
*The Diary of a Young Girl*

pp. 194–Epilogue

*Daily Objectives*

    A. To reflect on the questions Anne asks regarding war, privations, and human instincts
    B. To reflect with Anne on racial and religious attitudes
    C. To consider the statements "All children must look after their own upbringing" and "For in its innermost depths youth is lonelier than old age"

*Discussion Questions*

1. On page 197, Anne asks some questions about war, peace and destruction. Could we ask the same questions today? Compare the current world situation with the time of Anne's diary. What are the similarities and differences?
2. Anne says the little man is as guilty as the politicians for the war. Otherwise people of the world would rise up in

revolt. In what ways can the little man express his dislike of a government's policies? Give examples of methods used in this country to demonstrate dislike.

3. How would you define the words *prejudice, scapegoat* and *anti-Semitism*? Are these words applicable to our society today? Give examples.

4. Why is it unfair to belittle a group of people on the basis of their race, religion or nationality?

5. Is it possible to achieve freedom, truth and right when people are prejudiced toward each other? How can an individual overcome his personal prejudices toward his fellow-man?

6. How does the above question relate to the statement, "All children must look after their own upbringing"?

7. Do you agree that the "final forming of a person's character lies in his own hands"? Explain your answer.

8. Why is it that youth is lonelier than old age? What does this mean when you consider youth's attempts to change fixed, old ideas? How could this statement relate to a young person attempting to change his social attitudes?

9. Briefly describe your feelings about Anne Frank as you finished the book.

*Enrichment Activities*

1. Collect some information on the history and present status of the war in Vietnam from newspapers and magazines. How is the civilian population being affected by this war? See if you can find any organizations or individuals who are attempting to help the civilians of Vietnam. Make a booklet of the articles and pictures.

2. Collect articles from magazines and newspapers on any group of people seeking full civil rights. Make a scrapbook or poster display of these articles.

3. Investigate the history of "civil disobedience" and its use in this country as well as overseas to change laws, customs and attitudes. Make an oral or written report to be presented to the class.

4. Select a minority group and find out all you can about the history and current status of that group.

5. Read a book on the three major religions of the United States and make a chart comparing basic beliefs.

6. Look in the reference book *Who's Who* and compile a list of famous people who are members of minority groups.

7. Draw a map of the United States and label those areas of the country where there are large pockets of minority

groups. Find out the reasons a large minority population occupies these areas.

8. Rewrite your own epilogue for this book. Were you satisfied with the ending? If not, how would you have preferred the epilogue to read?

9. Write a review of this book pretending it will be submitted to a newspaper or magazine.

10. Write a character sketch of Anne Frank or any other member of the Secret Annexe

# QUOTATIONS

## from *Anne Frank: The Diary of a Young Girl*

143

"Lazyness may appear attractive, but work *gives* satisfaction." 226
"A quiet conscience makes one strong." 227
"All children must look after their own upbringing." 230
"The final forming of a person's character lies in his own hands." 230

## ONE HUNDRED WORDS

degradation
enhance
albeit
emigrated
pogroms
capitulation
succession
prohibited
devour
ardent
blithely
speculation
florin
pondered
inventiveness
absurd
accompany
stimulant
accordingly
fanatic
*vix satis*
conditionally
superfluous
overawed
stifled
sufficiently
W.C.
oppressive
phenomenon
hypochondria
piqued
waxed—waned
lorries

enthralling
ingenious
surreptitiously
reprimands
lenient
unassuming
urchins
herald (verb)
hypercritical
calamity
staid
loathe
relentless
aggressor
emancipation
saboteurs
hemorrhage
abdominal
distorted
ventilated
incendiary
precaution
siege
duodenal
clandestine
shamming
grouser
oculist
petrified
indignant
seething
het up
wrath

professed
monopolized
pedantic
smoldering
droning
extremity
subsided
dispersed
proficient
calculating
coquetry
irrevocable
envies
tranquillity
impenetrable
implore
recede
nib
celluloid
consolation
cremated
condole
mania
refrain
beseeched
brusquely
diligently
pensive
delve
furbelows
intuition
wretched
reproaches
despondency

# APPENDIX

*Sample from the* Guide to Periodical Literature

ANTI-SEMITISM

Unforgiving; concerning survey findings of Charles Y. Glock and Rodney Stark. Newsweek 67:66 My 2 '66

Anguish of the Jews, by E. H. Flannery, review Sat R 48:34 Ju 19 '65 A. L. Sachar

Anti-Semitic noises: Austria, Newsweek 67:46 Mr 14 '66

CIVIL RIGHTS

New turn? Alabama trials: Brewster, Liuzzo, and Reeb cases. Sr Schol 87:4-5 Ju 7 '66

Protectors: trial of Klansmen accused of harassing Negroes: Athens. Time 88:20 Ju 8 '66

Whitewashed court: cases involving the shooting and murder of civil rights workers on trial in Hayneville, Ala. Time 88:36 O 7 '66

JEWS

### Arabs

Diary of the Sinai campaign, by M. Dayan. Time 87:111 + Je 24 '66 review

Ancient hatred builds toward war; struggle for water. G. DeCarvalho Life 58:44 + Je 18 '65

Storm troopers; terrorist group of Palestinian Arabs. Time 85:31A 31B Je 18 '65

### Denmark

Denmark's heroic week, Sr Schol 89:3 O 7 '66

### History

Jews in their land; ed. by D. Ben-Gurion. Sat R 49:26 Au 20 '66

PERSECUTION

Worst that ever happened—Poland with editorial comment. Sat Eve Post 239:29-33+, 112 O 22 '66

Blood accusation, by M. Samuel. Newsweek 68:100-1 Au 22 '66

Was silence the only solution? G. Lewy. Sat R 49:26-7 My 21 '66

Forgive them not, for they knew what they did: Warsaw ghetto. A. M. Rosenthal. il N Y Times Mag p. 50-1+ O 24 '65 Discussion p 22 N 7 '65

Et tu Tito? Yugoslav report on Stalin's concentration camps. Time 85:27 F 19 '65

## WAR CRIMINALS

Last prisoner of Spandau: R. Hess, P. Shabecoff N Y
Times Mag p 28–9+ Au 28 '66

Case against Eichman continues. A. L. Fein Sat R 49:27
+ Ju 2 '66

Looking backward: Auschwitz. Newsweek 66:39–40
Au 30 '65

## LESS-THAN-A-DOLLAR LIST
## OF
## RELATED READING

| | | | |
|---|---|---|---|
| Anderson, M. | *My Lord, What a Morning* | Avon | .60 |
| Bahm, A. | *The World's Living Religions* | Dell | .75 |
| Beckhard, A. | *Albert Einstein* | Avon | .50 |
| Bocca, G. | *The Adventurous Life of Winston Churchill* | Avon | .50 |
| Brickhill, P. | *The Great Escape* | Crest | .50 |
| Buck, P. | *My Several Worlds* | PB | .75 |
| Carr, W. | *JFK: An Informal Biography* | Lance | .50 |
| Congdon, D. | *Combat: European Theater —World War II* | Dell | .60 |
| ——— | *Combat: The War with Germany* | Dell | .60 |
| Day, C. | *Life with Father* and *Life with Mother* | WSP | .60 |
| Delarue, J. | *The Gestapo* | Dell | .75 |
| Dimont, M. | *Jews, God and History* | Sig | .95 |
| Fischer, L. | *Gandhi* | Ment | .60 |
| Frank, A. | *Tales from the House Behind* | Ban | .50 |
| Gaer, J. | *How the Great Religions Began* | Sig | .60 |
| ——— | *What the Great Religions Believe* | Sig | .60 |
| Gilbreth, F., and Carey, E. | *Cheaper by the Dozen* | Ban | .50 |
| Hart, M. | *Act One* | Sig | .75 |

146

| Heimler, E. | Concentration Camp | Pyr | .50 |
|---|---|---|---|
| Hersey, J. | The Wall | PB | .75 |
| Hirsch, P. | Great Untold Stories of World War II | Pyr | .50 |
| Howarth, D. | D Day | Pyr | .50 |
| Hudson, V. | O Ye Jigs & Juleps! | Macf | .60 |
| Jarman, T. | The Rise and Fall of Nazi Germany | Sig | .75 |
| Knight, C. | We Were There at the Normandy Invasion | G&D | .50 |
| Landis, B. | World Religions | Duttn | .95 |
| Landis, J., and Landis, M. | Teen-agers Guide for Living | Tower | .50 |
| Levi, P. | Survival in Auschwitz: The Nazi Assault on Humanity | Cllr | .95 |
| Lewis, C. | Cassius Clay | Macf | .60 |
| Martin, R., and Harrity, R. | World War II: A Photographic Record of the War in Europe from D-Day to V-E Day | GM | .60 |
| Morton, F. | The Rothschilds | Crest | .75 |
| Needham, I. | Biographies of Great Composers | High | .75 |
| New York Times | Churchill: In Memoriam | Ban | .75 |
| Roosevelt, E. | This Is My Story | Dolp | .95 |
| Ross, F., and Hills, T. | Great Religions by Which Men Live | Prem | .60 |
| Ryan, C. | The Longest Day | Crest | .75 |
| Schroter, H. | Stalingrad | Bal | .75 |
| Schultz, J. | My Life as an Indian | Prem | .60 |
| Shirer, W. | Berlin Diary | Pop | .95 |
| Smith, H. | The Religions of Man | PL | .85 |
| Uris, L. | Exodus | Ban | .95 |
| ——— | Mila 18 | Ban | .95 |
| Van Wagenen, B. | Ways of Life in Africa | High | .75 |
| Washington, B. | Up from Slavery | Dell | .45 |
| Wouk, H. | Marjorie Morningstar | Sig | .95 |
| Wright, R. | Black Boy | Sig | .75 |

# READING LIST

## OF

## 1,000 PAPERBACK BOOKS

| | | | |
|---|---|---|---|
| Adamson, J. | Born Free | Ban | .75 |
| ——— | Forever Free | Macf | .75 |
| ——— | Living Free | Ban | .75 |
| Addams, C. | Addams and Evil | PB | .50 |
| ——— | Drawn and Quartered | PB | .50 |
| ——— | Homebodies | PB | .50 |
| ——— | Monster Rally | PB | .50 |
| ——— | Nightcrawlers | PB | .50 |
| Adler, B. | Dear President Johnson | Avon | .40 |
| ——— | The Ghost Wore White | G&D | .50 |
| ——— | The Kennedy Wit | Ban | .60 |
| ——— | Kids' Letters to President Kennedy | PB | .35 |
| ——— | The Mystery of the Ruby Queens | G&D | .50 |
| ——— | The Secret of Black Cat Gulch | G&D | .40 |
| ——— | The Yellow Warning | G&D | .40 |
| Adler, I. | Thinking Machines | Sig | .60 |
| Agee, J. | A Death in the Family | Avon | .75 |
| Agnew, D. | Undercover Agent: Narcotics | Macf | .50 |
| Aldrich, B. | A Lantern in Her Hand | G&D | .50 |
| Allen, B. | The Riddle in Red | G&D | .50 |
| Anderson, W. | My Lord, What a Morning | Avon | .60 |
| Andrews, R. | The Quest of the Snow Leopard | G&D | .50 |
| Annixter, J. and P. | Buffalo Chief | Dell | .35 |
| Annixter, P. | Swiftwater | SBS | .50 |
| Anon. | Superman | Sig | .50 |
| Armer, A. | Screwball | G&D | .50 |
| Arthur, B. and B. | The Stranger | Avon | .40 |
| ——— | Walk Tall, Ride Tall | Sig | .40 |
| Asimov, I. | The Currents of Space | Lance | .75 |
| ——— | The End of Eternity | Lance | .50 |
| ——— | Naked Sun | Lance | .50 |

| | | | |
|---|---|---|---|
| ——— | Pebble in the Sky | Ban | .50 |
| ——— | The Rest of the Robots | Pyr | .50 |
| ——— | Search for the Elements | Prem | .60 |
| ——— | Second Foundation | Avon | .60 |
| ——— | The Stars Like Dust | Lance | .50 |
| Bagnold, E. | National Velvet | G&D | .50 |
| Baker, W. | Departure Deferred | Macf | .50 |
| Baldwin, F. | Three Women | Dell | .50 |
| Baldwin, J. | Blues for Mr. Charlie | Dell | .60 |
| ——— | The Fire Next Time | Dell | .50 |
| ——— | Go Tell It on the Mountain | Dell | .60 |
| ——— | Nobody Knows My Name | Dell | .50 |
| ——— | Notes of a Native Son | Ban | .60 |
| Ball, J. | Judo Boy | Nova | .50 |
| Barlow, R. | Black Treasure | G&D | .50 |
| ——— | The Danger at Mormon Crossing | G&D | .50 |
| ——— | Fire at Red Lake | G&D | .45 |
| ——— | Stormy Voyage | G&D | .50 |
| Barr, D. | How and Why Wonder Book of Primitive Man | G&D | .59 |
| Barrett, W. | The Lilies of the Field | Pop | .40 |
| Barton, G. | Real Spies | Nova | .50 |
| Bassett, J. | In Harm's Way | Sig | .75 |
| Baum, L. | The Wizard of Oz | Airmt | .50 |
| Beach, E. | Run Silent, Run Deep | PB | .50 |
| ——— | Submarine! | Sig | .60 |
| Benedict, S. | Tales of Terror and Suspense | Dell | .45 |
| Benner, R. and S. | Sex and the Teenager | Macf | .60 |
| Bennett, E. | I, Judy | Nova | .50 |
| ——— | Walk in the Moonlight | Nova | .40 |
| Bennett, G. | Great Tales of Action and Adventure | Dell | .40 |
| Bennett, J. | Jamie | Ban | .50 |
| Benson, S. | Junior Miss | WSP | .60 |
| ——— | Meet Me in St. Louis | Ban | .45 |
| Berenstain, S. and J. | Flipsville/Squaresville | Dell | .45 |
| Berrill, N. | The Living Tide | Prem | .60 |
| Bishop, J. | The Day Lincoln Was Shot | PL | .85 |
| ——— | A Day in the Life of President Kennedy | Ban | .50 |
| Blake, R. | 101 Elephant Jokes | Pyr | .40 |
| Bligh, W. | The Mutiny on Board H.M.S. *Bounty* | Sig | .60 |
| Bluestone, G. | The Private World of Cully Powers | Ace | .50 |
| Bolton, C. | Christy | G&D | .50 |

| Bonham, F. | Burma Rifles | Berk | .50 |
| —————— | War Beneath the Sea | Berk | .50 |
| Bonsall, G. | How and Why Wonder Book of Weather | G&D | .59 |
| Borland, H. | When the Legends Die | Ban | .60 |
| Boulle, P. | A Bridge over the River Kwai | Ban | .50 |
| Bowen, R. | Flight into Danger | Nova | .40 |
| —————— | Hot Rod Angels | Nova | .50 |
| —————— | Perfect Game | Nova | .45 |
| Bradbury, R. | Dandelion Wine | Ban | .60 |
| —————— | Fahrenheit 451 | Bal | .50 |
| —————— | The Illustrated Man | Ban | .50 |
| —————— | The Machineries of Joy | Ban | .60 |
| —————— | The Martian Chronicles | Ban | .60 |
| —————— | Medicine for Melancholy | Ban | .60 |
| —————— | R Is for Rocket | Ban | .50 |
| Braithwaite, E. | To Sir, With Love | Pyr | .60 |
| Brand, M. | Dead or Alive | Pop | .50 |
| —————— | The Gambler | PB | .50 |
| —————— | The Garden of Eden | PB | .50 |
| —————— | Gentle Gunman | PB | .50 |
| —————— | Hired Guns | PB | .35 |
| —————— | The Stranger | PB | .50 |
| —————— | White Wolf | PB | .35 |
| Brand, O. | Folksongs for Fun | Berk | .75 |
| Brean, H. | How to Stop Smoking | PB | .35 |
| Brickhill, P. | Escape or Die | Pyr | .60 |
| —————— | The Great Escape | Crest | .50 |
| Brinley, B. | Rocket Manual for Amateurs | Bal | .75 |
| Buchan, J. | The 39 Steps | Pop | .40 |
| Buck, F. and Anthony, E. | Wild Cargo | Lance | .50 |
| Buck, P. | Fighting Angel | PB | .50 |
| —————— | The Good Earth | PB | .50 |
| —————— | The Hidden Flower | PB | .50 |
| Bunn, M. | Gus Wilson's Model Garage | Berk | .45 |
| Burgess, A. | The Inn of the Sixth Happiness | Ban | .50 |
| Burnford, S. | The Incredible Journey | Ban | .50 |
| Burroughs, E. | The Beasts of Tarzan | Bal | .50 |
| —————— | The Chessmen of Mars | Bal | .50 |
| —————— | Escape on Venus | Ace | .40 |
| —————— | The Eternal Savage | Ace | .40 |
| —————— | A Fighting Man of Mars | Ace | .40 |
| —————— | The Gods of Mars | Bal | .50 |
| —————— | Jungle Tales of Tarzan | Bal | .50 |
| —————— | The Lad and the Lion | Bal | .50 |

| | | | |
|---|---|---|---|
| ———— | The Land of Hidden Men | Ace | .40 |
| ———— | Llana of Gathol | Bal | .50 |
| ———— | The Mad King | Ace | .40 |
| ———— | The Master Mind of Mars | Bal | .50 |
| ———— | The Monster Men | Ace | .40 |
| ———— | The Moon Maid | Ace | .40 |
| ———— | The Mucker | Bal | .75 |
| ———— | Out of Time's Abyss | Ace | .40 |
| ———— | The People That Time Forgot | Ace | .40 |
| ———— | A Princess of Mars | Bal | .50 |
| ———— | The Return of Tarzan | Bal | .50 |
| ———— | Savage Pellucidar | Ace | .40 |
| ———— | The Son of Tarzan | Bal | .50 |
| ———— | The Swords of Mars | Bal | .50 |
| ———— | Synthetic Men of Mars | Bal | .50 |
| ———— | Tanar of Pellucidar | Ace | .40 |
| ———— | Tarzan and the Ant Men | Bal | .50 |
| ———— | Tarzan and the Castaways | Bal | .50 |
| ———— | Tarzan and the City of Gold | Ace | .40 |
| ———— | Tarzan and the Forbidden City | Bal | .50 |
| ———— | Tarzan and the Foreign Legion | Bal | .50 |
| ———— | Tarzan and the Golden Lion | Bal | .50 |
| ———— | Tarzan and the Jewels of Opar | Bal | .50 |
| ———— | Tarzan and the Leopard Men | Bal | .50 |
| ———— | Tarzan and the Lion Man | Ace | .40 |
| ———— | Tarzan and the Lost Empire | Bal | .50 |
| ———— | Tarzan and the Madman | Bal | .50 |
| ———— | Tarzan at the Earth's Core | Ace | .40 |
| ———— | Tarzan, Lord of the Jungle | Bal | .50 |
| ———— | Tarzan of the Apes | Bal | .50 |
| ———— | Tarzan, the Invincible | Ace | .40 |
| ———— | Tarzan the Magnificent | Bal | .50 |
| ———— | Tarzan the Terrible | Bal | .50 |
| ———— | Tarzan the Untamed | Bal | .50 |
| ———— | Tarzan Triumphant | Ace | .40 |
| ———— | Thuvia, Maid of Mars | Bal | .50 |
| ———— | The War Chief | Bal | .50 |
| ———— | The Warlord of Mars | Bal | .50 |
| Busch, H. | U-Boats at War | Bal | .50 |
| Butters, D. | Heart's Design | Berk | .40 |
| Cadell, E. | I Love a Lass | Berk | .45 |
| Cain, A. | Young People and Drinking: The Use and Abuse of Beverage Alcohol | Dell | .40 |
| Caldwell, E. | This Very Earth | Sig | .50 |

| | | | |
|---|---|---|---|
| Caldwell, T. | The Strong City | Pyr | .75 |
| Campbell, R. | Drag Doll | Nova | .50 |
| Canaway, W. | A Boy Ten Feet Tall | Bal | .50 |
| Canfield, D. | The Bent Twig | G&D | .75 |
| Carr, H. | Confidential Secretary | Berk | .45 |
| Carroll, L. | Alice's Adventures in Wonderland and Through the Looking Glass | Airmt | .50 |
| Carson, J. | The Coach Nobody Liked | Dell | .50 |
| ———— | Hotshot | Dell | .50 |
| Carson, R. | The Sea Around Us | Sig | .60 |
| ———— | Silent Spring | Crest | .75 |
| ———— | Under the Sea Wind | Sig | .60 |
| Carter, R. | Those Devils in Baggy Pants | Sig | .60 |
| Catton, B. | Stillness at Appomattox | PB | .75 |
| Cavanna, B. | Accent on April | Berk | .50 |
| ———— | Angel on Skis | Berk | .50 |
| ———— | The Boy Next Door | Berk | .50 |
| ———— | A Date for Diane | Berk | .50 |
| ———— | Diane's New Love | Berk | .50 |
| ———— | Fancy Free | Berk | .50 |
| ———— | The Scarlet Sail | Berk | .45 |
| ———— | 6 on Easy Street | Berk | .50 |
| ———— | Spurs for Suzanna | SBS | .50 |
| ———— | A Time for Tenderness | Berk | .50 |
| ———— | Toujours Diane | Berk | .50 |
| Cerf, B. | The Laugh's on Me | PB | .35 |
| ———— | Out on a Limerick | PB | .35 |
| Cerf, B. and P. | Stories Selected from the Unexpected | Ban | .50 |
| Chamberlain, W. | Combat General | SBS | .45 |
| ———— | Hellbent for Glory | pbl | .60 |
| Charnwood, Lord | Abraham Lincoln | PB | .35 |
| Churchill, R. and B. | Guide to Glamour and Personality | Nova | .50 |
| Clark, D. | To Goof or Not to Goof | Crest | .40 |
| Clarke, A.C. | Challenge of the Sea | Dell | .50 |
| ———— | Childhood's End | Bal | .60 |
| ———— | Earthlight | Bal | .50 |
| ———— | Profiles of the Future | Ban | .75 |
| ———— | Reach for Tomorrow | Bal | .50 |
| ———— | Tales of Ten Worlds | Dell | .50 |
| Clavell, J. | King Rat | Crest | .75 |
| Cleary, B. | Beaver and Wally | Berk | .50 |
| Coe, G. | How and Why Wonder Book of Fish | G&D | .59 |
| Colby, C. | Strangely Enough | SBS | .35 |
| ———— | Weirdest People in the World | Pop | .50 |

| Collins, F. | FBI in Peace and War | Ace | .50 |
|---|---|---|---|
| Collins, W. | Moonstone | Pyr | .75 |
| Colman, H. | A Crown for Gina | Pyr | .45 |
| ———— | Dangerous Summer | Ban | .45 |
| ———— | Julie Builds Her Castle | Dell | .50 |
| Comics, E. | Tales of the Incredible | Bal | .50 |
| Congdon, D. | Combat: European Theater —World War II | Dell | .60 |
| ———— | Combat: Pacific Theater —World War II | Dell | .60 |
| ———— | Combat: The War with Germany | Dell | .60 |
| ———— | Combat: War with Japan | Dell | .60 |
| Conklin, G. | Great Stories of Space Travel | G&D | .50 |
| ———— | Giants Unleashed | G&D | .50 |
| ———— | Invaders of Earth | G&D | .60 |
| ———— | The Supernatural Reader | Cllr | .95 |
| ———— | 13 Great Classics of Science-Fiction | GM | .50 |
| Conot, R. | Ministers of Vengeance | Ban | .95 |
| Conrad, J. | Lord Jim | Ban | .50 |
| Considine, B., and Ruth B. | The Babe Ruth Story | SBS | .50 |
| Coolidge, O. | Hercules and Other Tales from Greek Myths | SBS | .35 |
| Coombs, C. | Adventure Stories | PB | .50 |
| ———— | The Mystery of Satellite Seven | G&D | .50 |
| Cooper, J. | The Deerslayer | WSP | .60 |
| ———— | The Last of the Mohicans | Airmt | .50 |
| ———— | The Pathfinder | WSP | .60 |
| ———— | The Pioneers | Airmt | .60 |
| ———— | The Prairie | Airmt | .60 |
| Copland, A. | What to Listen for in Music | Ment | .60 |
| Corbett, J. | Man-Eaters of Kumaon | Ban | .60 |
| Corbin, W. | Deadline | G&D | .50 |
| ———— | High Road Home | G&D | .50 |
| Cottrell, L. | The Horizon Book of Lost Worlds | Dell | .75 |
| ———— | Wonders of the World | G&D | .50 |
| Cousteau, J., and Dugan, J. | The Living Sea | PB | .75 |
| Cousteau, J., and Dumas, F. | The Silent World | PL | .75 |
| Cousy, B. | Basketball Is My Life | JLP | .50 |
| Craig, M. | Marsha | Berk | .50 |
| ———— | Now That I'm Sixteen | Berk | .50 |
| ———— | Trish | Berk | .50 |

| | | | |
|---|---|---|---|
| Crane, S. | The Red Badge of Courage and 4 Great Stories | Dell | .50 |
| Curie, E. | Madame Curie | PB | .75 |
| Dana, R. | Two Years Before the Mast | Pyr | .35 |
| Daniels, J. | War Party | Sig | .50 |
| Davenport, B. | Deals with the Devil | Bal | .50 |
| Davis, Mac | Baseball's Unforgettables | Ban | .50 |
| Davis, Maxine | Sex and the Adolescent | Perm | .50 |
| | Sexual Responsibility in Marriage | Dell | .95 |
| DeFoe, D. | Robinson Crusoe | Dell | .40 |
| DeJong, D. | By Marvelous Agreement | Berk | .40 |
| Dennis, P. | Auntie Mame | Pop | .75 |
| Dern, P. | Orchids for a Nurse | Lance | .40 |
| Dickens, C. | A Tale of Two Cities | Sig | .50 |
| Donovan, R. | P.T. 109 | Crest | .50 |
| Dooley, T. | Deliver Us from Evil | Sig | .60 |
| —— | Doctor Tom Dooley, My Story | Sig | .50 |
| —— | The Edge of Tomorrow | Sig | .60 |
| —— | The Night They Burned the Mountain | Sig | .60 |
| Dorian, E. | The Twisted Shadow | Berk | .45 |
| —— | Mystery on Graveyard Head | Berk | .50 |
| Dorman, M. | We Shall Overcome | Dell | .75 |
| Doss, H. | The Family Nobody Wanted | SBS | .50 |
| Douglas, L. | Magnificent Obsession | PB | .50 |
| —— | The Robe | PB | .75 |
| Douglass, Frederick | Narrative of the Life of Frederick Douglass, Slave | Dolph | .95 |
| Doyle, A. C. | The Adventures of Sherlock Holmes | Berk | .60 |
| —— | The Hound of the Baskervilles | Berk | .50 |
| —— | Great Stories of Sherlock Holmes | Dell | .50 |
| —— | The Lost World | Berk | .50 |
| —— | A Study in Scarlet and The Sign of Four | Berk | .50 |
| —— | The Valley of Fear | Berk | .50 |
| Dreiser, T. | An American Tragedy | Sig | .95 |
| Duberman, M. | In White America | Sig | .60 |
| DuBois, W. | The Souls of Black Folk | Crest | .60 |
| du Jardin, R. | Boy Trouble | Berk | .50 |
| —— | Double Date | Berk | .45 |
| —— | A Man for Marcy | Berk | .50 |
| —— | One of the Crowd | Berk | .50 |
| —— | The Real Thing | Berk | .50 |
| —— | Wedding in the Family | Berk | .50 |

| | | | |
|---|---|---|---|
| Dumas, A. | The Count of Monte Cristo | Ban | .75 |
| Du Maurier, D. | Rebecca | PB | .50 |
| Durrell, G. | The Whispering Land | Berk | .60 |
| ———— | Zoo in My Luggage | Berk | .60 |
| Duvall, E. | The Art of Dating | PB | .50 |
| Edmonds, W. | Chad Hanna | Ban | .75 |
| ———— | Drums along the Mohawk | Ban | .75 |
| Edwards, F. | Strange People | Pop | .50 |
| ———— | Strange World | Ace | .50 |
| ———— | Stranger than Science | Ace | .50 |
| ———— | Strangest of All | Ace | .50 |
| Ehrmann, W. | Premarital Dating Behavior | Ban | .75 |
| Ellis, H. | On Life and Sex | Sig | .60 |
| Ellison, R. | Invisible Man | Sig | .95 |
| Emery, A. | County Fair | Berk | .45 |
| ———— | First Love, True Love | Berk | .45 |
| ———— | First Orchid for Pat | Berk | .45 |
| ———— | Hickory Hill | Berk | .45 |
| ———— | Married on Wednesday | Berk | .45 |
| ———— | Scarlet Royal | SBS | .35 |
| ———— | Senior Year | SBS | .50 |
| Essien-Udom, E. | Black Nationalism | Dell | .75 |
| Everett, W. | First Command | Bal | .50 |
| Falkner, J. | Moonfleet | G&D | .50 |
| Fallon, M. and Saunders, J. | Muscle Building for Beginners | Arc | .95 |
| Fast, H. | April Morning | Ban | .50 |
| Felsen, H. | The Crash Club | Ban | .50 |
| ———— | Davey Logan, Interne | Berk | .45 |
| ———— | Hot Rod | Ban | .50 |
| ———— | Rag Top | Ban | .50 |
| ———— | Road Rocket | Ban | .50 |
| ———— | Street Rod | Ban | .50 |
| ———— | To My Son, the Teen-Age Driver | Ban | .50 |
| Ferber, E. | So Big | Avon | .60 |
| Fichter, G. | Snakes | Gold | .25 |
| Fiennes, R. | Man, Nature and Disease | Sig | .75 |
| Fisher, C. | The Blue Mustang | PB | .35 |
| ———— | The Brass Command | PB | .50 |
| ———— | Santa Fe Passage | PB | .45 |
| ———— | The Tall Men | PB | .50 |
| ———— | Yellow Hair | PB | .35 |
| ———— | Yellowstone Kelly | PB | .45 |
| Fleming, I. | Casino Royale | Sig | .60 |
| ———— | The Diamond Smugglers | Dell | .50 |
| ———— | Diamonds Are Forever | Sig | .60 |
| ———— | Doctor No | Sig | .60 |
| ———— | For Your Eyes Only | Sig | .60 |

| | | | |
|---|---|---|---|
| ———— | From Russia, With Love | Sig | .60 |
| ———— | Goldfinger | Sig | .60 |
| ———— | Live and Let Die | Sig | .60 |
| ———— | The Man with the Golden Gun | Sig | .60 |
| ———— | Moonraker | Sig | .60 |
| | On Her Majesty's Secret Service | Sig | .60 |
| ———— | Thunderball | Sig | .60 |
| | You Only Live Twice | Sig | .60 |
| Floren, L. | Deputy's Revenge | pbl | .45 |
| Fordham, P. | The Robber's Tale | Pop | .50 |
| Forester, C. | The African Queen | Ban | .60 |
| ———— | The Gun | Ban | .50 |
| ———— | The Ship | Ban | .45 |
| ———— | Sink the Bismarck! | Ban | .50 |
| Fowles, J. | The Collector | Dell | .75 |
| Francis, H. | Big Swat | Sig | .50 |
| Frank, A. | The Diary of a Young Girl | PB | .50 |
| Freedman, Nancy and Benedict | Mrs. Mike | Ban | .50 |
| Frick, C. | Comeback Guy | VoyB | .60 |
| Friedenberg, E. | The Vanishing Adolescent | Dell | .50 |
| Funk, W., and Lewis, N. | 30 Days to a More Powerful Vocabulary | WSP | .60 |
| Furman, A. | Ghost Stories | PB | .50 |
| ———— | Romance Stories | PB | .50 |
| Furneaux, R. | The World's Strangest Mysteries | Ace | .50 |
| Gaddis, T. | Birdman of Alcatraz | Sig | .60 |
| Gaer, J. | How the Great Religions Began | Sig | .60 |
| Gaines, W. | Brothers Mad | Bal | .50 |
| ———— | It's a World, World, World, World Mad | Sig | .50 |
| ———— | The Mad Sampler | Sig | .50 |
| ———— | The Self-Made Mad | Sig | .50 |
| Gallagher, R., and Colvin, J. | Words Most Often Misspelled and Mispronounced | WSP | .60 |
| Gallico, P. | The Hurricane Story | Berk | .50 |
| Gamow, G. | A Planet Called Earth | Ban | .75 |
| Gann, E. | Fate Is the Hunter | Crest | .75 |
| Garagiola, J. | Baseball Is a Funny Game | Ban | .60 |
| Garrison, J. | Come Walk with Love | pbl | .50 |
| Gasser, H. | How to Draw and Paint | Dell | .75 |
| Gault, W. | Drag Strip | Berk | .50 |
| ———— | Speedway Challenge | Berk | .50 |
| ———— | Thunder Road | Berk | .50 |

156

| Geis, D. | How and Why Wonder Book of Dinosaurs | G&D | .59 |
| Gelinas, P. | How and Why Wonder Book of Coins and Currency | G&D | .59 |
| Gibson, Althea | I Always Wanted to Be Somebody | PL | .60 |
| Gibson, W. | The Miracle Worker | Ban | .50 |
| Gilbreth, F., and Carey, E. | Cheaper by the Dozen | Ban | .50 |
| Gipson, F. | Hound-Dog Man | PL | .50 |
| ———— | Old Yeller | PL | .50 |
| ———— | Savage Sam | PB | .35 |
| Glazer, T. | New Treasury of Folk Songs | Ban | .60 |
| Golden, H. | Mr. Kennedy and the Negroes | Crest | .60 |
| Goodman, I. | Stan Musial | Macf | .50 |
| Goodman, R., and Lewin, D. | New Ways to Greater Word Power | Dell | .40 |
| Gordons, The | That Darn Cat | Ban | .50 |
| Graham, F. | Bowling Secrets from the Stars | Macf | .50 |
| Graham, L. | South Town | Sig | .50 |
| Gregory, D. | From the Back of the Bus | Avon | .60 |
| Gregory, D., and Lipsyte, R. | Nigger | PB | .75 |
| Grey, Z. | The Last of the Plainsmen | Ban | .45 |
| Grider, G., and Sims, L. | War Fish | Pyr | .50 |
| Griffin, J. | Black Like Me | Sig | .60 |
| Guttmacher, A. | Pregnancy and Birth | Sig | .60 |
| Haas, B. | KKK | Rgncy | .50 |
| ———— | Look Away, Look Away | PB | .75 |
| Hailey, A., and Castle, J. | Runway Zero-Eight | Ban | .45 |
| Hall, A. | Beauty Queen | Nova | .40 |
| Halliday, B. | Call for Mike Shane | Dell | .40 |
| ———— | The Corpse That Never Was | Dell | .40 |
| ———— | Shoot to Kill | Dell | .45 |
| Hamilton, D. | Line of Fire | GM | .40 |
| ———— | Mad River | GM | .40 |
| ———— | Murderers' Row | GM | .50 |
| ———— | Steel Mirror | GM | .50 |
| ———— | The Wrecking Crew | GM | .50 |
| Hamilton, E. | Mythology | Ment | .75 |
| Hammett, D. | The Glass Key | Dell | .50 |
| ———— | The Maltese Falcon | Dell | .50 |
| ———— | The Thin Man | Dell | .50 |
| Hanle, D. | The Hairdo Handbook | Dell | .75 |
| Hano, A. | Willie Mays | G&D | .50 |

| Hansberry, L. | Raisin in the Sun and The Sign in Sidney Brustein's Window | Sig | .60 |
| Harkins, P. | The Day of the Drag Race | Berk | .50 |
| —————— | Argentine Road Race | Berk | .50 |
| —————— | Young Skin Diver | Berk | .50 |
| Harte, B. | The Outcasts of Poker Flat and Other Tales | Sig | .50 |
| Haufrecht, H. | 'Round the World Folksing | Berk | .75 |
| Hawthorne, N. | The Scarlet Letter | Dell | .50 |
| Haycraft, H. | The Boys' Book of Great Detective Stories | Berk | .50 |
| —————— | The Boys' Second Book of Great Detective Stories | Berk | .50 |
| Hechinger, G. and F. | Teen-Age Tyranny | Crest | .50 |
| Heinlein, R. | Assignment in Eternity | Sig | .50 |
| —————— | The Door into Summer | Sig | .50 |
| —————— | Green Hills of Earth | Sig | .50 |
| —————— | The Man Who Sold the Moon | Sig | .50 |
| —————— | The Menace from Earth | Sig | .50 |
| —————— | Orphans of the Sky | Sig | .50 |
| —————— | Podkayne of Mars | Avon | .50 |
| —————— | The Puppet Masters | Sig | .50 |
| Heller, Jack | Jokesmith's Jubilee | SBS | .35 |
| Heller, Joseph | Catch–22 | Dell | .75 |
| Hellmuth, J. | A Wolf in the Family | Sig | .75 |
| Herndon, B. | The Humor of JFK | GM | .50 |
| Hersey, J. | Here to Stay | Ban | .75 |
| —————— | Hiroshima | Ban | .50 |
| —————— | The Wall | PB | .75 |
| Herzog, M. | Annapurna | PL | .50 |
| Heyerdahl, T. | Aku-Aku | PB | .75 |
| —————— | Kon-Tiki | PB | .75 |
| Highland, H. | How and Why Wonder Book of Planets and Interplanetary Travel | G&D | .59 |
| Hilton, J. | Lost Horizon | PB | .50 |
| —————— | Random Harvest | PB | .50 |
| Himes, C. | Pinktoes | Dell | .75 |
| —————— | The Primitive | Sig | .60 |
| —————— | The Third Generation | Sig | .75 |
| Hirsch, P. | Fighting Eagles | Pyr | .45 |
| —————— | Great Untold Stories of World War II | Pyr | .50 |
| —————— | Killer Subs | Pyr | .50 |
| Hitchcock, A. | Anti-Social Register | Dell | .50 |
| —————— | A Hangman's Dozen | Dell | .75 |

| | | | |
|---|---|---|---|
| ——— | Hold Your Breath | Dell | .50 |
| ——— | More Stories My Mother Never Told Me | Dell | .50 |
| ——— | More Stories Not for the Nervous | Dell | .50 |
| ——— | Noose Report | Dell | .50 |
| ——— | Once Upon a Dreadful Time | Dell | .50 |
| ——— | Witches' Brew | Dell | .50 |
| Holt, V. | Mistress of Mellyn | Crest | .60 |
| Holzer, H. | Ghost Hunter | Ace | .50 |
| ——— | Ghosts I've Met | Ace | .60 |
| Horsley, F. | The Hot Rod Handbook | JLP | .75 |
| Hoss, N. | How and Why Wonder Book of Stars | G&D | .59 |
| Hot Rod editors | Supertuning | Sig | .95 |
| Howarth, D. | D Day | Pyr | .50 |
| ——— | We Die Alone | Ace | .50 |
| Hughes, L. | African Treasure | Pyr | .50 |
| Hugo, V. | The Hunchback of Notre Dame | Ban | .60 |
| Hulme, K. | The Nun's Story | PB | .50 |
| Hunt, I. | Across Five Aprils | G&D | .50 |
| Hunter, Edward | Brainwashing | Pyr | .50 |
| Hunter, Evan | The Blackboard Jungle | PB | .50 |
| Hunter, J. | The Blue Max | Ban | .75 |
| Hurkos, P. | Psychic | Pop | .60 |
| Hurwood, B. | Monsters and Nightmares | BB | .50 |
| Huxley, A. | Brave New World | Ban | .75 |
| Hyler, N. | How and Why Wonder Book of Rocks and Minerals | G&D | .59 |
| Hyman, M. | No Time for Sergeants | Sig | .60 |
| Icenhower, J. | The Scarlet Raider | Nova | .40 |
| Irving, W. | The Legend of Sleepy Hollow | WSP | .60 |
| Jackson, C. | Stock Car Races | Sig | .50 |
| Janis, R. | The Beautiful Americans | Dell | .60 |
| Jensen, A. | How and Why Wonder Book of Mushrooms, Ferns and Mosses | G&D | .59 |
| Johnston, W. | Get Smart! | G&D | .60 |
| Jones, E. | High Gear | Ban | .50 |
| Jones, J. | The Pistol | Sig | .50 |
| Judd, F. | The Green Cameo Mystery | Berk | .45 |
| Juster, H. | Clothes Make the Man | Macf | .75 |
| Kane, B. | Batman | Sig | .50 |
| ——— | Batman vs. the Joker | Sig | .50 |
| ——— | Batman vs. the Penguin | Sig | .50 |
| Kantor, M. | Andersonville | Sig | .95 |

| | | | |
|---|---|---|---|
| ——— | If the South Had Won the Civil War | Ban | .45 |
| Karloff, B. | Boris Karloff's Favorite Horror Stories | Avon | .50 |
| Kata, E. | A Patch of Blue | Pop | .50 |
| Kaufman, B. | Up the Down Staircase | Avon | .95 |
| Keen, M. | How and Why Wonder Book of Chemistry | G&D | .59 |
| ——— | How and Why Wonder Book of the Human Body | G&D | .59 |
| ——— | How and Why Wonder Book of Prehistoric Mammals | G&D | .59 |
| ——— | How and Why Wonder Book of Wild Animals | G&D | .59 |
| Keller, H. | The Story of My Life | Dell | .50 |
| Kennedy, J. | The Burden and the Glory | Pop | .75 |
| ——— | Profiles in Courage | PL | .65 |
| Ketcham, H. | Dennis the Menace, Ambassador of Mischief | Crest | .40 |
| ——— | Dennis the Menace, Happy Half Pint | Crest | .40 |
| ——— | Dennis the Menace, Household Hurricane | Crest | .40 |
| ——— | Dennis the Menace, Make-Believe Angel | Crest | .40 |
| ——— | Dennis the Menace Rides Again | Crest | .40 |
| ——— | Dennis the Menace— Teacher's Threat | Crest | .40 |
| ——— | Dennis the Menace vs. Everybody | Crest | .40 |
| ——— | Dennis the Menace, Who Me? | Crest | .40 |
| ——— | In This Corner . . . Dennis the Menace | Crest | .40 |
| ——— | Wanted, Dennis the Menace | Crest | .40 |
| Ketcham, H., and Harmon, B. | Babysitter's Guide by Dennis the Menace | Crest | .50 |
| King, H. | The Exploration of the Universe | Sig | .75 |
| King, M. | Strength to Love | PB | .50 |
| ——— | Stride toward Freedom: The Montgomery Story | PL | .75 |
| ——— | Why We Can't Wait | Sig | .60 |
| Kipling, R. | Captains Courageous | Dell | .40 |
| ——— | The Jungle Books | Sig | .50 |
| ——— | Kim | Dell | .40 |
| Kjelgaard, J. | Big Red | SBS | .50 |

160

| | | | |
|---|---|---|---|
| Knebel, F., and Bailey, C. | No High Ground | Ban | .50 |
| ———— | Seven Days in May | Ban | .95 |
| Knight, C. | How and Why Wonder Book of Rockets and Missiles | G&D | .59 |
| Knight, D. | In Deep | Berk | .50 |
| ———— | Mind Switch | Berk | .50 |
| Knowles, J. | A Separate Peace | Ban | .75 |
| Koehler, C. and A. | How and Why Wonder Book of Ants and Bees | G&D | .59 |
| Krepps, R. | Stagecoach | GM | .40 |
| Krich, A. | Facts of Love and Marriage for Young People | Dell | .50 |
| Kytle, E. | Willie Mae | Sig | .50 |
| Lacy, E. | Sleep in Thunder | G&D | .50 |
| Lamb, H. | Genghis Khan, Emperor of All Men | Ban | .60 |
| Lambert, G. | Duke Ellington | Prpta | .95 |
| Lambert, J. | Dreams of Glory | G&D | .50 |
| ———— | Friday's Child | G&D | .50 |
| ———— | Practically Perfect | G&D | .50 |
| ———— | The Reluctant Heart | G&D | .50 |
| ———— | The Star-Spangled Summer | G&D | .50 |
| Landers, A. | Ann Landers Talks to Teen-Agers About Sex | Crest | .40 |
| ———— | Since You Ask Me | Crest | .50 |
| Landis, J. and M. | Teen-Agers Guide for Living | Tower | .50 |
| Laumer, K. | Galactic Diplomat | Berk | .50 |
| Lawrence, J., and Lee, R. | Inherit the Wind | Ban | .50 |
| Lawrence, M. | Along Comes Spring | Berk | .40 |
| Lawson, D. | United States in World War II | G&D | .50 |
| Lear, E. | The Nonsense Books of Edward Lear | Sig | .75 |
| Leasor, J. | Where the Spies Are | Sig | .60 |
| LeCarré, J. | The Spy Who Came in from the Cold | Dell | .75 |
| Lederer, W., and Burdick, E. | The Ugly American | Crest | .60 |
| Lee, B. | JFK: Boyhood to White House | Crest | .50 |
| Lee, H. | To Kill a Mockingbird | Pop | .60 |
| Leiber, F. | The Night of the Wolf | Bal | .50 |
| ———— | Tarzan and the Valley of Gold | Bal | .75 |
| ———— | The Wanderer | Bal | .75 |
| Leinster, M. | The Aliens | Berk | .50 |

| | | | |
|---|---|---|---|
| ——— | Checkpoint Lambda | Berk | .50 |
| ——— | The Other Side of Nowhere | Berk | .50 |
| ——— | Time Tunnel | Pyr | .50 |
| Lerner, A. | My Fair Lady | Sig | .60 |
| Lewis, C. | Cassius Clay | Macf | .60 |
| Lewis, N. | How to Become a Better Reader | Macf | .95 |
| ——— | Rapid Vocabulary Builder | G&D | 1.00 |
| ——— | Word Power Made Easy | PB | .50 |
| Ley, W. | Satellites, Rockets and Outer Space | Sig | .60 |
| Liebers, A. | Wit's End | G&D | .50 |
| Linkletter, A. | Kids Sure Rite Funny! | Crest | .40 |
| Little, P. | Love in Style | pbl | .50 |
| Lomax, L. | The Negro Revolt | Sig | .75 |
| ——— | When the Word Is Given . . . | Sig | .60 |
| London, J. | The Call of the Wild | Airmt | .50 |
| ——— | Sea Wolf | Ban | .50 |
| ——— | South Sea Tales | Pyr | .50 |
| ——— | White Fang | Airmt | .50 |
| Long, A. | Ricardo of the Lion Heart | Sig | .50 |
| Lorand, R. | Love, Sex and the Teenager | Pop | .60 |
| Lord, W. | Day of Infamy | Ban | .50 |
| ——— | A Night to Remember | Ban | .60 |
| Loring, E. | I Take This Man | Ban | .50 |
| ——— | Look to the Stars | Ban | .50 |
| ——— | Love Came Laughing By | Ban | .50 |
| ——— | My Dearest Love | Ban | .45 |
| ——— | Shadow of Suspicion | Ban | .50 |
| ——— | Stars in Your Eyes | Ban | .50 |
| ——— | With This Ring | Ban | .50 |
| Low, D. | How and Why Wonder Book of Sea Shells | G&D | .59 |
| Low, E. | Hold Fast the Dream | G&D | .50 |
| Lutz, G. | Outcast Gun | GM | .40 |
| Lyon, W. | Batman vs. the Fearsome Foursome | Sig | .50 |
| MacDonald, J. | End of Night | GM | .50 |
| MacLean, A. | Ice Station Zebra | Crest | .60 |
| ——— | The Guns of Navarone | WSP | .60 |
| Maddox, H. | How to Study | Crest | .60 |
| Mantle, M. | Quality of Courage | Ban | .50 |
| Marquand, J. | Point of No Return | Ban | .95 |
| ——— | Last Laugh, Mr. Moto | Berk | .50 |
| ——— | The Last of Mr. Moto | Berk | .50 |
| ——— | Think Fast, Mr. Moto | Berk | .50 |
| Martin, B. | Miracle at Carville | Dday | .85 |
| Martin, G. | The Bells of St. Mary's | Ban | .50 |

| Martin, R. | World War II: A Photographic Record of the War in the Pacific from Pearl Harbor to V-J Day | GM | .60 |
|---|---|---|---|
| Martin, R., and Harrity, R. | World War II: A Photographic Record of the War in Europe from D-Day to V-E Day | GM | .60 |
| Mathewson, R. | How and Why Wonder Book of Birds | G&D | .59 |
| ———— | How and Why Wonder Book of Reptiles and Amphibians | G&D | .59 |
| Maxwell, G. | People of the Reeds | Pyr | .75 |
| ———— | Ring of Bright Water | Crest | .60 |
| ———— | The Rocks Remain | Crest | .60 |
| May, E. | The Wasted Americans | Sig | .60 |
| McCarthy, J. | Brother Juniper at Work and Play | PB | .35 |
| ———— | Inside Brother Juniper | PB | .35 |
| ———— | More Brother Juniper | Dday | 1.00 |
| ———— | Well Done, Brother Juniper | PB | .45 |
| ———— | The Whimsical World of Brother Juniper | PB | .35 |
| McCormick, W. | The Five Man Break | Nova | .40 |
| McCoy, H. | They Shoot Horses, Don't They? | Avon | .60 |
| McCullers, C. | The Member of the Wedding | Ban | .60 |
| McCulloch, M. | Second Year Nurse | SBS | .45 |
| McCutchan, P. | Bluebolt One | Berk | .50 |
| ———— | The Dead Line | Berk | .50 |
| ———— | Redcap | Berk | .50 |
| ———— | Warmaster | Berk | .50 |
| McDaniel, D. | The Man from U.N.C.L.E. #4: The Dagger Affair | Ace | .50 |
| ———— | The Man from U.N.C.L.E. #6: The Vampire Affair | Ace | .50 |
| McDonald, L. and Ross, Z. | The Stolen Letters | Pyr | .45 |
| McKay, C. | Home to Harlem | PB | .50 |
| Mead, M. | People and Places | Ban | .60 |
| Medearis, M. | Big Doc's Girl | Pyr | .45 |
| Melville, H. | Billy Budd | SBS | .45 |
| ———— | Moby Dick | Sig | .75 |
| Merriam, R. | The Battle of the Bulge | Bal | .60 |
| Michener, J. | The Bridge at Andau | Ban | .50 |
| ———— | The Bridges at Toko-Ri | Ban | .50 |
| ———— | Hawaii | Ban | 1.65 |

| | | | |
|---|---|---|---|
| ———— | Return to Paradise | Ban | .75 |
| ———— | Sayonara | Ban | .75 |
| ———— | Tales of the South Pacific | PB | .50 |
| Michener, J. and Day, A. | Rascals in Paradise | Ban | .75 |
| Miers, E. | How and Why Wonder Book of the Civil War | G&D | .59 |
| Miksch, W. | The Addams Family Strikes Back | Pyr | .50 |
| Miller, A. | Fury | G&D | .50 |
| Miller, R. | Impossible—Yet It Happened! | Ace | .40 |
| Miller, W. | The Cool World | Crest | .40 |
| ———— | The Siege of Harlem | Crest | .60 |
| Mitchell, J. | The Amazing Mets | G&D | .50 |
| ———— | Sandy Koufax | G&D | .50 |
| Monahan, J. | Masterpieces of Surprise | HPC | .75 |
| Monsarrat, N. | The Cruel Sea | PB | .75 |
| ———— | The Ship That Died of Shame | PB | .35 |
| Montagu, E. | The Man Who Never Was | Ban | .50 |
| Montgomery, R. | Yellow Eyes | SBS | .35 |
| Moore, R. | The Green Berets | Avon | .95 |
| Morehead, A. | The Official Rules of Card Games | Crest | .60 |
| Morris, E. | The Flowers of Hiroshima | M&M | 1.75 |
| Morris, L. | Masterpieces of Adventure | HPC | .75 |
| ———— | Masterpieces of Humor | HPC | .75 |
| Morris, R. | Masterpieces of Horror | HPC | .75 |
| ———— | Masterpieces of Mystery and Detection | HPC | .75 |
| ———— | Masterpieces of Suspense | HPC | .75 |
| Morrow, E. | Black Man in the White House | Macf | .60 |
| Moss, S., and Purdy, K. | All But My Life | Ban | .75 |
| Mowat, F. | Dog Who Wouldn't Be | Pyr | .45 |
| ———— | Never Cry Wolf | Dell | .50 |
| Nash, O. | The Pocket Book of Ogden Nash | PB | .50 |
| Nathan, R. | Portrait of Jennie | Pop | .35 |
| Nathanson, E. | The Dirty Dozen | Dell | .95 |
| Nickerson, J. | Circle of Love | Nova | .40 |
| Nolan, W. | Men of Thunder | Ban | .50 |
| Nolan, W. and Beaumont, C. | When Engines Roar | Ban | .50 |
| Nordhoff, C., and Hall, J. | Falcons of France | Ban | .60 |
| ———— | Men Against the Sea | PB | .50 |

| | | | |
|---|---|---|---|
| —————— | Mutiny on the Bounty | PB | .50 |
| | Pitcairn's Island | PB | .35 |
| Nordholt, J. | The People That Walk in Darkness | Bal | .75 |
| North, S. | Rascal | Avon | .60 |
| Norton, A. | Catseye | Ace | .40 |
| —————— | Daybreak | Ace | .40 |
| —————— | The Defiant Agents | Ace | .45 |
| —————— | Huon of the Horn | Ace | .40 |
| —————— | Judgment on Janus | Ace | .40 |
| —————— | Key Out of Time | Ace | .40 |
| —————— | Lord of Thunder | Ace | .40 |
| —————— | Night of Masks | Ace | .40 |
| —————— | Ordeal in Otherwhere | Ace | .40 |
| —————— | Sea Siege and Eye of the Monster | Ace | .40 |
| —————— | Shadow Hawk | Ace | .50 |
| —————— | The Sioux Spaceman | Ace | .40 |
| —————— | Star Born | Ace | .45 |
| —————— | Star Gate | Ace | .45 |
| —————— | The Stars Are Ours! | Ace | .45 |
| —————— | Storm Over Wallock | Ace | .40 |
| —————— | Three Against the Witch World | Ace | .40 |
| —————— | The Time Traders | Ace | .40 |
| —————— | Witch World | Ace | .40 |
| —————— | Year of the Unicorn | Ace | .40 |
| Notkin, J. | How and Why Wonder Book of Science Experiments | G&D | .59 |
| Notkin, J. and Gulkin, S. | How and Why Wonder Book of Beginning Science | G&D | .59 |
| —————— | How and Why Wonder Book of Electricity | G&D | .59 |
| Nourse, A. | Raiders from the Rings | Pyr | .40 |
| | Tiger by the Tail | Macf | .50 |
| O'Connor, P. | The Black Tiger | Berk | .50 |
| | Black Tiger at Indianapolis | SBS | .45 |
| —————— | Mexican Road Race | Berk | .50 |
| | Treasure at Twenty Fathoms | Berk | .50 |
| Ogan, M. and G. | Devil Drivers | Nova | .50 |
| —————— | A Place for Ingrid | Nova | .45 |
| Ogilvie, E. | Becky's Island | Berk | .50 |
| Olson, G. | The Bucket of Thunderbolts | Pyr | .45 |
| —————— | Three Men on Third | G&D | .50 |
| Oram, J. | The Man from U.N.C.L.E. #3: The Copenhagen Affair | Ace | .50 |
| Orczy, Baroness | The Scarlet Pimpernel | Pyr | .50 |

165

| Orr, J. | Baseball's Greatest | | |
| | Players Today | JLP | .50 |
| Orwell, G. | Animal Farm | Sig | .75 |
| ———— | 1984 | Sig | .75 |
| Osborne, E. | How to Deal with Parents | | |
| | and Other Problems | G&D | .50 |
| O'Sullivan, J. | 100 Ways to Popularity | Ace | .50 |
| Owen, F. | Baseball Stories | PB | .50 |
| Packard, V. | The Human Side of Animals | PB | .50 |
| Pangborn, E. | Davy | Bal | .75 |
| Papashvily, | | | |
| G. and H. | Anything Can Happen | PL | .50 |
| Parkman, F. | Oregon Trail | Airmt | .50 |
| Partch, V. | Crazy Cartoons by Vip | GM | .40 |
| Patten, L. | Deputy From Furnace Creek | Lance | .40 |
| ———— | Flame in the West | Berk | .45 |
| ———— | The Odds Against Circle L | Ace | .40 |
| | Outlaw Canyon | Berk | .40 |
| ———— | Prodigal Gunfighter | Berk | .50 |
| Pearson, J. | John F. Kennedy | Gold | .25 |
| Phillifrent, J. | The Man from U.N.C.L.E. | | |
| | #5: The Mad Scientist | | |
| | Affair | Ace | .50 |
| Pinney, R. | Wild Animal Pets | Gold | .50 |
| Pinto, O. | Spy Catcher | Berk | .60 |
| Poe, E. | Eight Tales of Terror | SBS | .50 |
| | Fall of the House of Usher | | |
| | and Other Tales | Sig | .50 |
| Pohl, F. | Slave Ship | Bal | .50 |
| Pohl, F. and | | | |
| Kornbluth, C. | Space Merchants | Bal | .50 |
| Poncins, G. de | Kabloona | Pop | .50 |
| Porter, M. | Keeper Play | G&D | .50 |
| | Overtime Upset | G&D | .45 |
| ———— | Winning Pitcher | G&D | .50 |
| Pyle, E. | Brave Men | Pop | .75 |
| Pyle, H. | Men of Iron | Airmt | .50 |
| Quarles, B. | The Negro in the | | |
| | Making of America | Cllr | .95 |
| Queen, E. | To Be Read before | | |
| | Midnight | Pop | .50 |
| Quentin, P. | My Son the Murderer | Avon | .50 |
| Raab, E. | American Race Relations | | |
| | Today | Anch | .95 |
| Randall, C. | Amos Flagg—High Gun | GM | .40 |
| ———— | Amos Flagg—Lawman | GM | .40 |
| | Amos Flagg Rides Out | GM | .40 |
| Rathjen, C. | Wild Wheels | G&D | .50 |

| Rawicz, S. and Downing, R. | The Long Walk: A Gamble for Life | PL | .60 |
|---|---|---|---|
| Raymond, J. | Your Military Obligations and Opportunities | Cllr | .95 |
| Reading Laboratory | Double Your Reading Speed | Crest | .60 |
| Redding, J. | On Being Negro in America | Chart | 1.35 |
| Reeder, R. | West Point Yearling | Berk | .50 |
| | West Point Plebe | Berk | .50 |
| Reid, E., and Demaris, O. | The Green Felt Jungle | PB | .75 |
| Reid, P. | Escape from Colditz | Berk | .60 |
| Remarque, E. | All Quiet on the Western Front | Crest | .60 |
| Reynolds, Q. | Officially Dead | Pyr | .40 |
| | 70,000 to One | Pyr | .50 |
| | They Fought for the Sky | Ban | .50 |
| Ribakove, S. and B. | Folk-Rock: The Bob Dylan Story | Dell | .50 |
| Richter, C. | The Light in the Forest | Ban | .50 |
| | The Sea of Grass | Ban | .50 |
| Robbin, I. | How and Why Wonder Book of Guns | G&D | .50 |
| Robbins, H. | Never Love a Stranger | PB | .75 |
| | A Stone for Danny Fisher | PB | .75 |
| Roberts, Keith | The Furies | Berk | .50 |
| Roberts, Kenneth | Captain Caution | Crest | .75 |
| Roberts, M. | Get With It, Joan | Nova | .50 |
| Roberts, S. | Co-ed in White | Ace | .35 |
| | Hootenanny Nurse | Ace | .35 |
| Robinson, M. | Bright Island | G&D | .50 |
| Rohmer, S. | The Day the World Ended | Ace | .40 |
| | Drums of Fu Manchu | Pyr | .50 |
| | The Hand of Fu Manchu | Pyr | .50 |
| | The Island of Fu Manchu | Pyr | .50 |
| | The Mask of Fu Manchu | Pyr | .50 |
| | The Yellow Claw | Pyr | .50 |
| Rood, R. | How and Why Wonder Book of Insects | G&D | .59 |
| Rostand, E. | Cyrano de Bergerac | Ban | .60 |
| Rosten, L. | Captain Newman, M.D. | Crest | .60 |
| Ruark, R. | Horn of the Hunter | Crest | .75 |
| | Poor No More | Crest | .95 |
| | Uhuru | Crest | .95 |
| Ruppelt, E. | Report on Unidentified Flying Objects | Ace | .50 |
| Russell, E. | Men, Martians and Machines | Berk | .50 |
| Russell, R. | To Catch an Angel | Pop | .60 |
| Ryan, C. | The Longest Day | Crest | .75 |

| | | | |
|---|---|---|---|
| Sakai, S.,<br>Caidin, M., and<br>Saito, F. | Samurai | Bal | .50 |
| Sale, R. | The Oscar | PB | .75 |
| Salinger, J. | The Catcher in the Rye | Ban | .75 |
| Salisbury, H. | The Shook-Up Generation | Crest | .50 |
| Sands, B. | My Shadow Ran Fast | Sig | .60 |
| Saroyan, W. | The Human Comedy | Dell | .60 |
| ———— | My Name Is Aram | Dell | .60 |
| Saudek, R. | Eight Courageous<br>Americans | Ban | .60 |
| Schaefer, J. | Shane | Ban | .50 |
| Scharff, R. | How and Why Wonder<br>Book of Oceanography | G&D | .59 |
| Schultz, J. | My Life as an Indian | Prem | .60 |
| Schulz, C. | For the Love of Peanuts! | Crest | .40 |
| ———— | Fun with Peanuts! | Crest | .40 |
| ———— | Good Grief, Charlie Brown! | Crest | .40 |
| ———— | Here Comes Charlie Brown | Crest | .40 |
| ———— | Here Comes Snoopy | Crest | .40 |
| ———— | Hey, Peanuts! | Crest | .40 |
| ———— | Very Funny, Charlie Brown | Crest | .40 |
| ———— | We're on Your Side,<br>Charlie Brown | Crest | .40 |
| ———— | What Next, Charlie Brown? | Crest | .40 |
| ———— | The Wonderful World of<br>Peanuts | Crest | .40 |
| ———— | You Are Too Much,<br>Charlie Brown | Crest | .40 |
| Scoggin, M. | Chucklebait | Dell | .50 |
| Scott, J. | The Art of Being a Girl | G&D | .50 |
| Scott, R. | God Is My Co-Pilot | Bal | .50 |
| Self, M. | How and Why Wonder<br>Book of Horses | G&D | .59 |
| Senje, S. | Escape! | VoyB | .60 |
| Serling, R. | More Stories from the<br>Twilight Zone | Ban | .45 |
| ———— | New Stories from the<br>Twilight Zone | Ban | .45 |
| ———— | Stories from the<br>Twilight Zone | Ban | .45 |
| Sewell, A. | Black Beauty | Airmt | .50 |
| Shakespeare, W. | Othello | WSP | .45 |
| Sheckley, R. | Pilgrimage to Earth | Ban | .50 |
| Shelley, M. | Frankenstein | Dell | .45 |
| Short, L. | Branded Man | Dell | .45 |
| ———— | Marauder's Moon | Dell | .45 |
| ———— | Ramrod | Pop | .50 |
| Shotwell, L. | Roosevelt Grady | G&D | .50 |

| | | | |
|---|---|---|---|
| Shulman, I. | The Amboy Dukes | Ban | .60 |
| ——— | Children of the Dark | Pop | .35 |
| ——— | West Side Story | PB | .50 |
| Shulman, M. | I Was a Teen-Age Dwarf | Ban | 50 |
| ——— | Rally Round the Flag, Boys! | Ban | .75 |
| Shute, N. | On the Beach | PL | .60 |
| Sillitoe, A. | The Loneliness of the Long Distance Runner | Sig | .60 |
| Silverberg, R. | Empires in the Dust | Ban | .60 |
| ——— | Sunken History | Ban | .50 |
| Simak, C. | Time Is the Simplest Thing | Crest | .60 |
| ——— | Way Station | Macf | .60 |
| Simmons, H. | So You Think You Know Baseball | Crest | .40 |
| Sims, E. | American Aces | Bal | .50 |
| ——— | Greatest Fighter Missions | Bal | .60 |
| Sinclair, U. | The Jungle | Airmt | .60 |
| ——— | The Gnomobile | G&D | .50 |
| Singer, K. | Spies Who Changed History | Ace | .50 |
| Sire, G. and J. | Something Foolish, Something Gay | Berk | .50 |
| Slaughter, F. | Fort Everglades | PB | .50 |
| Sloane, E. | How Can You Forecast the Weather | Prem | .60 |
| Smith, B. | A Tree Grows in Brooklyn | Pop | .75 |
| ——— | Joy in the Morning | Ban | .75 |
| Smith, C. | Great Science Fiction Stories | Dell | .50 |
| Smith, D. | The Quarterbacks | JLP | .50 |
| Smith, N. | Faster Reading Made Easy | Pop | .75 |
| Smith, R. | Baseball's Hall of Fame | Ban | .75 |
| Smythe | Andy Capp Sounds Off | GM | .40 |
| ——— | Meet Andy Capp | GM | .40 |
| ——— | What Next, Andy Capp? | GM | .40 |
| Sneider, V. | Teahouse of the August Moon | Sig | .60 |
| Sorensen, V. | Plain Girl | VoyB | .50 |
| Soubiran, A. | The Doctors | Pop | .75 |
| Soule, G. | The Mystery Monsters | Ace | .60 |
| Spock, B. | Baby and Child Care | PB | .50 |
| Stanford, D. | The Red Car | SBS | .35 |
| ——— | Ski Town | Nova | .45 |
| Steiger, B. | Strange Guests | Ace | .50 |
| ——— | Strangers from the Skies | Nova | .60 |
| Steinbeck, J. | Cannery Row | Ban | .50 |
| ——— | East of Eden | Ban | .95 |
| ——— | The Grapes of Wrath | Ban | .95 |
| ——— | Of Mice and Men | Ban | .60 |
| ——— | The Pearl | Ban | .50 |

| | | | |
|---|---|---|---|
| ———— | The Red Pony | Ban | .50 |
| | Tortilla Flat | Ban | .60 |
| Stern, P. | Great Ghost Stories | WSP | .60 |
| Stewart, M. | Madam, Will You Talk? | Crest | .60 |
| | The Moon-Spinners | Crest | .60 |
| ———— | Nine Coaches Waiting | Crest | .60 |
| Stevenson, R. L. | The Black Arrow | Dell | .45 |
| ———— | Kidnapped | Dell | .40 |
| ———— | Treasure Island | Dell | .40 |
| Stevenson, R. L. and others | Ghosts and Things | Berk | .50 |
| Stoker, B. | Dracula | Dell | .60 |
| Stolz, M. | The Day and the Way We Met | G&D | .50 |
| ———— | Hospital Zone | Berk | .50 |
| ———— | Student Nurse | Berk | .50 |
| Stowe, H. | Uncle Tom's Cabin | PL | .75 |
| Strang, R. | Target: Tomorrow | Dell | .50 |
| Stuart, I. | The Satan Bug | Pop | .50 |
| Sturgeon, T. | More Than Human | Bal | .50 |
| ———— | Rare Breed | GM | .50 |
| ———— | Some of Your Blood | Bal | .50 |
| ———— | A Touch of Strange | Berk | .50 |
| ———— | Voyage to the Bottom of the Sea | Pyr | .50 |
| Sullivan, G. | Famous Auto Racing Thrills | Nova | .50 |
| ———— | Peace Corps Nurse | Nova | .45 |
| Summers, J. | Trouble on the Run | G&D | .50 |
| Sutton, F. | How and Why Wonder Book of the Moon | G&D | .59 |
| ———— | How and Why Wonder Book of the North American Indians | G&D | .59 |
| ———— | How and Why Wonder Book of Our Earth | G&D | .59 |
| ———— | How and Why Wonder Book of World War II | G&D | .59 |
| Suyin, H. | A Many Splendored Thing | Sig | .75 |
| Tabor, M. | Battle of the Bulge | Pop | .50 |
| Tegner, B. | Bruce Tegner's Complete Book of Self-Defense | Ban | 1.00 |
| Thane, E. | Tryst | G&D | .50 |
| Thomas D. | Dog Stories | PB | .50 |
| ———— | Horse Stories | PB | .50 |
| Thomas, H. | Better English Made Easy | Pop | .60 |
| Thomas, L. | Raiders of the Deep | Nova | .75 |
| Thompson, H. | Art of Being a Successful Student | WSP | .45 |
| Tiger, J. | I Spy | Pop | .50 |

| | | | |
|---|---|---|---|
| Trapp, M. | The Story of the Trapp Family Singers | Dday | .95 |
| Tregaskis, R. | Guadalcanal Diary | Pop | .40 |
| | Vietnam Diary | Pop | .75 |
| Trevor, E. | The Flight of the Phoenix | Avon | .75 |
| Trevor-Roper, H. | The Last Days of Hitler | Cllr | .95 |
| Trumbull, R. | Raft | Pyr | .45 |
| Tunis, J. | The Kid Comes Back | SBS | .50 |
| ———— | The Kid from Tomkinsville | Berk | .45 |
| ———— | Schoolboy Johnson | Berk | .45 |
| ———— | Silence over Dunkerque | Berk | .50 |
| ———— | World Series | Berk | .50 |
| ———— | Young Razzle | Berk | .45 |
| Tunley, R. | Kids, Crime and Chaos | Dell | .50 |
| Turnbull, A. | The Bishop's Mantle | Avon | .75 |
| Twain, M. | The Adventures of Huckleberry Fin | WSP | .45 |
| ———— | The Adventures of Tom Sawyer | WSP | .45 |
| ———— | Connecticut Yankee in King Arthur's Court | WSP | .45 |
| Uhnak, D. | Policewoman | Macf | .60 |
| Unger, A. | Datebook's Complete Guide to Dating | Nova | .50 |
| ———— | First Dates and Other Disasters | Sig | .50 |
| Unger, A., and Berman, C. | What Girls Want to Know About Boys | G&D | .50 |
| Untermeyer, L. | A Concise Treasury of Great Poems | PB | .75 |
| Uris, L. | Battle Cry | Ban | .95 |
| ———— | Exodus | Ban | .95 |
| Van Every, D. | A Company of Heroes: The First American Frontier, 1775–1783 | Ment | .75 |
| Van Vogt, A. | Destination: Universe! | Berk | .50 |
| ———— | The Mind Cage | Tower | .60 |
| ———— | Mission to the Stars | Berk | .50 |
| ———— | The Violent Man | Avon | .75 |
| Verne, J. | Around the World in 80 Days | SBS | .45 |
| ———— | A Journey to the Center of the Earth | Airmt | .50 |
| ———— | The Mysterious Island | SBS | .50 |
| ———— | 20,000 Leagues Under the Sea | Ban | .60 |
| Verrill, A. | The Strange Story of Our Earth | Prem | .50 |

| | | | |
|---|---|---|---|
| Viereck, P. | The Summer I Was Lost | Sig | .50 |
| Villiers, A. | Great Sea Stories | Dell | .45 |
| Vivian, E. (intro. by) | Robin Hood | Airmt | .50 |
| Wadsworth, L. | The Bamboo Key | G&D | .50 |
| ———— | The Puzzle of the Talking Monkey | G&D | .50 |
| Walden, A. | My Sister Mike | Berk | .50 |
| ———— | When Love Speaks | Berk | .45 |
| ———— | Where Is My Heart? | Berk | .40 |
| Waldman, F. | The Challenger | G&D | .50 |
| Waldron, T., and Gleeson, J. | The Frogmen | Berk | .50 |
| Wallace, L. | Ben Hur | Ban | .50 |
| Wallant, E. | The Pawnbroker | Macf | .50 |
| Walters, H. | First on the Moon | G&D | .50 |
| Ward, R., and Yates, B. | Rodger Ward's Guide to Good Driving | PL | .75 |
| Warren, R., and Erskine, A. | Six Centuries of Great Poetry | Dell | .75 |
| Washington, B. | Up from Slavery | Ban | .60 |
| Weber, L. | Beany and the Beckoning Road | Berk | .50 |
| ———— | Beany Malone | Berk | .50 |
| ———— | Leave It to Beany | Berk | .50 |
| ———— | Meet the Malones | Berk | .50 |
| Webster, J. | Daddy Long Legs | G&D | .60 |
| Weir, R. | Star and the Flame | Sig | .50 |
| Wells, H. G. | The First Men in the Moon | Airmt | .50 |
| ———— | Inexperienced Ghost and Nine Other Stories | Ban | .50 |
| ———— | The Invisible Man | Berk | .50 |
| ———— | The Island of Dr. Moreau | Berk | .50 |
| ———— | The Time Machine | Berk | .50 |
| ———— | The War of the Worlds | Berk | .50 |
| Wells, L. | Brand of Evil | Berk | .40 |
| West, J. | Cress Delehanty | WSP | .60 |
| Westheimer, D. | Von Ryan's Express | Sig | .75 |
| Wharton, V. | The Coming of Flame | Dell | .35 |
| White, B. | Betty White's Teen-Age Dance Book | Perm | .50 |
| White, T. | Sword in the Stone | Dell | .50 |
| Whitehouse, A. | Fighters in the Sky | Nova | .50 |
| ———— | The Years of the Sky Kings | Nova | .75 |
| Whitney, P. | Black Amber | Crest | .50 |
| ———— | Blue Fire | Ban | .60 |
| ———— | The Highest Dream | SBS | .60 |
| ———— | Mystery of the Hidden Hand | G&D | .50 |
| ———— | The Quicksilver Pool | Ace | .50 |

| | | | |
|---|---|---|---|
| ——— | Thunder Heights | Ace | .50 |
| Whittington, H. | The Man from U.N.C.L.E. #2: The Doomsday Affair | Ace | .50 |
| Wibberley, L. | The Mouse on the Moon | Ban | .50 |
| ——— | The Mouse That Roared | Ban | .50 |
| Wilde, O. | The Picture of Dorian Gray | Dell | .35 |
| Wilder, T. | Our Town: A Play in Three Acts | CN | .95 |
| Wilkerson, D., and Sherrill, J. and E. | The Cross and the Switchblade | Pyr | .50 |
| Williams, E. | The Tunnel Escape | Berk | .50 |
| Williams, O. | Immortal Poems of the English Language | WSP | .75 |
| ——— | The Mentor Book of Major British Poets | Ment | 1.25 |
| ——— | The New Pocket Anthology of American Verse | WSP | .75 |
| ——— | Pocket Book of Modern Verse | WSP | .75 |
| ——— | The Silver Treasury of Light Verse | Ment | .95 |
| Williams, O., and Honig, E. | The Mentor Book of Major American Poets | Ment | 1.25 |
| Wilson, H. | The Hundred Steps | Nova | .40 |
| Wister, O. | The Virginian | PB | .35 |
| Wouk, H. | The City Boy | Dell | .60 |
| Wright, R. | Black Boy | Sig | .75 |
| ——— | Native Son | Sig | .75 |
| ——— | The Outsider | PL | .95 |
| ——— | Uncle Tom's Children | PL | .60 |
| ——— | White Man, Listen | Anch | .95 |
| Wylie, P. and Balmer, E. | After Worlds Collide | pbl | .50 |
| | When Worlds Collide | pbl | .50 |
| Wyndham, L. | Beth Hilton: Model | G&D | .50 |
| Wyss, J. | Swiss Family Robinson | Dell | .40 |
| Young, D. | Rommel, Desert Fox | PL | .65 |

## Publishers and Symbols

Ace    Ace Books and Ace Star Books, 1120 Avenue of the Americas, New York, N. Y. 10036

Airmt    Airmont Publishing Co., Inc., 22 E. 60th Street, New York, N. Y. 10022

Anch    Anchor Books, Doubleday & Co., Inc., 277 Park Avenue, New York, N. Y. 10017

Arc    Arco Publishing Co., Inc. 219 Park Avenue South, New York, N. Y. 10003

Avon    Avon Book Div., The Hearst Corp., 959 Eighth Avenue, New York, N. Y. 10019

Bal    Ballantine Books, Inc., 101 Fifth Avenue, New York, N. Y. 10003

Ban    Bantam Books, Inc., 271 Madison Avenue, New York, N. Y. 10016

Berk    Berkley Publishing Corp., 200 Madison Avenue, New York, N. Y. 10016

Chart    Charter Books, Bobbs-Merrill Co., Inc., 4300 W. 62nd Street, Indianapolis, Ind. 46206

Cllr    Collier Books, 60 Fifth Avenue, New York, N. Y. 10003

CN    Harper & Row *see* PL

Crest    Crest Books, Fawcett Publications, Inc., Greenwich, Conn. 06830

Dday    Doubleday & Co., Inc., 277 Park Avenue, New York, N. Y. 10017

Dell    Dell Publishing Co., Inc., 750 Third Avenue, New York, N. Y. 10017

Dolp    Dolphin Books and Dolphin Masters, Doubleday & Co., Inc., 277 Park Avenue, New York, N. Y. 10017

Duttn    Dutton Paperbacks, E. P. Dutton & Co., Inc., 201 Park Avenue South, New York, N. Y. 10003

G&D    Grossett & Dunlap, Inc., 51 Madison Avenue, New York, N. Y., 10010

GM    Gold Medal Books, Fawcett Publications, Inc., Greenwich, Conn. 06830

Gold    Golden Press, Inc., 850 Third Avenue, New York, N. Y. 10022

High    Highlights for Children, Inc., 2300 W. Fifth Avenue, Columbus, Ohio 43216

HPC    Hart Publishing Co., 510 Avenue of the Americas, New York, N. Y. 10011

JLP    J. Lowell Pratt & Co., Pubs., 15 East 48th Street, New York, N. Y. 10017

Lance    Lancer Books, 185 Madison Avenue, New York, N. Y. 10016

| | |
|---|---|
| M&M | Marzani & Munsell, Inc., 100 West 23rd Street, New York, N. Y. 10011 |
| Macf | Macfadden Books, Macfadden-Bartell Corp., 205 East 42nd Street, New York, N. Y. 10017 |
| Ment | Mentor Books *see* NAL |
| NAL | New American Library of World Literature, Inc., 1301 Avenue of the Americas, New York, N. Y. 10019 |
| Nova | Nova Books, Universal Publishing & Distributing Corp., 800 Second Avenue, New York, N. Y. 10017 |
| PB | Pocket Books, Inc., 630 Fifth Avenue, New York, N. Y. 10020 |
| pbl | Paperback Library, Inc., 260 Park Avenue South, New York, N. Y. 10010 |
| Perm | Permabooks *see* PB |
| PL | Perennial Library, Harper & Row, Publishers, 49 E. 33rd Street, New York, N. Y. 10016 |
| Pop | Popular Library, Inc., 355 Lexington Avenue, New York, N. Y. 10017 |
| Prem | Premier Books, Fawcett Publications, Inc., Greenwich, Conn. 06830 |
| Prpta | Perpetua Books, A. S. Barnes & Co., Inc., 8 East 36th Street, New York, N. Y. 10016 |
| Pyr | Pyramid Books, Pyramid Publications, Inc., 444 Madison Avenue, New York, N. Y. 10022 |
| Rgncy | Regency Books, Box 1247, Evanston, Ill. 60204 |
| SBS | Scholastic Book Services, 900 Sylvan Avenue, Englewood Cliffs, N. J. |
| Sig | Signet Books *see* NAL |
| Tower | Tower Publications, Inc., 185 Madison Avenue, New York, N. Y. 10016 |
| VoyB | Voyager Books, Harcourt Brace & World, Inc., 757 Third Avenue, New York, N. Y. 10017 |
| WSP | Washington Square Press, Inc., 630 Fifth Avenue, New York, N. Y. 10020 |

# *Part Two*

# HOOKED ON RESEARCH

## By Elton B. McNeil, Ph. D.

"I haven't got much time now," I said to the man standing in the doorway of my office. I didn't want to be rude to a colleague—even if he was from the English Department—but the fact was that I *didn't* have much time. After an hour and a half of the time I didn't have, I watched him leave my office and I realized I'd been had by an expert. I was hooked on *English in Every Classroom*.

Dan Fader is a former poolroom hustler who cares as much about kids as a child psychologist, which he isn't, and as much about language as a Renaissance scholar, which he is. He's also one of the great idea-pushers of our time. Brushing aside my objections as though he hadn't heard them—and he probably hadn't—he pursued me from one excuse to another. What he wanted was nothing less than my unqualified commitment to spend part of the next three years testing his idea that kids could learn to *like* to read and write. What I wanted was to be left alone with my own writing, teaching, and responsibilities as director of graduate programs in psychology at the University of Michigan. By the time he left my office I had agreed to test his thesis. Without Fader, the idea is persuasive. With him, it's irresistible.

Irresistible though the idea seemed at the time, the more I thought about my commitment to test the premises and practices of *English in Every Classroom,* the more uneasy I became. I had spent many years laboring in clinical and educational settings with socially and culturally deprived children, and I found it difficult to believe that anything so simple as Fader's idea could make a significant difference in their behavior. I was reasonably certain that they could not read and write with pleasure unless some of their other problems were solved first. But the more I read what Fader wrote and listened to what he said, the less certain I became. Today I have quantitative proof of the quality my instincts responded to three years ago. The fact is that Fader's educational theory is as sound as his pool game.

During the six months following our initial meeting, I designed a program of research calculated to answer the most pressing questions raised by the theory of *English in Every Classroom*. From the beginning I realized that these answers were bound to be imperfect, for the techniques of psychology are not adequate to measure completely the changes in attitude aimed at by Fader's program. But this necessary imperfection bothered me less than the fact that this project had come alive just as I had abandoned hope for the classic and traditional forms of conducting psychological research.

I have no particular objection to the methods psychologists use, since they represent a massive improvement over the hit-and-miss subjective techniques of the past. What bothers me most about the stage to which psychological research has evolved is that we psychologists seem increasingly unable to answer simple questions. We have become very much like the man who was asked, "How's the weather?" and proceeded to answer with a statistically complex meteorological observation and prediction.

My feeling that research psychologists have become obsessively concerned with technique at the expense of purpose is a personal issue that forced me to set conditions on the nature of the conduct and reporting of this research. My desire is to return research to something of its previous state, to have it become again, in part at least, a personal document that focuses its energies largely on the business of telling people, in an intelligible way, how the weather is.

As the form of this research report will indicate, neither Professor Fader nor I was willing to settle for a traditional report directed to those who face the problem of adapting our findings to the challenges of school and classroom. Our sole objective was to make our answers to the questions we raised useful to all those who must convert them into workable plans of action involving real human beings. The freshness, newness and basic simplicity of the idea of *English in Every Classroom* make demands of their own. I hope that I have been able to meet those demands in this report.

# A GOOD STEW MUST BE STIRRED CONSTANTLY

We had stirrers aplenty because the fragrance of the stew proved to be irresistible to all who smelled it cooking. There is no reasonable way to distinguish who stirred most, who stirred least or who stirred with greater vigor. This project rapidly became a group rather than an individual effort and involved an amazingly long list of persons—more than a hundred—who contributed to its success. Despite this large number, the research assistants most closely connected with the project, Robert Goyer and Stephen Yelon, deserve special mention, and additional acknowledgment of the valuable work of Professor Morton H. Shaevitz, of the Psychology Department of the University of Michigan, is required.

When the project was barely a year old, Professor Shaevitz worked untiringly to modify existing testing instruments and to devise new ones better suited to find answers to the complex questions we were asking. In company with a number of colleagues representing various disciplines and research approaches, he hammered the final research design into workable form. We are indebted to him and to the host of colleagues whose ideas became part of our own thinking about how best to accomplish a difficult task.

There is a fantasy in our culture that the intellectual heroes of research thrive on the joys of unadulterated data. The hard truth is that most good research (and some that is bad) is grueling work not much different in its demands from any other labor requiring limitless attention to minutiae. The glamor of research is in the eye of the distant beholder. It is seldom visible to the researcher frustrated by unpredictable human beings who won't stand still long enough to be studied.

## WHO'S HOOKED AND HOW DO YOU TELL?

We began with the assumption that *English in Every Classroom* had an unusually good chance of failure. Our research report, we calculated, might be devoted to intricate explanations of why it didn't work even though it had seemed like such a good idea. We had chosen an almost impossible terrain on which to do battle and we could hardly count on anything better than the bare survival of a few of our ideas. I know at least one hundred research settings less hostile to the basic premises of Fader's plan for literacy, but this was the battle site he had chosen and I was stuck with it.

The trouble is that "hooked" has a variety of meanings when applied to young people for whom reading, writing, teachers, books and schools add up to nothing more than bitter failure. Response to such a program is certain to be uniquely individual and best recorded by collecting hundreds of highly personal case histories. These individual testimonials would contain the real heart of the experiment; unfortunately, anecdotes have never been an acceptable substitute for the more objective kinds of information that testing provides. We had to discover who got hooked, where the hook found its mark, and the depth to which it penetrated. We were aware that some young people learn the pleasures of the written word despite the crippling influence of the worst kinds of educational experience, and we were also aware that some can resist all blandishments. Furthermore, we realized that we needed to compare changes issuing from the program of *English in Every Classroom* with the natural, self-induced and accidental changes that time alone brings to a comparable group of human beings.

One inch away from the edge of a cliff may be a significant distance to a man walking in the dark, just as a linear mile may be an insufficient distance from the center of a bomb burst. Under the new program, microscopic gains in reading and writing by an educational loser might be greatly significant when contrasted to the regression of a similar child subjected to traditional methods. Thus a "control group" was necessary to the experiment. In another mid-western training school, we found a population of counterparts to the students at B.T.S.—boys similarly enmeshed in the toils of the law, burdened by similar social histories, and characterized by their rejection of everything that school is and represents. This training school became our control, while the program of *English in Every Classroom* was actually initiated in the W. J. Maxey Boys' Training School (B.T.S.) at Whitmore Lake, Michigan.

Selection of our control group (CG) marked the end of the beginning. We had matched populations available for study, we had measuring devices that looked good on paper, and we had all the confidence and enthusiasm that usually characterize a new venture. What follows here is a guided tour through the results of placing boys, books, newspapers, magazines *and* teachers in continuous contact.

# THE RAW MATERIAL

What were the fundamental characteristics of the boys who made up our experimental and control samples? The boys at B.T.S. averaged fifteen years and seven months of age while their control counterparts were four months younger. From youngest to oldest, the boys ranged from twelve to seventeen.

Racially: The overall sample was divided between Negro and white students with fewer white subjects in the control group than at Whitmore Lake. This possible bias in the sample is explored as a separate factor in our analysis. We have no reason to suspect that this differential representation by race is significant, since the sample is weighted heavily in both institutions in favor of membership in the lower socio-economic classes. Our experience has led us to believe that social class, rather than race, is the prime determinant of the individual's attitude and behavior toward reading, writing and speaking the language of the middle class. Comparisons of white and Negro boys at the two training schools may clarify the relationship of race and social class to literacy. They will be cited where they seem to influence our research findings.

### Racial Distribution by School

| School | Negro | White |
|--------|-------|-------|
| Whitmore Lake | 31 | 29 |
| Control Group | 21 | 10 |

Intellectually: A high-jumper with both legs amputated at the knees probably has no greater handicap than the prospective student entering school competition equipped with limited intelligence. Smart kids have always done disproportionally better than dumb kids in a formal educational setting, but we have also learned that it is awfully difficult to tell who's smart and who's dumb if our sole measure is the traditional intelligence test.

As every educator has learned the hard way, intelligence tests may measure the basic intellectual capacity of middle-class white children, but such tests are at best only very rough assessments of *probable* academic success for lower-class

183

white and Negro children. Intelligence tests are inadequate measures of the mental capacity of lower-class children because such tests are so heavily weighted with knowledge gained only by participation in the world of the middle class. Though no one knows the intelligence of lower-class white or Negro children, our crude measures can tell us something of their probable response to a traditional education.

An intelligence test can be a threat and a promise of failure or it can be a showcase for the display of intellectual capacity. It can be a difficult task that is accomplished with verve, or it can be middle-class punishment visited on lower-class victims. For want of better devices, we used these inadequate indices as measure of the basic equipment our children brought to the fray. An average of five I.Q. points separated the boys in the CG from those at B.T.S. (approximately the number of Full Scale I.Q. points allowed for on the Wechsler to compensate for testing error). The Full Scale I.Q.'s of the B.T.S. sample average 95 and those in the CG average 90. Both scores are below the hypothetical statistical average of 100, and this fact sets an additional limit to our expectations regarding reading, writing, and literate attainment. (Appendix, Table 1)

The relevance of skin color to intelligence that is measured by tests standardized on white middle-class youngsters is inescapable here. Being Negro is, on the average, a condition that assures one of a lower score on any test of intelligence currently in use. Such is the case with the boys we studied. Whether the Full Scale Intelligence quotient or its Verbal or Performance subparts are used as measures, the Negro child does less well throughout our sample. If we accept the Wechsler Intelligence Test as a representation of functional abstract and symbolic intelligence, then our Negro children are less well equipped in this way than are the white. The Negro child in the CG had a Full Scale I.Q. of 85.57 and the Negro in B.T.S. scored 87.59. The white boys in the CG scored 98.91 for a Full Scale I.Q. and their counterparts at B.T.S. scored 104.60.

A rank-ordering of the boys in our sample from highest to lowest scores on individual intelligence tests is as follows:

1. White boys at B.T.S.
2. White boys in the CG
3. Negro boys at B.T.S.
4. Negro boys in the CG

Despite these differences in measured intellect, statistical comparison of the Whitmore Lake boys as a whole with the total CG sample of boys disclosed *no* over-all significant difference in intelligence.

184

In the analysis of our tests and measures and the interpretation of the research findings, we are primarily interested in determining how the boys at B.T.S. differed from the boys in the CG before and after the experiment. To reach scientifically reliable conclusions we must view each finding in terms of the qualifications imposed on it by age, intelligence and race. This is an important research step to take since we need to know which children are most and least receptive to the program of *English in Every Classroom* and what characteristics identify each of them.

Age differences in the two samples must also be noted. Our typical subject at B.T.S. was 188.81 months old while the typical CG boy was 183.50 months old. It is reasonable to assume that some effect of this average age difference of five months between the samples is possible.

# A CATALOGUE OF TESTS AND MEASURES

There is no exciting way to describe the variety of measures we used to assess the progress of our pilgrims to literacy in the two training schools. Some of the tests and measures were modifications of research instruments proved effective in other settings with different children. We adapted, altered and modified traditional instruments to meet the demands of a particularly difficult testing situation. Here we have grouped our research instruments in terms of the psychological and behavioral phenomena they were designed to tap. All catalogues are wearisome reading; the one that follows here merely hopes to convey the range and kind of devices employed in assessing this program for the teaching of reading and writing in the schools.

*Intellectual Performance*

Most of our children were administered individual intelligence tests at the time of their commitment to one or the other of the two correctional institutions. These tests served as a rough indicator of potential response to educational designs within the institutions and, indeed, we suspect that assignment to the CG school or B.T.S. was, in some part, a function of how bright the child was. B.T.S. has the deserved reputation of being a model correctional institution in the State of Michigan and a bright child (if he is free of other grossly disqualifying characteristics) has a greater likelihood of being assigned to B.T.S. than to other correctional institutions within the state.

We used both individual intelligence tests (the Wechsler Intelligence Scale for Children) and scores on the Stanford Achievement Test as indicators of intellectual capacity. Scores on subparts of the Stanford having the greatest relevance to our study included those on language, word meaning, paragraph meaning, and spelling. Though we were unable to repeat the Wechsler for a significant number of children as they were released from incarceration, we do have Stanford Achievement Test scores for enough boys, both before and after the experiment, to warrant statistical analysis. On the average, eight months elapsed between intelligence tests or achievement tests.

## In the Eye of the Beholder—the Teacher

We sought to measure certain values and beliefs which affect teachers' attitudes toward their pupils, since their view of the children they teach profoundly affects the pattern of educational and human interaction that takes place between them. On the *Teacher's Behavior Rating Sheet,* for example, we presented each teacher with pairs of words often used to describe pupils and asked for an estimate of the degree to which one or another of these words fit a particular student. A sample of the form used appears in Illustration 1, which follows.

### Illustration 1

#### Teacher's Behavior Rating Sheet

Below you will find pairs of words or phrases which can be used to describe people. Each pair is separated by seven spaces. Please put an X in the space that best describes the student you are rating.

For example, if the student is really very much like either one of the words, you would put the X on the line to the extreme left or right as follows:

agile    X
      — — — — — — —    awkward

or

agile    — — — — — — X —    awkward

You would choose an intermediate position in accordance with how you feel about the particular student being described.

You will be rating a number of students, but do not try for balance. For example, it is possible that *all* the students in your particular class are agile or that all of them are awkward. You would rate them accordingly.

Be sure to check every item. Use only one check mark

187

for each pair of words or phrases. Mark each item quickly. Your first impressions or immediate feelings are best.

| | | |
|---|---|---|
| dishonest | — — — — — — — | honest |
| bad | — — — — — — — | good |
| inattentive | — — — — — — — | attentive |
| unaggressive | — — — — — — — | aggressive |
| adjusted | — — — — — — — | disturbed |
| energetic | — — — — — — — | lazy |
| devious | — — — — — — — | forthright |

From teacher ratings of these opposite word pairs, it was possible to construct the following broad stereotypes:

### The Angel

The angelic student is one the teacher describes as honest, good, energetic, attentive, unaggressive, forthright and well adjusted. Even in a population of delinquent boys in a training school there are some who roughly approximate this model.

### The Devil

The devil is everything the angel is not. The devilish student is dishonest, bad, lazy, inattentive, aggressive, devious and disturbed. Few students are described completely in such terms, but our sample contains boys who have a startling resemblance to that portrait.

### The Mixed Type

Only grade-B Western movies persist in dividing human beings into two classes—the good guys and the bad guys. In real life there are many shades of gray between those who wear white hats and those who swear black oaths. Where teachers reported mixed views of a child, we cast him into this category.

On a *Teacher's Evaluation Form* additional ratings were gathered to assess such dimensions as:

The pupil's capacity to form interpersonal relationships
The pupil's emotional adjustment

The pupil's attitude toward school and motivation for
school work.

Each of these broad categories was constructed by compiling a series of ratings of individual items, to form a total score. Thus, for example, "the pupil's emotional adjustment" is a composite based on teacher ratings of the pupil's frustration tolerance, his attitudes toward limits set in the classroom, his general emotional adjustment, his degree of self-control, and his ability to contemplate consequences before acting.

The *Teacher's Evaluation Form* also provided us with estimates of:

The pupil's sense of self-worth and self-esteem

The pupil's tendency to become withdrawn

The pupil's relationship to the teacher

The pupil's attention span in school

The pupil's reaction to failure

All these aspects of the teacher's view of her pupils were deemed important to the kind of educational and human interaction most likely to take place in the classroom. In any research project you have to make decisions and choices; these elements were our choices.

The *Teacher's Evaluation Form* provided for ratings on the same kind of seven-point scale used for the *Teacher's Behavior Rating Sheet* but the descriptive adjectives used differed somewhat. The *Teacher's Evaluation Form* is exemplified in the following illustration.

*Illustration 2*

*Teacher's Evaluation Form*

For each statement below, place an X in the space that best describes the person you are rating. Even though you may be unsure about some of the categories, do not leave any items blank.

1. Pupil's capacity to form interpersonal relationship with peers.

   High    — — — — — — —    Low

2. Pupil's capacity to form interpersonal relationships with adults.

   Low    — — — — — — —    High

3. Evidence of anxiety

Little — — — — — — — Overwhelm-
apparent                                    ing and
                                            debilitating

4. Frustration tolerance

Becomes upset easily                        Rarely
when things                                 becomes
happen — — — — — — — upset

5. Sense of self-worth and self-esteem

Feels adequate                              Feels inade-
and                                         quate and
competent — — — — — — — worthless

6. Attitude toward classroom limits

Rebels — — — — — — — Accepts

7. General emotional adjustment

Good — — — — — — — Poor

8. Tendency to become withdrawn from people and things
   around him

High — — — — — — — Low

9. Relationship to teachers

Wants to be                                 Rejects all
accepted                                    overtures
and liked — — — — — —

10. Attention span in school

Needs constant                              Capable of
reminders and                               sustained
direction — — — — — — — work

11. Amount of self-control

Well                                        Frequent
controlled — — — — — — — breakdowns

190

12. Attitude toward school

Negative — — — — — — — Positive

13. Motivation for school work and learning

High — — — — — — — Low

14. Reaction to failure

Gives up in anger or
gives up after denying
concern    — — — — — — —
Tends to
work harder
for mastery

15. Acts without considering the consequences

Usually — — — — — — — Rarely

## In the Eye of the Beholder—The Pupil

Teachers' eyes and pupils' eyes do not always see the same events in the same light. It was therefore equally important for us to obtain before-and-after measures of pupils' views in both our experimental and control samples of young men.

We began by asking each pupil to tell us how much he liked (a lot or a little) "being in a school that has a library," "learning how to read and write well," "reading books and magazines" and "writing about things." The pupils' responses were converted into a single measure or score of *Attitude Toward Literacy*. This form includes eight items as follows:

### Illustration 3

### "How Much Do You Like" Form

Since all people are different, they like different things and they like them in different amounts. We would like to learn *How Much You Like* certain things about school. The way to mark this section is this: the more you like something, the more points you give it. The things you like very little, you mark 1. The things you like very much, you mark 7. You can choose any number from 1 to 7. Mark the number you choose by *drawing a circle* around it.

A. Playing games or sports at school

    like a little    1  2  3  4  5  6  7    like a lot

B. Being in a school that has a library

    like a little    1  2  3  4  5  6  7    like a lot

C. Learning how to read and write well

    like a little    1  2  3  4  5  6  7    like a lot

D. Learning about people and places

    like a little    1  2  3  4  5  6  7    like a lot

E. Learning about arithmetic or mathematics

    like a little    1  2  3  4  5  6  7    like a lot

F. Being where there are many others my own age

    like a little    1  2  3  4  5  6  7    like a lot

G. Reading books and magazines

    like a little    1  2  3  4  5  6  7    like a lot

H. Writing about things

    like a little    1  2  3  4  5  6  7    like a lot

Seeking an alternative way to test feelings toward books and school, we gave a *Behavioral Rating Form* to each student and asked him to indicate which of fifty-one items were "like me" or "not like me." Illustration 4 depicts the experimental form we employed.

*Illustration 4*

*Behavioral Rating Form*

Please mark each statement in the following way:
If the statement describes how you usually feel, put a check in the column "LIKE ME." If the statement *does not*

describe how you usually feel, put a check in the column
"NOT LIKE ME."

There are no right or wrong answers.

LIKE ME    NOT LIKE ME

EXAMPLE: I'm a hard worker._____

LIKE ME    NOT LIKE ME

1. I spend a lot of time thinking
   and wondering. _____

2. I'm pretty sure of myself._____

3. I often wish I was
   someone else. _____

4. I'm easy to like._____

5. I find it very hard to talk in front
   of the class. _____

6. I wish I was younger._____

7. I'd change a lot of things about
   myself if I could._____

8. I can make up my mind without too
   much trouble._____

9. I'm a lot of fun to be with._____

10. I'm proud of my school work. _____

11. Someone always has to tell me
    what to do._____

12. It takes me a long time to get used
    to anything new._____

13. Lots of times I'm sorry for the
    things I do._____

14. I'm popular with kids my own age._____

15. I'm doing the best work I can._____

16. I give in very easily._____

17. I can usually take
    care of myself._____

18. I'm pretty happy._____

19. I would rather play with kids
    younger than me._____

20. I like to be called on in class._____

21. I understand myself._____

22. It's pretty tough to be me._____

23. Things are all mixed up in my life._____

24. Kids usually follow my ideas._____

25. I'm not doing as well in school
    as I'd like to._____

26. I can make up my mind
    and stick to it._____

27. It's better to be a girl
    than a boy._____

28. I have a low opinion of myself._____

29. I don't like to be with
    other people._____

30. I often feel upset in school._____

31. I often feel ashamed of myself._____

32. I'm not as nice looking
    as most people._____

33. If I have something to say,
    I usually say it._____

34. Kids pick on me a lot._____

35. My teacher makes me feel
    I'm not good enough._____

36. I don't care what happens to me._____

37. I don't do things very well._____

38. I get upset easily
    when I'm scolded._____

39. Most people are better liked
    than I am._____

40. I often get discouraged in school._____

41. Things usually don't bother me._____

42. I can't be depended upon._____

43. Books are things I like
    to have around._____

44. I read a newspaper almost
    every day._____

45. I like to write things down when I
think about them._____

46. I usually read something when I have
some free time._____

47. I get pretty nervous when I have to
explain something._____

48. I hate books._____

49. There are lots of magazines I am
interested in._____

50. Writing is something I can
do without._____

51. It's better to be a grown-up
than a kid._____

By combining responses to items clearly related to one another, we devised a series of composite pupil views.

*The Literacy Lover,* for example, is a boy who indicates that he likes to have books around, likes to write things down when he thinks of them, usually reads something when he has free time, finds lots of magazines he is interested in, and does not consider writing unimportant. The *Literacy Hater* is a boy whose attitudes caused him to reverse all or most of these responses.

Literacy tends to be an abstract concept to most children despite attempts to translate it into everyday terms. Using other items in the *Behavioral Rating Form,* we established *School Lover* and *School Hater* categories. A *School Hater* tells us he "is not proud of his school work," "does not like to be called on in class," "feels upset in school," "thinks his teacher makes him feel he is not good enough" and "often gets discouraged in school." And of course the *School Lover,* by comparison, feels that in school he has found a home away from home.

It is obviously important for us to know something of the attitudes with which students in our experimental and control samples view the classroom both at the beginning and the end of their exposure to *English in Every Classroom.* But school is not all books and learning. School is the sum total of the work of the child and the forge on which he hammers out his self-image and self-esteem. Using several of the fifty-one items of the *Behavioral Rating Form,* we assembled a single score that would tell us something of the pupil's view of himself. A young man with a positive self-image and high self-esteem, for example, would report to us that he saw himself as a person who is "sure of himself, is easy to like, is a lot of fun to be with, is popular with kids his own age, can take care of himself, is happy, understands himself, has friends who follow him, and doesn't usually let things bother him." The reverse of this image is a loser who expects catastrophe in the academic world and has little hope for social or interpersonal success.

An additional measure of academic attitude was our form entitled *How Do You Feel About Things in Class?* This elaborate questionnaire includes thirty items, all of which addressed themselves to the issue of anxiety in the classroom. The students were asked to estimate the intensity of their feelings along four dimensions. The dimensions differed descriptively, *i.e.*, from "worry a lot" to "never worry," from "often" to "never," etc., for various items, but the intention was to sum up anxiety in many of its forms in order to achieve a total index of its amount. The pupils then were asked to indicate intensity of concern for the following thirty items:

## Illustration 5

### How Do You Feel About Things in Class?

I am going to be asking you some questions—questions different from the usual school questions, for these are about how you feel and so these questions have no right or wrong answers.

No one but myself will see your answers to these questions—not your teacher, principal or your parents. Read each question with me as I read the question aloud. You can answer each question by circling just *one* of the letters right below the question.

These questions are about how you think and feel and therefore have no right or wrong answers. People think and feel differently. The person next to you might answer a question in one way. You might answer the same question in another way, but both would be right because you feel differently about the matter.

Remember, I shall read each question, including the kinds of answers you can give. Wait until I finish reading the question and then answer. Give only one answer for each question.

1. Do you worry when the teachers say that they are going to ask you questions to find out how much you know about a subject?

2. Do you worry about whether you will be promoted, that is, passing from one class to the next class at the end of a year?

3. When the teacher asks you to answer questions in front

196

of the class, are you afraid that you are going to make some bad mistakes?

4. When teachers say that they are going to call on students to do some problems, do you hope they will call on someone else?

5. Do you dream at night that you are in school and cannot answer a teacher's question?

6. When you think you are going to be called on by a teacher, does your heart begin to beat fast?

7. When a teacher is explaining a hard subject, do you feel others in the class understand it better than you do?

8. Before you fall asleep do you worry about how well you are going to do in class the next day?

9. When a teacher asks you to write on the blackboard in front of the class, does your hand shake?

10. Do you worry more about school than other students?

11. When you are thinking about your school work for the next day, do you become afraid that you will get the answers wrong when a teacher calls on you?

12. If you are sick and miss class, are you afraid you will be way behind the other students when you return?

13. Do you dream at night that others in your class can do things better than you?

14. When you are thinking about your classwork for the next day, do you worry that you will do poorly?

15. When you think you are going to be called on by a teacher, do you get a funny feeling in your stomach?

16. If you do very poorly when a teacher calls on you, does it bother you and make you feel unhappy?

17. Do you ever dream that a teacher is angry because you don't know the material?

18. Are you afraid of school tests?

19. Do you worry before you take a test?

20. Do you worry while you are taking a test?

21. After you have taken a test, do you worry about how well you did on the test?

22. Do you dream at night that you did poorly on a test you had in school that day?

23. When you are taking a test does your hand shake?

24. When teachers say they are going to give the class a test, do you become afraid you'll do poorly?

25. When you are taking a difficult test, do you forget some things you knew well before you started taking the test?

26. Do you ever wish that you didn't worry so much about tests?

27. When teachers say they are going to give the class a test, do you get a nervous feeling?

28. While you are taking a test do you usually think you are doing poorly?

29. While you are on your way to school do you worry that you might have a test?

30. While you are taking a test do your hands ever feel sweaty?

From this test, a single measure was constructed based on the child's total anxiety score. Some children are made nervous by the classroom setting and others take it easily in their stride. We needed to distinguish between these two types and used this measure to accomplish our purpose. While the academically anxious child may worry about every aspect of the classroom encounter, there are those for whom the classroom is an arena designed to fit their personal specifications and they revel in it.

Finally, we adapted familiar test devices to form what has been given the rather pretentious title of a *Literary Attitude Scale* for children. This particular measurement is an adaptation of the semantic differential technique. On this scale, any object, feeling, attitude or behavior can be assessed along a variety of dimensions calculated to reveal the subject's fundamental feelings. Take *money* for example: Would you consider money very good or very bad, very weak or very strong, very interesting or very dull, very small or very big, very important or very unimportant? On such a set of rating scales we apprised ourselves of the value these children ascribed to literary efforts (reading and writing) and literary materials (newspapers, magazines, and books).

As an additional measure, we used the semantic differential style of questioning to allow the child to tell us about himself; *i.e.*, are you as a person good or bad, weak or strong, interesting or dull, small or big, important or unimportant? Using this research technique we probed for reaction to sixteen different items. Illustration 6 demonstrates the descriptive adjectives attached to each concept and is followed by a list of the items we explored.

## Illustration 6

### Literary Attitude Scale

*Example*

Money is

| very good | good | sort of good | not good or bad | sort of bad | bad | very bad |
|---|---|---|---|---|---|---|
| very weak | weak | sort of weak | not weak or strong | sort of strong | strong | very strong |
| very interesting | interesting | sort of interesting | not interest- ing or dull | sort of dull | dull | very dull |
| very small | small | sort of small | not small or big | sort of big | big | very big |
| very important | unimportant | sort of important | not important or unimportant | sort of unimportant | unimportant | very unimportant |

*Test Items (using above dimensions)*

1. Cars are
2. Television is
3. Classes are
4. Newspapers are
5. I am
6. Sports are
7. Writing is
8. Food is
9. This place is
10. Reading is
11. Tests are
12. Teachers are
13. Home is
14. Magazines are
15. Work is
16. Books are

Few of the traditional measures of intelligence and achievement seemed to us useful in assessing progress in our students. We needed something more than these, something more directly concerned with literacy. We therefore modified existing techniques to construct a test of *Verbal Proficiency*. The *Verbal Proficiency Test* was nothing more than an attempt to provoke our anti-literate boys into producing words and ideas. The test included instructions such as the following:

1. Write all the uses you can think of for tin cans, bottles or milk cartons.
2. Write all the things you think might happen if we could understand birds and animals, if people from Mars landed on the earth, or if we could read each other's minds.
3. Write all the things you would say if you tried to tell someone what kind of person you are.
4. Write the improvements you could make in such items as bicycles, chairs, telephones, beds, cars, and shoes.
5. Write all the words you can invent by using the letters in CREATION, GENERATION or MATURATION.

From these diverse assessments of literary production, we marked off measures of the number of words actually written and the number of separate ideas contained in these words. The scores on the various subtests were combined to achieve a total score reflecting the number of ideas and number of words produced by the student.

This, then, constitutes the catalogue of instruments, measures and techniques we employed to find out what was happening to the boys exposed to *English in Every Classroom* as compared with what happened to their peers, who were given a more traditional education. Other methods, other devices and other techniques might well have been used to assess what was happening, but the ones we selected seemed to us most likely to serve our purposes.

Our primary concern was to study our subjects, to assess the effects of the program, as contrasted with its absence, and to communicate the results in as direct and uncomplicated a fashion as possible. Thus, what follows here is our *interpretation* of our research results in a form relieved wherever possible of the burden of statistics and technical jargon. Two methods have been used to keep the text intact and readable and yet to maintain statistical accuracy. First, the bulk of the tabular material has been placed in an appendix to be referred to if statistical detail is sought. Second, only the broad differences between B.T.S. and CG are tabled. The detailed statistical subanalyses of the findings by age, race and I.Q. are reported in descriptive terms, but most of the tabular form of the material is not included. These details are recorded in full in the extended report furnished to the United States Office of Education and are available on request. To include this entire level of statistical analysis here would be tedious and irrelevant to the scope of this book, and would require the reproduction of more than 130 separate tables.

# TWO YEARS OF TESTING

## The Self—Its Image and Its Esteem

When a child turns his eyes inward he gets an image of himself—of who and what he is—and he reacts intellectually and emotionally to his judgment of what he sees. With his inner eye he takes the measure of himself—his characteristics, his physique, his looks, his style of life—and compares this self-view, for better or for worse, with the way others see him. His view of himself is also constructed of reflected appraisals, i.e., the kind of person other people think he is. What do I think I am? What do others think I am? What do I want to be? Such are the questions asked of the self; in the answers to these questions we find a wellspring of motivation for human behavior.

The quest for a sense of identity continues throughout every man's life. Suppose, for a moment, that the seeker discovers an identity like this one:

> I am a fifteen-year-old Negro boy who has been in a lot of trouble with the police. Finally, one time they caught me, they took me away from my family and sent me to this training school. All the boys here are tough and have got busted by the police, too. People think I am pure bad and don't trust me. My mother's ashamed of me, the neighbors don't like me, and kids at home are told to stay away from me because I'm "trouble." White folks don't treat me fair and they don't like me. Everybody thinks I am dumb and no-account and they think I am going to end up in Jackson Prison for the rest of my life. Maybe they're right.

Such a self-image makes its possessor unlikely to look to literacy as a means of changing his life. Hope and prospect are functions of how you value yourself and of the importance you attach to seeing yourself as you think you are. Education and self-worth are necessary complements to one another.

We asked the teachers to evaluate the sense of self-worth and self-esteem of each of their pupils. We asked the teacher to tell us whether a child feels adequate and competent, inadequate and worthless, or somewhere between these extremes.

202

There was no statistically significant difference between teacher estimates of self-esteem at B.T.S. and in the CG at the beginning of the experiment. The self-esteem of the boys in the CG was somewhat higher when we began, but it deteriorated during the year, while that of the boys at B.T.S. rose, until, according to the teachers, it matched the original starting position of those in the control group. In other words, self-esteem rose among the boys at B.T.S. while it was falling in the CG (Table 2, Entry D).

The details of this change are instructive. When the experiment began, high self-esteem characterized the youngest and the brightest of the Negro boys in the CG. They valued themselves more highly than older boys of either race at either school. By the end of the school year this promising state of affairs ceased to exist. Superior self-esteem traded partners and became the possession of the older boys at both schools and, significantly, the particular pride of the brightest ones at B.T.S. At the end of the year, those with the highest self-esteem were the older, brighter, white boys at B.T.S.

One year in a penal training school must maim the psychological well-being of the young, bright Negro, for he ends this period of intended rehabilitation with his view of himself greatly diminished. The significant early advantage posted by the young in the CG, compared with the young in B.T.S., disappears in post-test evaluations. Pre- and post-test comparisons between schools by high and low I.Q. display a marked, significant shift (Tables 25 and 26).

## The Self Through the Child's Eyes

We asked the children to tell us how they viewed themselves. In the *Behavioral Rating Form* (Table 3) and in the *Literary Attitude Scale* (Table 4) they could tell us who and what they were. When we began to examine *English in Every Classroom,* the least bright in the CG possessed, on both measures, a superior view of themselves (Table 15). The same finding appeared for the Negroes in both groups. In fact, being a Negro in the CG was better than being a Negro in B.T.S. if self-image is taken as the criterion. And a Negro in the control school had a better self-concept than white boys at either institution (Table 17).

When the smoke of a year in a training school had cleared, those with the highest self-esteem were found to be the boys in the B.T.S. population (Table 3, Entry C; Table 4, Entry B) and a positive self-image was most apparent in the brightest among them (Table 16). The Negro boys in the CG maintain their superiority of self-view when compared with the general run of white boys at the same school, but both the Negroes and the whites at B.T.S. do even better in maintaining self-esteem (Table 18). It is clear that the two schools have a different effect on their charges' views of themselves; it is also clear that this view is not a function of the age of the boys tested. We believe this self-view is crucial to each child's ability to respond to the world of words. Something of a positive nature took place in B.T.S. that was missing in the CG. A part of this positive influence was *English in Every Classroom*.

## The Child as the Teacher Sees Him

One kind of truth about classroom and pupils can be seen through the eyes of the teacher. Her view of the classroom world is an essential one because it contains the key to educational success or failure. In time every student comes to understand that the teacher is the master of the class and is the dispenser of reward, punishment, success and failure. Education is basically a process of child–teacher interaction and, given the form in which it is fashioned, any child at any given time has teachers who may or may not understand him, appreciate him, help him, encourage him or teach him.

Teachers reach conclusions about children following very brief and superficial contacts with them and these conclusions are, unfortunately, emotional and cognitive stereotypes. Children extend similar treatment to teachers, but since teachers are vested with the ultimate educational authority, their stereotypes are the more dangerous. In common with all teachers, the teachers in both the CG and B.T.S. stereotyped their pupils and, perceiving surface rather than depth, reacted to them accordingly.

We asked the teachers about "devils" and "angels," for example, and discovered that the angelic student was white, bright and older than the average at both institutions. What is most important is that this educational view of children was *invisible* when the semester *began* and only became apparent at the conclusion of our experiment. In this single academic year the stereotype for teacher discrimination of good versus bad students reared its ugly head to the detriment of Negro, less bright and younger pupils. It is our conviction that the teachers' classroom responses to individual children followed closely the outlines of these stereotypes, but we cannot prove it scientifically. We also suspect that what we discovered in these detention homes is a reasonable facsimile of events in our national public school system, but we are again without adequate proof that this is true.

204

Inferential corroboration is available, however. We asked teachers at both schools to rate the general emotional adjustment of each child and to judge his response to the establishment of limits on his classroom behavior. The boys judged best adjusted by teachers when the experiment began were, at both schools, predictably, white, and the ranks of the best adjusted were populated most significantly by boys at Whitmore Lake (Table 2, Entry B).

Being smarter than the average of the group made no difference in the initial ratings of teachers, but it came into its own after a year. Somehow, being smarter was confused with being better adjusted by the teachers in both schools. This is an error of judgment that seems to be repeated over and over again in the history of education.

If you are seeking a good adjustment rating from your teacher, be white. To a significant extent, white was right for pupils in both schools. It may be that skin color will prove to be an insurmountable obstacle as long as our teacher population is as predominantly white as it is at present. It might also be that our teachers are responding to some inevitable facts of life and that they are responding honestly. In our schools as they are presently constituted, white pupils have an advantage denied to their colored peers. Though both explanations are defensible, our observations suggest that being Negro carries with it the penalty of misunderstanding by white teachers.

What about teacher estimates of these children's interests, reactions and attitudes more immediately and directly concerned with literacy? When we asked teachers to tell us about the child's attitude toward school, they consistently reported that older and brighter children have the best attitudes. What little influence race has on this issue favors the white rather than the Negro child, but even this distinction disappeared by the end of the experiment. The clearly reliable finding is that teachers see bright students as better oriented to school. Perhaps this evaluation is both accurate and reasonable. After all, who else should respond best to confrontation with the mysteries of symbolism and abstraction? In this respect, geographical location makes less difference than measured intelligence. Teachers like smarter rather than dumber students and they view them as better disposed toward school.

Teachers' attitudes and beliefs about pupils may be most significant when things are going badly. What happens to the student who is experiencing failure? Does he give up in anger, does he insist that he "doesn't care, anyway," or does he work harder to master the problem that confronts him? The child's reaction to failure, as the teacher sees it at the

205

beginning and end of our experiment, ought to be a reasonable indicator of the child's "learning how to learn" in the course of the year.

When *English in Every Classroom* was first installed, the boys at B.T.S. responded best to failure and buckled down to work harder and did better when academic catastrophe threatened (Table 2, Entry G). The age of the child at Whitmore Lake was not related to digging-in rather than quitting, but it was evident at the beginning of the experiment that a good response appeared most often in the bright and white boys at B.T.S. Being Negro, being less bright and being in the control school group combined to make "working harder" an alien reaction to failure.

At the conclusion of our experiment, the boys in the CG were reported to have improved slightly in their reaction to failure, while those at B.T.S. showed a slight loss in maturity of response to failure (Table 2, Entry G). Both sets of differences were slight and it was no longer possible to make a significant distinction between boys at the two schools. The advantages of intelligence and race disappeared by the end of our study. It was as if these protections were inadequate defenses against the continued onslaught of failure as symbolized by incarceration. Both young and old at B.T.S. scored better at the conclusion of the experiment than the young at the CG. Intelligence ceases to be a significant factor at the conclusion of the experiment, as does the advantage of being white. The reaction to failure becomes almost totally uniform during the year the boys spend in training schools.

## Literacy and the Attitude of the Child

There are a number of perfectly respectable, more-or-less scientific definitions of the word "attitude." But most of them are so stiff and stuffy that what we mean to convey by the term attitude gets carried away in a flood of jargon. I once told a delinquent boy that I was worried about his "attitude" toward the crime to which he had admitted (professors talk funny even when they try not to). He replied, "I don't know what a attitude is, but it's how I feel, baby. The hell with them." The "them," of course, was all the members of middle-class society who bugged him by their insistence that he should not do what he regularly did.

Perhaps we need no better definition of attitude than "it's how I feel, baby," for that's the level at which an attitude is experienced by its possessor and we must start where they are rather than where we wish them to be. How our subjects feel about reading, writing, the classroom and things properly belonging to it is of vital interest to us. If literacy "feels bad," we must improve its feeling before we can accomplish any meaningful training at all. If we can influence the feelings people have, we can make fundamental changes in their view of the world.

It is conceivable that even if none of our subjects display a change in literary habits and energy investment in the acts of reading and writing, we could yet proclaim ourselves victors in the battle. If how they *feel* about reading and writing can be nudged into a new posture, we may have achieved the stance needed to move their whole outlook on the world. Once a child stops fighting the system, he can divert his energy into making it work for him to get what he wants and needs.

Our scales were designed to reflect two aspects of attitude toward literacy: (1) the child's attitude toward literary effort on his part, i.e., reading or writing; and (2) the child's attitude toward literary material, i.e., books, newspapers and magazines.

At the beginning of the experiment, the boys' attitudes toward their own literary efforts (Table 4, Entry C) were statistically indistinguishable by age, I.Q. or race, although the boys at B.T.S. had slightly more positive feelings than the boys in the control group. In the brief period of exposure a number of differences did appear and all of them fitted our original hypotheses about the impact of *English in Every Classroom:* they all favored the Whitmore Lake setting. The attitude of the B.T.S. boys improved and they kept their edge over the boys in the CG. In particular, in both schools the older boys showed the greatest improvement in attitude (significant at the .05 level). Literary effort had greater meaning for them than it did for the younger boys, particularly for those in the CG. Uniquely, being smarter or dumber and being Negro or white made little difference on this measure when the experiment was finished.

When the children were asked to express their attitude toward books, magazines and newspapers (Table 4, Entry D), intelligence played no part at all either before or after the initiation of *English in Every Classroom* at B.T.S. At the beginning, there was a clear-cut age difference in the schools (significant at the .05 and .01 levels). The younger boys at Whitmore Lake were happier about these instruments of literacy than were the older boys at the same school or the younger boys in the control group. Both the CG and B.T.S. had increased their interest in reading materials by the end of the experiment, but our findings favored the boys at B.T.S., whether young or old.

Initially, the white boys at Whitmore Lake felt better about the materials but this was not a significant difference. When the experiment was concluded, the significant finding was that the white boys at both institutions had more positive attitudes than their Negro comrades, with those of the white boys in the CG significantly more favorable than those of Negroes at the same school.

Reviewing the data, we can only conclude once again that the white–Negro differential response reflects the depth of our educational dilemma. In a variety of subtle ways the fact of skin color gets hopelessly entangled with notions about literacy. In the self-image of the child, in the teacher's view of him, and in his attitude toward education, the unbright, non-white child is so handicapped that massive educational reorganization may be necessary to help him. Getting him hooked on books may be a beginning but it is only that. The educational climate within our schools and within ourselves as teachers must be modified to meet the needs of the Negro student if we are to alter the way he feels about school and basic literacy.

In our next attempt to study attitude, we brought various items together to form the dimensions of "literacy lovers–literacy haters" and "school lovers–school haters." In the beginning, school lovers and school haters were distinguishable along only one dimension—race. Surprisingly, the Negro students at both institutions brought with them the most positive attitude toward school and the tasks of education. Age and intelligence were not significant forces in shaping this attitude. The results at the conclusion of the experiment wiped out this initially significant difference in attitude. On an uneven pattern, the attitude to school of the white boys improved slightly while the attitude of the Negro boys deteriorated. As a consequence of one year at these two training schools, no significant difference existed in the measurement of school lovers and school haters. All the boys in the sample occupied a position that could best be described as "alienated by the school experience." They didn't care much for school when they first arrived at the training center, and they didn't care much for it when they left.

Given a choice between books and schools, the children in our sample prefer books. Though our book lovers had only a modest passion for the written word, they clearly preferred it to school. As you might anticipate, the book lovers were, on the average, the older and brighter children at B.T.S. The older boys retained their interest in books at the end of the experiment, but intelligence ceased to contribute to this interest.

The questionnaire we titled "How Do You Feel About Things in Class?" actually addressed itself to the level of anxiety each child experienced as he thought about himself and education. We asked each child how much he worried about such things as tests, being promoted, reciting before the class, giving wrong answers, and being behind in his homework. Summarizing the answers to thirty such questions allowed us to compare the academic "worry scores" of boys in the two schools.

These scores were almost identical at the beginning of the experiment for the boys in both institutions. By the end of the school year, the boys in the CG were more worried about the educational process than they had been at the beginning of the year (Table 5). The reverse was true of the boys in B.T.S. The average boy there was significantly less anxious about school at the end of the experiment than he was at its inception.

Watching these changing levels of anxiety about education in the two schools was like witnessing a race in which the two runners left the starting line at the same time but one ran backward while the other ran forward. By the end of the race, the boys in the CG were farther back than they had been at the start. Had no anxiety reduction taken place for the B.T.S. boys, they would still have won the race. As it was, they were clearly more comfortable with things educational as a result of their experience in the training school.

Who became more anxious and who less? At the beginning, age didn't matter at either school (Table 19). On the average, all the boys at Whitmore Lake came to worry less, whether young or old, than those in the control group (Table 20). Being in the brighter half of the student body and being at B.T.S. proved to be twice good for those seeking relief from school pressures (Table 21). If you were sent to the CG, by the end of the experiment, your chances of worrying less about school were in direct proportion to the strength of your intellect (Table 22). At first, white boys in B.T.S. were less anxious than white boys in the CG; more surprisingly, Negro boys in the control group were less nervous about school than were white boys at the same institution (Table 23). By the time the experiment was completed, white children at B.T.S. felt better about school than their CG counterparts, both white and Negro (Table 24). Even more remarkably, the Negro children at Whitmore Lake felt considerably less anxious about school than both white and Negro boys in the other school.

Does *English in Every Classroom* really provide this relaxation of academic tension for the child exposed to its practices? We think it does. In part, we are convinced that providing the opportunity for children to get hooked on books is important and, in part, we know from observation that *English in Every Classroom* provides a new sense of excitement and enthusiasm for despairing teachers confronted with the hitherto hopeless task of forcing literacy upon unresponsive consumers. Teachers of reading and writing find new vigor and meaning in this English program because it returns teaching to where the kids *are* and removes it from the esoteric realm of where they *ought to be*. *English in Every Classroom* offers an educational rationality that produces in children a measurable relaxation of distress about school and its problems. Perhaps this is enough to demand of any educational innovation.

Measurements of attitudes by paper and pencil tests given in a group setting are far from infallible indicators of the way children really feel. If actions do speak louder than words, then we may look to the following measures of performance to discover which offers the greater promise—what the boys actually do on tests of literacy or their own expressions of how they feel about it.

### Verbal Proficiency

The Verbal Proficiency Test was really five tests rolled into one. Each test asked the child to perform with words and ideas in a variety of related intellectual tasks. Using separate scores based on the number of ideas and number of words the child had at his command to meet each test, we compared the performances of the boys in the two respective groups.

Though the results are as we hoped they would be, they are nonetheless shocking, for they are impersonal reflections of the fate of living human beings exposed to a crippling educational and social environment. In this measure of ease with words and ideas, B.T.S. boys were not significantly different from those in the CG when our experiment began. It was in the tests conducted after a year of work with and without *English in Every Classroom* that meaningful differences came to be so painfully clear (Table 6).

As reported earlier, the level of anxiety about school and literacy increased for the CG boys while it decreased for the inmates of Whitmore Lake (Table 5). As we look at these performance measures we can understand why. As in the race we described, a race with only two entries, our control group did worse than run second—it finished farther back than its own starting point. In their ability to generate ideas, boys at B.T.S. gained significantly by the time of post-testing; in the CG, boys not only failed to gain, but fell behind their initial levels of performance (Table 6). When a count was made of the number of words used to meet testing situations, boys exposed to *English in Every Classroom* at Whitmore Lake took part in what can only be described as a runaway performance. While the B.T.S. boys performed so well, the boys in our control sample were unable even to maintain their unsatisfactory level of the year before (Table 6).

This is a pathetic report but it is consistent with other reports in scientific literature which record intellectual regression following an absence of cognitive stimulation. We could, realistically, have expected little else. Given intellectual deprivation in an overworked and understaffed institution, we can hardly expect pupils to hold their own in the battle for verbal survival.

The facts speak for themselves. A calculated program of intellectual stimulation has a measurable impact on its consumers—the children. Verbal Proficiency, measured in our fashion, reflects the kind and quality of program an educational institution is willing to invest in. Though a great many events other than *English in Every Classroom* occurred simultaneously with our program, we are convinced that what we attempted must find its reflection in the results we have reported.

In both the CG and B.T.S. production of ideas (Table 9) and numbers of words (Table 11) were related to the students' measured intelligence. What is of particular interest is that the influence of basic intellectual ability was evident, not at the beginning of the experiment, but at its conclusion (Tables 10 and 12). In the tests of number of ideas and number of words, a significant relationship with intelligence was revealed only at the end of the experiment. Using the Verbal Proficiency Test as our measure, it is clear that our best prospects for inducing changes in literate performance are to be found in the ranks of the brightest students. They are, of course, always our most promising prospects: in part, because measures of intelligence tap exactly those qualities best suited to deal with the symbols and abstractions of education, and, in part, because an intelligence test is in an odd way a measure of how far the child has already traveled in his journey toward literacy.

Much the same relationship exists between Verbal Proficiency and all the subsections of the Stanford Achievement Tests in the Whitmore Lake sample. The best achievers on the Stanford Achievement Test among the boys at Whitmore Lake turned out to be those who displayed the highest degree of verbal proficiency both before and after the research study. While these findings are hardly startling, they gain import when we note that measured achievement did not prove a saving grace for the boys in the control group. No significant relationship existed between high achievers and low achievers on the Stanford Achievement Test and the ability to produce ideas and words on the Verbal Proficiency Test. There is a reasonable basis for believing that the (typical) environment created in the control school suppresses the boys' verbal productivity to the point that their performance does not even reflect the differences in achievement they have already attained.

The only significant correlations with Verbal Proficiency for the CG boys were with their self-stated high valuation of literary efforts (writing and reading) and of literary materials (newspapers, magazines and books). Those who displayed the greatest production of ideas and words on our tests were the same self-avowed lovers of reading, writing and books whom we identified at the beginning of the project. At B.T.S., the child did not have to be deeply committed to things literary to produce an abundance of ideas and words at final testing time.

An additional check was run to verify these observations. The section of the Verbal Proficiency Test asking each child to construct new words (using the letters available in a stimulus word) produced long and short words in unequal numbers. We decided to count the average number of letters in each word manufactured by each child in both schools. The outcome of this primitive means of assessment confirmed our previous conclusion about what had transpired between the beginning and end of our experiment. While the boys at B.T.S. showed a 20 percent improvement in the length of words they could invent, the boys in the CG lost so much ground that they reduced by almost one-half the average length of words they could assemble from the stimulus word (Table 6). There are a number of possible explanations of this turn of events, but it is evident that language production of even this simple variety is a sensitive response of children to their educational experience.

As the brightest among the children at both schools progressed most in the production of words and ideas during the course of the experiment, so too the white students achieved more in the idea production than did the Negro population at Whitmore Lake. In the beginning of our program, white students at B.T.S. proved to be slightly superior to Negro boys in their own school as well as to Negroes in the CG in the production of ideas (Table 13), and this trend became even more pronounced when the experiment ended (Table 14). Interestingly, race played no part in determining proficiency with words either before or after the experiment. Our suspicion is that words are a more easily available currency than ideas and that ideas are more subject to erosion when exposed to the abrasion of cultural disadvantage. The symbolic mental manipulation of words is a vital tool in the production of new and different ideas, but it is only one of a number of essential tools.

An additional technique designed to assess changes in language comprehension and proficiency was the Stanford Achievement Test (Table 7). Our plan was to take advantage of the routine administration of this test at the time each child entered and left detention. This "routine" data collection, we discovered, was a hit-and-miss affair—more miss than hit. In particular, the boys in our CG sample often failed to take the post-test we needed to assess their progress in achievement in comparison with that of the boys at Whitmore Lake.

The part of the Stanford Achievement Test least subject to this erosion in numbers is the section assessing the pupils' capacity to comprehend paragraph meaning. The measure of paragraph meaning is, happily, a global measure of comprehension and understanding that relies on knowledge of the meaning of the individual words of which it is composed. It is, in most respects, an ideal tool for our purposes, since it is unconcerned with such trivia of achievement as, for instance, spelling proficiency.

The analysis of the before-and-after scores of the boys in B.T.S. and the boys in the CG restates an already familiar set of observations (Table 8). The boys at B.T.S. are superior to those in the CG at the beginning of the experiment. Though both groups improve over the course of the academic year, the boys at B.T.S. make more than twice the progress of their control group counterparts. Their capacity to absorb a paragraph's meaning has clearly improved and the improvement is substantial.

A revealing subanalysis of this finding is worth reporting. We divided the Stanford Achievement Test scores of all the boys into upper and lower halves to see if the best achievers fared better than those who achieved less well when the test was that of ferreting out paragraph meaning. We discovered that having a high or low standing in achievement at the beginning of the experiment had little relevance for predicting a boy's progress during the ensuing year. Both the high and low achievers at B.T.S. made positive and substantial gains by the end of the study, while progress of the boys of the CG ranged between slight gains and equally slight losses. When we reduced our sample to those boys on whom we had pre-

213

and post-achievement measures, it became apparent that the highest achievers at Whitmore Lake profited most from the year of schooling.

The results of the Verbal Proficiency Test and the Stanford Achievement Test were congruent with one another and confirmed our hopes when we designed the experiment initially: where it finally counts—in performance—*English in Every Classroom* was a vital part of the educational experience available to the boys at the Maxey School. Furthermore, these changes in performance were directly attributable to a *change in feeling* generated by a change in methods and materials employed in the teaching of English.

# APPENDIX

A brief explanation of statistical language might be helpful here in interpreting the meaning of tables and the levels of significance they report. Significance levels, i.e., .05, .01, .001, etc., refer to the expected probability in every 100 instances that such a statistical result could occur by chance. The level of probability one chooses to designate as significant is arbitrary, but conventional practice in the social sciences tends most often to use levels of .05, .01, and better as significant indicators of real and reliable differences between groups. Where such indications are not present, the abbreviation N.S. (not significant) is used.

The tables make use of "t" and "F" ratios in reporting our findings. "t" is a conventional test of the significance of statistical differences between groups, while "F" involves analysis and testing of variance differences between groups. Thus, in making comparisons of performance between students in the two schools at the beginning and end of the experiment, an F Ratio statistic is needed to compensate for the fact that the two populations of students may have had different scores on any measure at the beginning of the experiment. Simply put, the F Ratio answers this question: "Given the starting position of each group of students, which group gained most during the course of the experiment?"

Of the two groups of boys compared in the following tables, one group of subjects came from the W. J. Maxey Boys' Training School and is referred to as B.T.S. The control group was made up of boys from another midwestern training school and is designated by the initials CG.

### Table 1

#### Intelligence Quotient

|  | B.T.S. | CG | t Ratio |
|---|---|---|---|
| I.Q. |  |  |  |
| *Full Scale* | 94.83 | 90.16 | N.S. |
| Verbal | 93.24 | 87.33 | N.S. |
| Performance | 95.59 | 91.85 | N.S. |

N.S. = Not significant statistically.

N.B. In the following tables, "Pre" means at the beginning of the subject's stay in training school and "Post" means results obtained after the subject has been in training school a year.

Table 2

Pre and Post Teachers' Evaluation Form

| Teacher's Evaluation Form | B.T.S. | CG | t Ratio | F Ratio | Level of Significance |
|---|---|---|---|---|---|
| A. Pupils Interpersonal Capacity | | | | .09 | N.S. |
| Pre | 7.63 | 7.36 | N.S. | | |
| Post | 8.11 | 8.21 | N.S. | | |
| B. Emotional Adjustment and Classroom Response | | | | .41 | N.S. |
| Pre | 21.66 | 19.41 | N.S. | | |
| Post | 20.97 | 19.36 | N.S. | | |
| C. Attitude and Motivation to School | | | | 3.13 | N.S. |
| Pre | 8.34 | 7.90 | N.S. | | |
| Post | 7.19 | 8.08 | N.S. | | |
| D. Child's Sense of Self-Esteem | | | | 1.65 | N.S. |
| Pre | 3.66 | 4.10 | N.S. | | |
| Post | 4.10 | 3.85 | N.S. | | |
| E. Tendency to Withdraw | | | | .06 | N.S. |
| Pre | 3.97 | 4.26 | N.S. | | |
| Post | 3.76 | 3.87 | N.S. | | |
| F. Attention Span in School | | | | .13 | N.S. |
| Pre | 4.34 | 4.21 | N.S. | | |
| Post | 4.08 | 3.92 | N.S. | | |
| G. Reaction to Failure | | | | .22 | N.S. |
| Pre | 4.11 | 3.46 | .05 | | |
| Post | 3.89 | 3.56 | N.S. | | |

## Table 3

### Pre and Post Behavior Rating Form

| Behavior Rating Form | B.I.S. | CG | t Ratio | F Ratio | Level of Significance |
|---|---|---|---|---|---|
| A. Book Lovers and Book Haters | | | | .02 | N.S. |
| Pre | 2.76 | 2.49 | .05 | | |
| Post | 2.68 | 2.56 | N.S. | | |
| B. Positive and Negative Attitude Toward School | | | | .11 | N.S. |
| Pre | 2.02 | 2.13 | N.S. | | |
| Post | 2.18 | 2.15 | N.S. | | |
| C. Positive or Negative Self-Image | | | | 4.17 | .05 |
| Pre | 2.34 | 2.49 | N.S. | | |
| Post | 2.60 | 2.44 | N.S. | | |

Table 4

Pre and Post Literacy Attitude Scale

| Literacy Attitude Scale | B.T.S. | CG | t Ratio | F Ratio | Level of Significance |
|---|---|---|---|---|---|
| A. Attitude Toward Tests, Teachers and Classes | | | | .01 | N.S. |
| Pre | 130.68 | 128.21 | N.S. | | |
| Post | 133.77 | 133.08 | N.S. | | |
| B. Self-Image (I Am) | | | | .67 | N.S. |
| Pre | 24.95 | 24.92 | N.S. | | |
| Post | 26.26 | 25.59 | N.S. | | |
| C. Literacy Efforts | | | | 1.21 | N.S. |
| Pre | 59.16 | 57.23 | N.S. | | |
| Post | 60.55 | 58.72 | N.S. | | |
| D. Literacy Material | | | | .38 | N.S. |
| Pre | 85.26 | 83.49 | N.S. | | |
| Post | 87.29 | 85.59 | N.S. | | |

218

## Table 5

### Pre and Post Anxiety Score
### (How Do You Feel About Things in Class?)

| Anxiety Score | B.T.S. | CG | t Ratio | F Ratio | Level of Significance |
|---|---|---|---|---|---|
| Pre | 88.11 | 85.79 | N.S. | 17.29 | .001 |
| Post | 92.61 | 81.90 | .01 | | |

## Table 6

### Verbal Proficiency Test
Mean Pre and Post Scores: Number of Ideas, Number of Words and Number of Letters per Word

| VPT | B.T.S. | CG | F Ratio | Level of Significance |
|---|---|---|---|---|
| **Ideas** | | | | |
| Pre | 37.53 | 36.67 | 2.70 | .10 |
| Post | 39.68 | 34.18 | | |
| | | | | |
| **Words** | | | | |
| Pre | 140.66 | 138.49 | 3.20 | .07 |
| Post | 145.55 | 122.36 | | |
| | | | | |
| **No. of Letters Per Word** | | | | |
| Pre | 31.32 | 64.77 | | .001 |
| Post | 49.05 | 36.11 | | |

## Table 7

### Scholastic Aptitude Tests
Pre-test (Scores in Grade Equivalents)

| SAT | B.T.S. | CG |
|---|---|---|
| Language | 6.0 | 4.4 |
| Word Meaning | 7.2 | 5.8 |
| Paragraph Meaning | 7.0 | 5.5 |
| Spelling | 7.0 | 5.5 |

## Table 8

### Pre and Post Scholastic Aptitude Test: Paragraph Meaning

| Paragraph Meaning | B.T.S. | CG | t Ratio | Level of Significance |
|---|---|---|---|---|
| Pre | 69.88 | 55.77 | 2.77 | .01 |
| Post | 82.96 | 60.38 | 2.70 | .01 |

## Table 9

### Pre-test of t Ratios of I.Q. and Verbal Proficiency Test: Number of Ideas

|  | VPT Score | B.T.S. High I.Q. | B.T.S. Low I.Q. | CG High I.Q. | CG Low I.Q. |
|---|---|---|---|---|---|
| *B.T.S.* |  |  |  |  |  |
| High I.Q. | 40.21 |  | 2.03* | .71 | 1.33 |
| Low I.Q. | 31.47 |  |  | 1.06 | .52 |
| *CG* |  |  |  |  |  |
| High I. Q. | 36.81 |  |  |  | .52 |
| Low I.Q. | 34.00 |  |  |  |  |

*Significant at the .05 level.

## Table 10

### Post-test of t Ratios of I.Q. and Verbal Proficiency Test: Number of Ideas

|  | VPT Score | B.T.S. High I.Q. | B.T.S. Low I.Q. | CG High I.Q. | CG Low I.Q. |
|---|---|---|---|---|---|
| *B.T.S.* |  |  |  |  |  |
| High I.Q. | 42.64 |  | 2.36* | .71 | 3.07** |
| Low I.Q. | 30.95 |  |  | 1.59 | .69 |
| *CG* |  |  |  |  |  |
| High I.Q. | 41.33 |  |  |  | 2.14* |
| Low I.Q. | 27.63 |  |  |  |  |

*Significant at the .05 level.
**Significant at the .01 level.

## Table 11

### Pre-test of t Ratios of I.Q. and Verbal Proficiency Test: Number of Words

|  | VPT Score | B.T.S. High I.Q. | B.T.S. Low I.Q. | CG High I.Q. | CG Low I.Q. |
|---|---|---|---|---|---|
| *B.T.S.* |  |  |  |  |  |
| High I.Q. | 139.89 |  | .41 | .25 | .48 |
| Low I.Q. | 132.11 |  |  | .15 | .06 |
| *CG* |  |  |  |  |  |
| High I.Q. | 135.13 |  |  |  | .22 |
| Low I.Q. | 130.88 |  |  |  |  |

## Table 12

### Post-test of t Ratios of I.Q. and
### Verbal Proficiency Test: Number of Words

| | VPT Score | B.T.S. High I.Q. | B.T.S. Low I.Q. | CG High I.Q. | CG Low I.Q. |
|---|---|---|---|---|---|
| **B.T.S.** | | | | | |
| High I.Q. | 147.96 | | .97 | .39 | 2.64** |
| Low I.Q. | 128.21 | | | .48 | 1.77 |
| **CG** | | | | | |
| High I.Q. | 139.13 | | | | 2.09* |
| Low I.Q. | 94.44 | | | | |

*Significant at the .05 level.
**Significant at the .01 level.


## Table 13

### Pre-test of t Ratios of Race and
### Verbal Proficiency Test: Number of Ideas

| | VPT Score | B.T.S. White | B.T.S. Negro | CG White | CG Negro |
|---|---|---|---|---|---|
| **B.T.S.** | | | | | |
| White | 41.27 | | 1.81 | .17 | 1.52 |
| Negro | 34.03 | | | 1.29 | .16 |
| **CG** | | | | | |
| White | 40.29 | | | | 1.09 |
| Negro | 34.64 | | | | |


## Table 14

### Post-test of t Ratios of Race and
### Verbal Proficiency Test: Number of Ideas

| | VPT Score | B.T.S. White | B.T.S. Negro | CG White | CG Negro |
|---|---|---|---|---|---|
| **B.T.S.** | | | | | |
| White | 46.20 | | 3.00** | 1.08 | 3.13** |
| Negro | 33.56 | | | .97 | .18 |
| **CG** | | | | | |
| White | 39.38 | | | | 1.09 |
| Negro | 32.84 | | | | |

*Significant at the .05 level.
**Significant at the .01 level.

222

## Table 15

### Pre-test of t Ratios of I.Q. and Pupils' Behavior Rating Form: Self-Image

| | VPT Score | B.T.S. | | CG | |
| --- | --- | --- | --- | --- | --- |
| | | High I.Q. | Low I.Q. | High I.Q. | Low I.Q. |
| *B.T.S.* | | | | | |
| High I.Q. | 2.36 | | .07 | 1.67 | 2.86** |
| Low I.Q. | 2.37 | | | 1.54 | 2.53* |
| *CG* | | | | | |
| High I.Q. | 2.06 | | | | 4.28** |
| Low I.Q. | 2.81 | | | | |

*Significant at the .05 level.
**Significant at the .01 level.

## Table 16

### Post-test of t Ratios of I.Q. and Pupils' Behavior Rating Form: Self-Image

| | VPT Score | B.T.S. | | CG | |
| --- | --- | --- | --- | --- | --- |
| | | High I.Q. | Low I.Q. | High I.Q. | Low I.Q. |
| *B.T.S.* | | | | | |
| High I.Q. | 2.71 | | .67 | 3.30** | .17 |
| Low I.Q. | 2.58 | | | 2.09* | .53 |
| *CG* | | | | | |
| High I.Q. | 2.06 | | | | 2.75** |
| Low I.Q. | 2.69 | | | | |

*Significant at the .05 level.
**Significant at the .01 level.

## Table 17

### Pre-test of t Ratios of Race and Pupils' Behavior Rating Form: Self-Image

| | VPT Score | B.T.S. | | CG | |
| --- | --- | --- | --- | --- | --- |
| | | White | Negro | White | Negro |
| *B.T.S.* | | | | | |
| White | 2.23 | | 1.35 | 1.14 | 3.55** |
| Negro | 2.44 | | | 2.43* | 2.36* |
| *CG* | | | | | |
| White | 2.00 | | | | 4.73** |
| Negro | 2.76 | | | | |

*Significant at the .05 level.
**Significant at the .01 level.

223

## Table 18

### Post-test of t Ratios of Race and
### Pupils' Behavior Rating Form: Self-Image

| | VPT Score | B.T.S. | | CG | |
|---|---|---|---|---|---|
| | | White | Negro | White | Negro |
| **B.T.S.** | | | | | |
| White | 2.50 | | 1,16 | 2.16* | 1.11 |
| Negro | 2.69 | | | 3.28** | .05 |
| **CG** | | | | | |
| White | 2.00 | | | | 3.88** |
| Negro | 2.68 | | | | |

*Significant at the .05 level.
**Significant at the .01 level.

## Table 19

### Pre-tests of t Ratios of Age and Anxiety Score

| | Anxiety Score | B.T.S. | | CG | |
|---|---|---|---|---|---|
| | | Young | Old | Young | Old |
| **B.T.S.** | | | | | |
| Young | 84.33 | | 1.49 | .60 | .16 |
| Old | 91.03 | | | .86 | 1.53 |
| **CG** | | | | | |
| Young | 87.25 | | | | .75 |
| Old | 83.47 | | | | |

## Table 20

### Post-test of t Ratios of Age and Anxiety Score

| | Anxiety Score | B.T.S. | | CG | |
|---|---|---|---|---|---|
| | | Young | Old | Young | Old |
| **B.T.S.** | | | | | |
| Young | 92.07 | | .27 | 2.54* | 2.30* |
| Old | 93.03 | | | 2.72** | 2.44* |
| **CG** | | | | | |
| Young | 82.50 | | | | .30 |
| Old | 80.93 | | | | |

*Significant at the .05 level.
**Significant at the .01 level.

## Table 21
### Pre-test of t Ratios of I.Q. and Anxiety Score

| | Anxiety Score | B.T.S. High I.Q. | B.T.S. Low I.Q. | CG High I.Q. | CG Low I.Q. |
|---|---|---|---|---|---|
| **B.T.S.** | | | | | |
| High I.Q. | 90.14 | | 1.35 | 1.49 | .25 |
| Low I.Q. | 83.42 | | | .17 | 1.05 |
| **CG** | | | | | |
| High I.Q. | 82.63 | | | | |
| Low I.Q. | 88.81 | | | | 1.27 |

## Table 22
### Post-test of t Ratios of I.Q. and Anxiety Score

| | Anxiety Score | B.T.S. High I.Q. | B.T.S. Low I.Q. | CG High I.Q. | CG Low I.Q. |
|---|---|---|---|---|---|
| **B.T.S.** | | | | | |
| High I.Q. | 96.71 | | 2.52* | 5.22** | 2.46* |
| Low I.Q. | 87.47 | | | 2.37* | .33 |
| **CG** | | | | | |
| High I.Q. | 76.69 | | | | |
| Low I.Q. | 85.69 | | | | 1.57 |

*Significant at the .05 level.
**Significant at the .01 level.

## Table 23
### Pre-test of t Ratios of Race and Anxiety Score

| | Anxiety Score | B.T.S. White | B.T.S. Negro | CG White | CG Negro |
|---|---|---|---|---|---|
| **B.T.S.** | | | | | |
| White | 89.97 | | .80 | 1.82 | .22 |
| Negro | 86.38 | | | 1.16 | .59 |
| **CG** | | | | | |
| White | 80.07 | | | | |
| Negro | 89.00 | | | | 1.81 |

## Table 24

### Post-test of t Ratios of Race and Anxiety Score

|  | Anxiety Score | B.T.S. | | CG | |
| --- | --- | --- | --- | --- | --- |
|  |  | White | Negro | White | Negro |
| B.T.S. |  |  |  |  |  |
| White | 94.67 |  | 1.13 | 3.20** | 2.58* |
| Negro | 90.69 |  |  | 2.84** | 1.87 |
| CG |  |  |  |  |  |
| White | 78.71 |  |  |  | .94 |
| Negro | 83.68 |  |  |  |  |

*Significant at the .05 level.
**Significant at the .01 level.

## Table 25

### Pre-test of t Ratios and Teachers' Evaluation Form: Self-Esteem

|  | Esteem Score | B.T.S. | | CG | |
| --- | --- | --- | --- | --- | --- |
|  |  | High I.Q. | Low I.Q. | High I.Q. | Low I.Q. |
| B.T.S. |  |  |  |  |  |
| High I.Q. | 3.54 |  | .62 | 1.76 | .29 |
| Low I.Q. | 3.21 |  |  | 2.17* | .87 |
| CG |  |  |  |  |  |
| High I.Q. | 4.50 |  |  |  | 1.47 |
| Low I.Q. | 3.69 |  |  |  |  |

*Significant at the .05 level.

## Table 26

### Post-test of t ratios and of I.Q. and Teachers' Evaluation Form: Self-Esteem

|  | Esteem Score | B.T.S. | | CG | |
| --- | --- | --- | --- | --- | --- |
|  |  | High I.Q. | Low I.Q. | High I.Q. | Low I.Q. |
| B.T.S. |  |  |  |  |  |
| High I.Q. | 4.68 |  | 3.14** | 2.30* | 1.80 |
| Low I.Q. | 3.37 |  |  | .59 | .95 |
| CG |  |  |  |  |  |
| High I.Q. | 3.63 |  |  |  | .36 |
| Low I.Q. | 3.81 |  |  |  |  |

*Significant at the .05 level.
**Significant at the .01 level.

# "WHAT I DONE LAST SUMMER"

## by Elton B. McNeil

Each September millions of kids face the impossible task of describing, in three hundred words or less, what they did during the summer. From the teacher's point of view, the gambit is foolproof: every child does *something* every summer, and he usually remembers it with pleasure, although children themselves aren't very demanding judges of a summer's quality—a summer is a summer is a summer. You don't have to go to school, so it's good. You come back to school, you've got to write, and that's bad. But you write because *they* want you to. Maybe you write like Reggie S., a twelve-year-old Negro boy who lives at the St. Francis Home for Wayward Boys.

Reggie's police record began when he was eight. In four years he's been arrested nine times (the top of the iceberg) for a variety of crimes against society, including extortion, thefts, truancy, gang fighting, and breaking and entering. Reggie writes like this:

## What I Done Last Summer

Last summer they said if I was a good boy and behave myself for a change I could git to go to camp. I done all what they said as good as I could and they let me go. A couple things I done I thought they wouldn't send me but they did on account I promised not to do them no more and some other guys started it anyway.

The camp has all kinds of free stuff. You don't pay nothing to ride in the boats or jump on the tramp or go to the crap [craft] shop or drink all the milk you want. Sometimes they has chocolate milk or Kool-ade. When you go to bed they has snacks. They don't hit kids even if you cuss at them or fight them but they make you go into the session room and talk about what's making you act that way. The people ain't like regular Whiteys and when I called Mac a white soda cracker he said he didn't call me no race names so I can't call him none.

227

They say they don't whip us ever and they don't. I think they ought to beat on some of them kids who wreck stuff or smoke illegal when they ain't supposed to. I had a lot of fun and only trouble sometimes. The first day we was their they took us to the Ludington Liebarey and the liebareyan give us any two books we wanted to keep. They was tiny paper books we could stick in our pockets and trade at the liebarey for other books. We used to trade books and all them magazines with other guys and sometimes we could read to the guys in the cabin with a flashlight when we went to bed. I used to take my books to the waterfront and tell one of them sitting waterfront guys to put it under his butt so's nobody would swipe it.

They used to let us play with the typewriters in the liebarey and we could look at all the books and magazines we wanted. Even if books and things got a little wrecked they didn't mess on us. I want to go back to camp next year and be a counselor when I grow up. That's what I done last summer and I still got them books.

Fictional? Yes. Fanciful? No. Reggie's "theme" is an accurate account, composed in their own phrases, of the view children at a Fresh Air Camp have of their month-long stay. The camp is an outdoor clinical center devoted to training budding professionals in the clinical management of emotionally disturbed and/or delinquent boys. The counselors are selected from the ranks of clinical psychologists, psychiatric nurses, psychiatric social workers, and teachers of special education for the emotionally disturbed. They don't holler at kids. They try to understand them.

In my years as director of this training center we had never made a meaningful attempt to incorporate literacy as a part of our basic program. We ignored the intellectual side of emotional and delinquent problems because I had no faith in the available programs of educational improvement for such youngsters. But I must report now that the *Hooked on Books* idea of a new approach to achieving literacy has changed our camp. The Fresh Air Camp is as corrosive an acid test for a literacy program as man or devil could invent. The odds against it were incredible. Who could imagine children who never read anything willingly, turning to books and magazines in an environment free of adult interference and full of fun and games?

*The Odds Against Reading*

The typical summer camp is populated by healthy, well-adjusted offspring of affluent American middle-class parents who view Mother Nature as a peerless developer of independence, maturity and character in their children. If not quite all that, then at least fun for the child and freedom from children for the parents. Such campers generally have two sorts of reading material available to them—the backs of cereal boxes and clandestine comic books. The fact is that the typical American camper is carefully shielded from books while he is adventuring in the great outdoors. With very few exceptions (such as academic or scientific camps for the very bright or gifted child), the American camping movement is fundamentally anti-intellectual.

Camp directors and counselors are vaguely discomfited by the sight of a child absorbed with the stimulation to his inner life that the written word provides. A child lying quietly on his bunk bed, lost in a novel, smacks of the "introvert" and introvert means maladjusted in the outgoing, friendly, bustling, go-get-'em society of the summer camp. Why isn't he *doing something* instead of just lying there? The maxim is, "Campers who play together pay together." As any camp director knows, the kid who reads by himself is the one who doesn't come back.

The portrait is overdrawn, but it is an essentially accurate picture of the typical summer's hiatus from literacy of the middle-class child. Quadruple its intensity and you have a small idea of such a hiatus at the University of Michigan's Fresh Air Camp. The children whose patronage we solicit come from mental hospitals, detention homes, houses of correction, child guidance clinics, slum neighborhoods and juvenile courts. These subjects of our experiment in reading are perhaps best characterized as children who hate. They are children from the worst sections of Michigan's large metropolitan areas. They are school kick-outs, smash-outs, and flunk-outs, and they are the debris of our educational and social system. They are nonreaders, almost nonreaders, pretend readers (picture lookers), and a host of slow, slow, slow readers whose lips move with every word their finger points to. There are some adequate readers, but a very few.

Books are painfully alien to these children, who have read only when forced to by a teacher. Besides, camp is for fun, not for schooling; it's a place where all the cool guys go. At the top of the summer's agenda for most of these children is the attainment of power and leadership by force. The bespectacled, literate bookworm hardly fits the stereotype of a scabrous, irreverent, adult-defying leader whose credo is summarized in the Rule of the Golden Knuckle: "A punch in the mouth is worth a thousand words." From this improbable clay we were to mold a model of the reading nonreader. As one young man put it, succinctly and directly, "What you got that motha library for? My worker [psychiatric case worker] tole me I was coming here for a good time. He didn't say

229

nothin about no mothering books. He said I could swim across the lake if I want to."

Given those crushing odds, it seemed only fair to demand a choice of weapons. We selected an armament consisting of the following pieces:

1. The Ludington Library (an unused camp cabin) was stocked with an assortment of paperback books and magazines selected to interest children ranging in age from seven to fifteen.

2. On the first day of camp every child was taken to the library, allowed to browse, and to choose two books as a gift.

3. The camper was told that the books were his to keep and could be exchanged for any others in the library whenever the mood moved him.

4. Games, typewriters, crayons, paper, etc., were distributed on tables for the pleasure of the library's visitors. It was not a "quiet" library; it was an activity center.

5. The three librarians were instructed to participate actively with the children and to have fun with them even if it hurt.

6. The library was to be kept open at all hours when the children were not engaged in scheduled camp activities.

The library weapons were primed and ready to fire but a target was needed. The traditional notions of what a camp should do for children and how it should plan for them had to be violated. These violations took the following form:

1. Every morning and all day Sunday were times for free activity. This meant that during approximately thirty-six waking hours of the seven-day week the children were free to visit the library, to read, to sit or to stare vacantly into space.

2. The counselors were instructed not to bug the reading child or to coerce him into physical activity. Reading was officially designated a worthwhile activity.

3. The teacher-trainees among the counselors were brainwashed in seminars to keep them from reverting instinctively to the classic role of the teacher-who-teaches-the-children-to-respect-books-and-to-take-care-of-them-properly.

## Who's Hooked and Who's Not?

The battle was joined when the children arrived at camp and settled down to spend a summer month with us. The strategy was planned and we sat back to see what would happen. Our first observation post was set up in the library and we made notations of the length of time our restless charges spent in the Ludington Library and of what they did while there. Our library was not only a place to check out books, it was a setting in which a boy could look at magazines and other books, read, type, play games or just mess around. Records had to be kept inconspicuously to keep the children from feeling watched. For these children, a scheduled activity is an adult plan to be destroyed and a grown-up purpose to be defiled. Once some of our boys found a tree-vine just right for playing Tarzan. When the fighting started ("It's *my* turn!" "The hell it is!" etc.), we installed a counselor at the site to arbitrate the mayhem. Within a day the children had lost interest in the whole affair. We feared the same fate might befall a library staffed by compulsive record-keepers.

On a typical library morning, between one and sixteen campers (out of the seventy children in camp) visited the Ludington facility. Averaged over a month's time, this works out to about six campers occupying the library at any one moment during the three hours of its availability in the morning. To put this number in proper perspective, it must be recalled that these free mornings could be spent swimming, boating, fishing, hiking, exploring, playing games or making "stuff" in the craft shop. Furthermore, no limitations were placed on out-of-library trading of books. Counselors reported a great deal of unrecorded book swapping—perhaps more than took place inside the library. Several counselors testified that a book became popular in proportion to the length of time a boy took to read it. If a boy and a book appeared to be going together, that book was likely to be coveted by the boy's friends who could obtain it only at the price of some personal service ("O.K., if you'll give me your dessert tonight") or if it gained the reader some immediate gratification ("Can I use your swimmin' fins?"). Finally, there was no discernible difference in library patronage between the first and last parts of the summer month, but a rainy day was as great a stimulus as the urge to read.

One boy checked out eleven books, after being given his initial two, while some (ten in all) checked out no more books once the original two were in their possession. On the average, the first two books were traded for two more during the month's time (forty-three boys). In all, 224 books were obtained at the library by the sixty-two boys who frequented it on a semiregular basis. Consider for a moment how often you go to your local library and you have a rough basis for comparing the figures reported here. Given the nature of our camper population, I think this is an astounding record of voluntary traffic in books. Of course there was another kind of traffic, as our rate of book-crookery was predictably high. Nearly 100 books "disappeared" in one month. However, it could have been worse: for instance, *no* books might have been stolen!

231

Our observations made it apparent that something like a reading habit gets established for certain cabins and not for others. Our youngest cabin, in which the boys averaged eight years of age, traded a total of twenty-four books at the library during the month, with each cabin member exchanging at least two. The oldest boys traded only sixteen books during the same period. The younger boys consistently checked out more books than the older ones in all ten cabins in camp. It should be no surprise, then, to learn that *What's New, Charlie Brown?* and *Dennis the Menace* were the books most frequently issued. The books next in line are a wry commentary on our times—*The Man from U.N.C.L.E., Man in Flight, Voyage to the Bottom of the Sea,* and *Batman versus the Joker.* Witness the power of television! By contrast, *Mary Poppins* was, among these street-hardened young men, treated to the position of low eminence also accorded *Grimm's Fairy Tales.* One boy checked out a book entitled *Energy and Power* but returned it shortly with the cryptic comment that he "thought it was about something else."

A most fascinating and startling finding emerged from a careful study of casual comments the children made to the librarians. Since I was primarily interested in the campers' attitudes toward reading, I asked the librarians to record offhand observations the children might make about books and magazines. No comments were recorded for fifteen of the seventy children, but of the remaining fifty-five a grand total of twenty-seven reported at the beginning of the month they could not or would not read. These twenty-seven checked out a total of sixty-eight books during the month of the experiment. Maybe they just liked to feel the weight of a book in the back pocket of their jeans or maybe they wanted to show the other guys they were "with it." But, for book haters, they certainly spent a lot of time with books. I prefer to take their words with a grain of salt and to believe their behavior.

And so our unlikely readers came to terms with paperback books and magazines. They visited the library on their own free time, and spent fifteen minutes there on the average. Some boys breezed in and out in five minutes while others stayed as long as an hour and a half. While they were in the library, their most frequent activity was the trading of one book for another, but typing ran an extremely close second in interest. Reading books and just messing around were the third and fourth runner-ups in popularity, followed by idle thumbing of and glancing at books and magazines. A library is still a library, however liberal an interpretation the word may be given, and playing games in the library was of the least interest to boys surrounded by 300 acres of games-playing possibilities.

There was a marked increase in idle time spent in the

library during the last two weeks of the month-long camp session. It became apparent that the mere inert availability of reading material was not enough for children unaccustomed intellectually to self-direction. A positive, active program of reading and writing is necessary for children unused to surmounting obstacles simply because they are there. "To the stars through bolts and bars" is a middle-class slogan ranking with the homily "A job worth doing is worth doing well." When told of these strange philosophies, our campers only smile tolerantly and say, "Sure, baby. *You* believe it."

## To Library Is One Thing; to Read Is Another

A place for books that avoids resembling a traditional library can attract customers who don't usually shop in that part of town. Business may be brisk and children wise in the ways of the adult world may learn to say those library-kinds-of-things that so endear them to library-type adults. But do they read, or do they smile gracefully and later rip the covers from the books in some secret setting? We can report convincingly about book-cover ripping. Though paperbacks seem particularly susceptible to destruction with the least flick of the wrist, the event rarely took place. The books were husbanded and nurtured as prize possessions. Placed carefully in locked footlockers, slipped under pillows or guarded on request by adults in camp, the books survived as few other material objects did. Windows were broken by irate fists, chairs hurled in anger, doors kicked akimbo in rage, and staff bodies bruised in focused resentment. But books and magazines seldom were torn or damaged. We had hoped to gauge the average life span of these reading materials with such children as ours, only to discover that with proper care even these insubstantial items can probably live forever.

But what of reading as distinct from library behavior? The most popular time for immersion in literature proved to be the half-hour allotted to getting ready for bed. Sometimes, and much to our chagrin, reading was used as a means of provoking adults who were tired from the day's labors and more intent on sleep than developing interests in literacy. Our boys used whatever tool was available to get the job done; when they discovered the simple trick of reading only at the wrong time and the wrong place, they mastered it superbly. Shouts of "Don't turn out the damn lights, I'm readin!" rang through the camp and every literacy-loving adult found himself disemboweled by ambivalence. The lights always went out (after some reasonable compromise) but flipping the

233

light switch began to seem like an act destined to be recorded in history on the same pages as book-burning.

The next most appealing time to read was mealtime. We did not demand that the children devote their attention exclusively to mastication and digestion. Consequently, they read books before, during and after eating. Next in frequency of patronage were our planned Free Activity Periods each morning. Those who read, read longer in the free morning time but more children were reading at meals and bedtime than at any other time of the day. The accuracy of these counselor recordings of reading is attested to by the fact that for an entire month no child was listed as reading during the free swim time each afternoon. The greatest frequency of reading as well as the greatest length of time spent at this activity was recorded for one child who was confined to the infirmary with a severe case of poison ivy. As he said, "I been scratchin' and readin' all day."

There were, of course, avid readers in the group who turned to their books at any moment that activities slackened or became uninteresting. I heard one boy in a boat tow (five rowboats strung together and towed by a power boat) shout to slow down and stop rocking the boat so he could read. The portability and availability of books and magazines were invitations to such reading. Probably the last word in portability was expressed by two boys on a three-mile hike to the village of Hell (that's really its name), Michigan. A Negro boy was reading *Black Like Me* while being led by the hand by a white cabin mate as they hiked down the road. Their bargain was completed on the return trip when they switched positions.

Any figure reflecting the average time our typical camper devoted to reading during the average camp day would be meaningless and would obscure the important observation that reading is a highly idiosyncratic and personal event and that its motivation is not a mass phenomenon. Some times of day and social settings are more conducive to the act of reading than others, and this is clearly reflected in counselor observations of the children. Still, there are nonreaders to whom words are totally alien and there are avid readers to whom the time for reading is anytime and anyplace.

In the cabin of our very youngest children (aged seven and retarded three years, on the average, in reading skills) the eight members of the cabin devoted a total of two hours to reading during a two-week period of observation. All but twenty minutes of this reading time took place just before going to bed. By comparison, the reading rate of boys in the adjoining cabin (populated by eight-year-olds) doubled that of their younger friends. In a sample of the older boys in camp (three cabins in the Senior division), a total of twelve hours beyond library time was spent in reading by each cabin during the same two-week period. The sight of a teenager immersed in a book was a familiar one despite heavy involvement of older boys in activities of great variety and number. Most remarkably, I have seen older boys reading books even when the evening's activity was television viewing in the cabin.

In the middle age range (ten to twelve), we discovered a steady progression, on the average, in the frequency of reading in the camp setting. Reading appears to be an age-related phenomenon whose joys are learned by practice and whose pleasures increase with the growth of greater skill. Even these primitive children violate our expectations when the proper setting and supplies are provided for them. They don't read much, from the point of view of the literate middle-class child; they read an astounding amount compared with our usual stereotype of their literary interests.

## The Odds for Tomorrow

It is highly unlikely that the cerebral pleasures of reading will ever replace the unique sensations of gross bodily movement or the sensory experience of water, wind and just being alive. Yet, in this hopeless experiment, I think we managed to demonstrate a fundamental and meaningful fact about the relationship of children of action to the world of words.

If ever a deck was stacked against us, this was it:

1. Our subjects were selected from the youthful intellectual dregs of modern society; they were academic retards in every sense of the word. In the most congenial of circumstances and settings, little could be expected of them in the way of reading involvement.

2. We constructed a three-ring circus of outdoor activities to lure these deprived children away from the solitary pursuit of reading.

3. We asked harried counselors to make objective recordings of when, where and how much time each child spent reading.

4. We found no means to control or properly assess the exchange of reading materials between children. Even camp bathrooms were sometimes converted into temporary markets for bartering books.

The entire experiment was only a crude and approximate match to the traditional models of pure science and perfectly hygienic methodology. It was impressionistic in the extreme despite the sanctification of numbers, percentages and levels of significance, all duly recorded day after day. And I am certain it contains no more than a rough sampling of the total interaction with books that took place in our camp population. However, the absence of methodological perfection troubles me very little, for the quarry being tracked was an unusual species seldom cornered in nature.

One of our original assumptions was that if delinquent and emotionally disturbed boys could be induced to read at all, we would feel we had succeeded in our assigned task. If they were to substitute reading for the call of the outdoors, we could have achieved goals we barely dared hope for. So strenuous a test as this was necessary for a number of reasons, not the least because a massive superstructure of doubt about the capability of such social rejects looms ominously over our society. We had to prove that books and magazines could be made compatible with a variety of ways of life other than that of the middle class in our social structure. We wanted an acid test: we got more acidity than we had bargained for.

In the words packaged between the covers of paperbound books and magazines I think we have finally found a common and exciting ground for conversation and contact between the dominant and dominated socioeconomic groups in our society. Books and magazines are a drug that anyone can become addicted to. You are hooked on books, I'm hooked on books, and THEY can become hooked on books too. The clearest testimonial I know of is contained in the reaction of a teacher from a detention home in Detroit. While we were discussing the case of one child he had sent to camp, I mentioned some of the books the boy was reading. The teacher interrupted to point out, "But he can't read a word!" He should have added, "Except when he wants to."

# NOTES

# NOTES